"My Bank Manager didn't like the sound of it. But he still gave me a Small Business Loan."

At Lloyds Bank, the success of small businesses is one of our biggest concerns.

That's why we're doing the very best we can to make cash more easily available.

With our new Small Business loans, whatever your business, whatever your plans, we can lend you up to £15,000 right now. The loan comes with fixed interest at a most competitive rate.

And as an extra option you can also take out loan repayment insurance.

And if you're a new customer with an annual turnover of up to £100,000, you'll get a year free of all bank charges, even if you're overdrawn (provided that we have previously agreed your overdraft).

Like the sound of all that? Then come in and have a chat or ring us free on 0800 800 424.

Lloyds Bank
Small Business
Services

THE THOROUGHBRED BANK.

The Guardian
GUIDE TO
RUNNING A
SMALL BUSINESS

The **Guardian**
GUIDE TO
RUNNING A
SMALL BUSINESS

Revised Seventh Edition

Clive Woodcock

KOGAN
PAGE

Please note that from 6 May 1990 London telephone numbers will no longer
have the 01- local area code. Instead numbers will start with either 071- or
081. Readers should check with British Telecom after 6 May 1990 if in doubt.

First published in Great Britain in 1980 by
Kogan Page Limited, 120 Pentonville Road,
London N1 9JN
Second edition 1981, Third edition 1983, Fourth edition 1984,
Fifth edition 1986, Sixth edition 1987, Seventh edition 1988
Seventh edition reprinted with revisions 1990

British Library Cataloguing in Publication Data
The Guardian guide to running a small business —
7th ed.
  1. Small business—Great Britain
  —Management
  1. Woodcock, Clive
  658'022'0941   HD62.7

ISBN 0-7494-0181-8

Printed and bound in Great Britain by
Richard Clay, The Chaucer Press, Bungay

Contents

1.   Introduction   11

2.   The First Steps   16
    2.1 Drawing up a plan *16*
    2.2 Seeking advice *18*
    2.3 Planning the future *22*
    2.4 Going for growth *25*
    2.5 Tenants' rights *27*
    2.6 The need for records *29*
    2.7 Starting a co-operative *32*
    2.8 Telephone for cash *35*
    2.9 Slow payers *37*
    2.10 Early payment *40*
    2.11 Strategy *42*
    2.12 Making them pay up *46*

3.   Getting Organised   49
    3.1 'I leave that to my accountant' *49*
    3.2 Borrowing from a bank: presenting your case *55*
    3.3 Borrowing from a bank: how a bank manager assesses your case *58*
    3.4 Is an overdraft always relevant? *61*
    3.5 Controlling debtors *64*
    3.6 Managing stockholding *67*
    3.7 The relevance of planning in a small business *70*
    3.8 Budgeting for profit *73*
    3.9 Budgeting for cash *77*
    3.10 The relevance of management information systems in a small business *81*

4.   Sources of Finance   85
    4.1 Introduction *85*
    4.2 Cash to start *87*
    4.3 Finance for young people *89*
    4.4 Bank finance *92*

"MY BUSINESS IS MY LIFE."

When your business starts to grow, so do the headaches.

There are company cars to organise, invoices to chase, even pension schemes to arrange.

All niggly little jobs that interfere with the running of the company. At a time when it needs your utmost attention.

At Midland, we're well aware of this dilemma between running a company and managing it.

So we've put together a package to help called The Business Service.

As you might expect, it includes all kinds of finance. From loans to leasing.

But it's also an open invitation to come along and talk things over with us.

Of course, we can't run your company for you.

But we do have a range of products and services that can take a lot of the donkey work off your hands.

To find out more about The Business Service send the coupon to: Business Information Service, Midland Bank plc, PO Box 2, FREE-POST, Sheffield S1 1AZ.

Or telephone us on 0800 400469.

☐ Please send me details of The Business Service
☐ Please ask your Manager at

branch to contact me to discuss The Business Service

Name
(Mr/Mrs/Miss/Ms*)   (*delete as appropriate)

Address

Postcode

Telephone No.

I am/am not** an existing Midland customer.
(**delete as appropriate)

MIDLAND
The Listening Bank
© MIDLAND BANK plc 1989

4.5   Loan guarantee scheme   *95*
4.6   Co-operatives   *97*
4.7   Business Expansion Scheme   *99*
4.8   Exporting   *103*
4.9   Local authority aid   *105*
4.10 Venture capital   *108*
4.11 Technology   *131*
4.12 Factoring   *133*
4.13 Leasing   *137*
4.14 Help from government bodies   *140*

5. **Marketing**   **143**
5.1   The small firm's route to profits and
       performance   *143*
5.2   Information for marketing decisions   *147*
5.3   Products and planning   *150*
5.4   Sales promotion and advertising   *154*
5.5   The marketing dimension to price in the small
       firm   *156*
5.6   Exporting by small firms   *159*
5.7   Marketing and selling for the start-up firm   *161*
5.8   Distribution and the small firm   *164*
5.9   Marketing and the smaller service firm   *167*

6. **Planning the Office**   **170**
6.1   The organised office   *170*
6.2   Office accommodation   *173*
6.3   Legal requirements   *176*
6.4   Fitting out office space   *180*

7. **Franchising**   **183**
7.1   Introduction   *183*
7.2   Setting up a franchise   *190*
7.3   The franchise relationship   *194*
7.4   Tips for potential franchisees   *199*
7.5   Franchising for the future   *203*

8. **Employing People**   **207**
8.1   Helping the smaller business   *207*
8.2   Unfair dismissal   *209*
8.3   Constructive dismissal   *211*
8.4   Capability dismissal   *214*
8.5   Misconduct dismissals   *216*

8.6   Laying off workers *219*
8.7   Maternity rights *221*
8.8   Statutory sick pay *223*

9.   **Choosing a Computer**   **226**
   9.1   Introduction *226*
   9.2   Buying a micro *230*
   9.3   Computer security *234*
   9.4   Small business computer selection package *238*
   9.5   Information technology disasters *242*
   9.6   Where to go for help *245*
   9.7   Using networks *247*
   9.8   The Data Protection Act *250*

10.   **Health and Safety**   **253**
   10.1   Introduction *253*
   10.2   General legal requirements *255*
   10.3   Maintenance *257*
   10.4   Falls *259*
   10.5   Safety policies *261*
   10.6   Accidents *263*
   10.7   Safe systems of work *266*
   10.8   Safeguarding machinery *268*
   10.9   Fire *271*
   10.10   Industrial health *273*
   10.11   Noise *275*
   10.12   The role of the enforcing authorities *277*

11.   **Business Premises**   **280**
   11.1   The right property *280*
   11.2   Key to the right front door *282*
   11.3   Living 'over the shop' *284*
   11.4   Looking for new premises *286*
   11.5   Organising your property – the internal layout *288*
   11.6   Keeping on the right side of officialdom *290*
   11.7   Property tenure and small business need *293*
   11.8   Converting property to your own requirements *295*

12.   **Further Information**   **298**
13.   **Select Bibliography**   **301**
Index   **303**
Index of Advertisers   **312**

1
Introduction

CLIVE WOODCOCK

'Little oaks from some great acorns grow' is a variation on the old saying which should be appreciated not only by the budding small businessman but by the existing small firm, as it brings a touch of reality to a subject which is often described in euphoric terms. It recognises that a big idea does not necessarily develop into a big business, but can still grow into a sturdy and successful tree. It also recognises that small business in general cannot become a dominant force in the economy, but it can play an important balancing role by widening the options and providing an alternative source of employment and wealth creation.

Running a small business can, in practice, often seem like a game of snakes and ladders in which the snakes are everywhere and the ladders are reserved for the larger firms. The pitfalls in the way of small firms in their constant fight for survival are such that the wonder is not that Britain has a relatively low proportion of small businesses contributing to the economy, but that so many believe it worthwhile continuing. Running your own business is often presented as being a very attractive proposition – which of course it can be and often is – but anyone who embarks upon it should also be well aware that it is no soft option. It is a hard path to follow, but one which can be rewarding both financially and in terms of personal satisfaction.

Small firms have a high mortality rate, both in the UK and overseas. Such statistics as there are show that one firm in three fails in the first 12 months, while only one in five makes it to five years. The would-be small businessman must be aware of that record, but should not be depressed or discouraged by it.

In recent years there has been a mushrooming of activities designed to encourage the development of small firms. Indeed, it may be the case that there are now more small business advisers than small firms! The small business industry itself has boomed, but has there been any lasting boost to the independent sector of the economy? There has certainly been an apparent increase in the number of firms being started, though this has

to a considerable extent been balanced by the numbers going out of business because of the general lack of consumer demand.

There are also some fears that the quality of businesses which have been started in the past year or so may render them vulnerable when the economy recovers and new, more competitive firms emerge, or if it fails to do so substantially. That fear arises from the belief that the myriad incentives which are being offered around the country have led many people who are unsuited to running a business to set up on their own. Such businesses may run for a year or two before their problems begin to emerge, resulting in a swathe of bankruptcies which could match the levels of the depths of the recession, taking with them many inflated hopes and the large amount of redundancy money invested in them, and leaving a residue of disillusion with the idea of small business generally.

On the other hand the encouragement of greater numbers of firms to start should lead to more making their way through to survive and develop to the point where they make a useful contribution to economic growth. Such encouragement may also generate the entrepreneurial attitudes and the willingness to take risks which have so long been absent in a society where people have become accustomed to working for others, to being part of the bureaucratic system.

After the initial euphoria in which the small business idea was enveloped began to clear, a more realistic appreciation of the role which the independent business can play has grown. The fanciful view that small business was the panacea for unemployment problems has given way to the realisation that the impact of independent firms on the growth of jobs will happen only in the medium to long term. Little, fortunately, is now heard of fatuous pronouncements that if every small firm took on one more employee the jobless total would be halved. Most people now understand that if that happened most of the small firms concerned would instead go out of business.

Pessimists are, however, inclined to say that the small business boom has reached its peak and that the bubble will burst when the instant solutions expected fail to materialise. In fact, it is more likely that the growth of the small business industry itself will reach a plateau as the burst of activity of recent years is directed more specifically at identifying and solving problems rather than optimistically spraying grapeshot in all directions.

The 'small business' section of the *Guardian* has played an important part in establishing a realistic view of the role of the smaller business, providing a serious national forum for the discussion of policies for independent firms and disseminating a wider knowledge of their problems and strengths. The 'sign of the acorn', the well-known *Small Business Guardian* logo, made its appearance in April 1977, well before the small business bandwagon which has now developed began to roll.

It has also served another important purpose, that of providing a guide through the minefield which faces the bewildered small businessman as he tries to sort out the relevant parts of the mass of information and schemes which are now thrown at him. It has given businessmen the facts which can point them in the right direction, and offered advice on a wide range of topics in the clear, succinct and essentially practical articles which have appeared in the *Small Business Guardian* first on Fridays, now on Mondays, since the section's inception. They have dealt with subjects such as starting a new business, budgeting and cash flow, marketing, office planning, franchising, choosing a computer and employing people. They do not pretend to be fully comprehensive in scope or to provide the answer to every problem encountered in managing a small business, but together they provide the hard-pressed small businessman or woman with an easily assimilable outline of how problems can be approached, an indication of possible solutions, and a guide to where more detailed and expert advice can be obtained.

These articles, and some specially written, form the basis of this book. The book is widely used by practising and potential small businessmen and in educational institutions which run management courses for would-be and existing entrepreneurs. Where there are gaps in coverage it is hoped to fill these in the pages of the *New Business Guardian* – the new title of the section – every Monday and to incorporate them in future editions of this book. In the meantime it is hoped that the articles collected here will help the small business owner to avoid some of the many pitfalls in managing his or her business.

Would the reader please note that the London telephone area code changes on 6 May 1990, and 01 will become either 071 (central area) or 081.

2
The First Steps

2.1 Drawing up a plan

CLIVE WOODCOCK

While luck naturally plays its part, the main reason for the success of a business is that it has developed a sound strategy and persisted in implementing it, a course which can substantially reduce the high risks of failure. An important element in this strategy is the basic plan for the business and, if this is well thought out, it will not only clarify the path which has to be taken through the first year of the firm's existence, but it will also help considerably if a need to raise money for the venture should exist.

For many just beginning the idea of drawing up a plan seems rather daunting, but it is a simple process. The proposal should begin with personal details, such as schooling, any apprenticeship served, qualifications, experience, jobs done and positions held in industry or commerce. If other people are involved their function in the proposed business should be explained.

The next step is to explain the idea, invention, manufacturing method or service on which the business will be based. The crux of the idea should be given in the first few lines and not buried in a mass of words.

The potential market for the product should then be explained with as much support as possible from documents, statistics, or other written evidence from prospective buyers. If it has been possible to make a sample, some indication of market reaction to it should be given.

An area of weakness with many small businesses is selling, so the plan should go into some detail on how the product will be sold. If there are partners involved in the project, it is a good idea if one has some knowledge of, or skill at, selling.

A sales forecast then has to be made and should be supported with as much evidence as possible. Cautious realism should be the tone of the forecast, leaving a little in hand in case of emergencies. The forecast should not be for more than one year ahead, but there is no reason why the possible growth of the business beyond that should not be discussed in less precise terms.

The question of price is also an important one. If the product proposed is better and more expensive than similar ones already available, an explanation should be given as to why the market will prefer it or why a particular method of marketing will produce the forecast sales. A margin should be allowed in the price for agents, wholesalers or retailers, depending on how the product or service is sold. These margins are likely to be quite substantial as the selling costs of most products represent a substantial proportion of the price. New firms quite often start out by charging too little for their products and then have to go through the embarrassing process of explaining to customers why prices have to go up, or go out of business.

The costs of the whole operation must then be thoroughly detailed. If the business is manufacturing, these will include raw materials, components bought in, direct labour, supervision and inspection costs, wastage, fuel and any other overheads. Drawings of, for example, engineering products will need to be submitted along with any other appropriate manufacturing information so that independent checks can be made of the costings. An effective system of financial control is essential to the survival and success of any business and this should be discussed with an accountant and put into operation from the inception of the business.

The next step is to draw up a budget for overheads which do not arise from the manufacturing process itself, such as costs of selling, accounts, development, packing, plant depreciation, and interest charges. Once this has been done it will be possible to make some assessment of the likely profit of the business.

A small business should aim at making a return of at least 15 per cent on its turnover, which, as a rough guide, would leave 10 per cent after tax. If the returns are any less than this the owner/manager might just as well start giving away the bricks and mortar.

It should also be remembered that in addition to the proprietor paying himself a fairly meagre salary in the initial stages, it will probably be necessary for profits to be ploughed back into the business for a number of years in order to avoid borrowing too much money. Using your own funds is the cheapest way of expanding.

All the information now gathered together will give the budding entrepreneur the means to draw up a cash flow forecast. This will show how much money is coming in and going out of the business and, most important, when this is likely to arise, and enable the businessman to make appropriate plans for this contingency. It is a particularly useful tool of control when a business is starting out, as the flow of cash will be all in one direction – outwards. Several forecasts will probably be needed to arrive at the best arrangement to get the business moving and make sure that it is done with the minimum amount of cash. The forecast will also indicate whether the proposal is too ambitious, and may enable the project to be scaled down to one of more manageable proportions which has a greater chance of success.

Any other information in support of the proposal should then be written down, but only that which has been thoroughly thought out and tested. The plan is then ready to be typed out and presented to the prospective financier of the new small business.

2.2 Seeking advice

CLIVE WOODCOCK

At one time anyone needing advice about starting a business was automatically referred to the three wise monkeys: the bank manager, solicitor and accountant. Any one of these may have had the knowledge or ability to understand the needs of the prospective small businessman, but often their advice was either not sought or was ignored, or they gave advice which was either wrong or not relevant.

It is not really their role to act as a general business advice service. Few have the knowledge to do so effectively and many are disinclined to offer such a service. Their particular specialist knowledge is of great value and the prospective businessman still needs that advice. The fact that they are no longer regarded as sources of general advice enables them to concentrate on the work for which they are best suited rather than offer advice in areas where their knowledge is limited.

The role of adviser and signposting service has now passed to a number of organisations which are generally better able to carry it out because that is their principal function.

The first point of contact for someone wanting to start a business but with no knowledge of how to go about it will probably be the Small Firms Service sponsored by the Department of Employment. The DoE is directly responsible for the service in England, but operates through the Scottish Development Agency in Scotland and the Welsh Development Agency in Wales. In Northern Ireland a similar service is provided through the Department of Commerce by the Local Enterprise Development Unit.

The service can be contacted more easily from any telephone by dialling 100 for the operator and asking for Freefone Enterprise, for which, of course, no charge is made. The service, which has 11 regional centres in England, publishes a range of leaflets on their own services and on several aspects of running a business. Its most useful function is that it can put the prospective business operator in touch with a wide range of specialist advisers. These can range from the most appropriate people in government departments or local authorities, to chambers of commerce or the professionals in accountancy, law, property, finance and exporting. The signposting service is one of the most valuable for the person starting out in business and even the *New Business Guardian* finds that it frequently operates in this role.

The service is manned by civil servants, but they display great enthusiasm in trying to meet the demands of their clients. Although the service has come in for criticism, and there are variations in quality as there would be in any organisation which tried to span the country on such a diverse subject as small business, the general response is that it is a very useful facility which could be more widely used.

Where the officials of the service are themselves unable to help they can put the inquirer in touch with the Small Firms Counselling Service, which is also the responsibility of the Small Firms Division of the Department of Employment. There are some 50 area counselling offices around the country and the inquirer will usually not be too far from a counsellor. All counsellors are experienced businessmen, some still in business, some retired. The initial counselling session is free and the charge for subsequent sessions (limited to 10 days in any one year) is not high and frequently offers very good value for money.

The facilities of the Small Firms Service are not limited to urban areas, but are usually based in them. It is, therefore, worth remembering that the Council for Small Industries in Rural Areas (CoSIRA), now absorbed into the Rural Development Commission, offers very similar and usually more extensive facilities for businesses located, or planning to set up, in rural areas. CoSIRA's services are generally limited to towns and villages of up to 10,000 inhabitants, though there have been circumstances where this restriction has been waived, such as in the Staffordshire moorlands town of Leek where CoSIRA has been involved in projects even though the population is nearer 15,000. CoSIRA operates only in England and similar services are offered in Wales by the Development Board for Rural Wales and in Scotland by the Highlands and Islands Development Board and the Scottish Development Agency.

CoSIRA has organisers throughout England and information about the nearest point of contact can be obtained from its head office. Other useful names and addresses are given on pages 298–300.

The various offices of BSC (Industry), the job creation arm of British Steel, should not be forgotten in any area where there has been a closure of a steel plant. Information can be obtained from BSC (Industry) at Canterbury House, 2–6 Sydenham Road, Croydon CR9 2LJ (tel: 01-686 2311). British Coal has set up a similar organisation called British Coal Enterprise, at 14–15 Lower Grosvenor Place, London SW1W 0EX (tel: 01-630 5304). The Action Resource Centre also has regional offices, information on which can be obtained from the head office.

A rapidly growing source of information and advice for both new and existing small firms are local enterprise trusts – organisations usually set up by a number of private companies in an area, often in association with public authorities, to tackle problems in the communities in which those large firms operate. Most of their work so far has focused on economic problems, with job creation the main objective, and most have seen the encouragement of small firms as a way of achieving that objective.

The first of the local enterprise trusts to be established was Enterprise North which started life about a decade ago, bringing together panels of experienced local businessmen to provide help and advice for budding and existing entrepreneurs. Enterprise North has close links with the practically oriented Small Business Centre at Durham University Business School.

Another early trust was the Community of St Helens Trust in the Merseyside town known for its glass making. It was backed by a number of companies led by the Pilkington's glass group, the enlightened local authority, and financial institutions in the area. This has developed in a different way from Enterprise North in that it has a full-time director with a staff of secondees from industry and financial institutions who spend a great deal of their time solving problems for individual companies, charting paths through the maze of government regulations and forms needed to obtain state aid, suggesting ideas and discussing problems with clients.

Many of the other enterprise trusts, now numbering more than 240, which have since emerged, follow the pattern of these two. There are variations, both in structure and quality, but the latter should improve with experience.

A comprehensive list can be obtained from Business in the Community, an organisation established to encourage and assist the involvement of industrial and commercial concerns with local economic and social development. It can be contacted at 227A City Road, London EC1V 1LX (tel: 01-253 3716).

A useful publication listing sources of information for new and small firms and containing perhaps the most comprehensive list of local enterprise agencies is the directory of sources of information and advice, *The Small Business Guide* (BBC Publications), produced by Colin Barrow.

Many technical colleges, colleges of further education and polytechnics, as well as the universities and business schools, run a wide range of courses for new and developing small firms, and full use should be made of them. Businessmen are right to be wary of the academics who have become involved in the small business scene, but there is also much to be learnt from the disciplines which they have to teach. Those disciplines can make the process of running a business easier, and many of the courses also make use of experienced businessmen and former participants in courses which provide a practical leavening of the theory.

2.3 Planning the future

JAMES CURRAN AND JOHN STANWORTH

How many people would start a long car journey without a route map? How many would build a house extension without drawings and a detailed estimate of costs?

Running a business is infinitely more hazardous than the first and much more prolonged than the second – the uncertainties continue as long as the business survives – yet many owner-managers manage day-to-day with few or any plans for the future.

An overall plan, however, not only reduces risks but makes the enterprise better able to cope with the unforeseen. Planning is also the hallmark of the businesses which take off successfully and of the long-term survivors – those who dig themselves in profitably and survive the winds of insecurity year after year.

Some owner-managers get it right almost instinctively, without much forward planning. But what is sometimes grandly called 'corporate strategy' cuts the odds against failure. Planning, in an appropriate form for the small firm, means being especially conscious of certain aspects of the business and using some fairly simple and often inexpensive techniques.

It also means paperwork and some administration, the very things that many private business owners hoped to avoid by working for themselves. It becomes easier over time and the benefits justify putting up with the tedious parts. Who knows, planning could even have its own attractions, especially for those who have minds that like solving puzzles.

The most commonly mentioned small firm problem is finance. Many firms are under-financed when they set up and then overtrade thereafter. Some enter highly competitive areas because these are cheap to enter, but lack of initial finance and low profit margins put the business under constant pressure and allow little time for planning.

This has sometimes been exacerbated by government subsidising new start-ups which simply push older businesses to the wall in highly competitive, densely populated sectors such as retailing.

This underlines rule number one – planning should start as early as possible. Find a market niche where there is a real advantage over others in terms of product or service.

New products or services or some combination are a key to successful start-up as well as being essential to the successful established enterprise. What the successful small firm is always trying to do is to distance itself from other firms in the market, and that has to be a constant of the planning process, whatever the age of the firm.

Marketing is just another way of saying that a good product or service does not sell itself. Potential customers can only buy what they know exists. Marketing need not be expensive – direct calls and targeted mail shots, for instance, can cost relatively little and may be much more effective than conventional blanket advertising.

For the established firm, analysing previous orders and inquiries is important. Where did the caller hear of the business, and if the business does not supply what he wants, should it be doing so? Regular personal contacts with customers and looking for new products/services to add to the present range equally cost little.

Elbow room for planning and moving the firm into a more exploitable market is linked to financial control and budgeting. Businesses are usually more financially stretched at start-up and when undergoing change than at any other time. New orders need to be sought and funded.

It can take months to search out the market, negotiate orders, produce them and finally receive payment from the customer. Financial control also means clear terms of payment and checking the credit records of customers (word of mouth can be a good source).

Large firms sometimes feel that they have little to lose in upsetting a small supplier by late payment. Often small firms are reluctant to demand payment for fear of losing future orders. However, it is worth remembering that in large firms functions are usually departmentally split. Little may be lost by upsetting the accounts department since the ordering department may never even be aware that the bill is being chased. Let the accounts department know that you are small and that you need payment to service other orders – the person at the other end is human too.

Start-up and later growth often need outside capital. Find out what a business plan looks like, since this is the language of the bank manager and increases the chances of getting a loan. The techniques of drawing up a business plan are not that mind-bending and the discipline is a safety check on the basic start-up idea or on how the established business is operating.

Remember, banks are not the only source of finance – other sources may offer additional benefits. Equipment suppliers give loans and a continuing supply of technical advice, often free. Venture capital funds often offer finance plus continuing management advice – they want to protect their investment and maximise their returns.

Some owners are reluctant to borrow from more sophisticated sources than their local bank. They are afraid that it will mean a loss of independence, that they will be back 'working for someone else'. But running a bigger business and making a bigger cake offers compensations: less than 100 per cent of a bigger cake can be worth more than 100 per cent of a smaller cake.

Thinking of the future means thinking of where the business needs to be in x years' time. Independence can be long term as well as short term, and nobody lives for ever. A business too weak to survive beyond its owner is not much good to its employees or much of a memorial to the vision and skills of its founder.

2.4 Going for growth

JOHN STANWORTH AND JAMES CURRAN

In running a small enterprise, time is the ever-present enemy. The owner-manager is the firm's major asset – using that asset to maximum advantage involves a planned and fully thought through use of time. It means, in other words, the same careful planning as applied to finance and marketing.

Periodically, keeping a diary of daily activities for a week or so is more than helpful. Often this is a source of surprises – it not only tells you where your time goes but throws up suggestions about how it might be used more profitably. Priorities have to be selected, especially when the work load becomes overwhelming, as it does from time to time in any busy enterprise. Should you be doing this or that task yourself at all? Costing out your time may show that employing somebody else produces more profit than doing it yourself because you could use your time to earn more than they cost. Remember, employees do not have to be bought whole – part-time workers may be more effective.

Owner-managers are often tempted to hire mirror images of themselves. But that may simply duplicate present personal strengths and weaknesses. It might be smarter to find somebody who is good at the tasks which the owner-manager finds most frustrating or boring. An employee may not only be better at the job than the owner-manager – he may also be cheaper. The object is to free the owner to do things which he or she does best, including planning.

Activities such as dealing with routine telephone inquiries, bookkeeping and other paperwork are important but the owner-manager can use time more effectively doing other things. What is important is to ensure that any new job is clearly defined and a good working relationship is built up with the occupant. Informal relations are attractive – 'we are all friends here' – and an easy atmosphere is an asset, but a lack of clarity about what people are responsible for is a recipe for trouble.

All the above is doubly important when the time for hiring specialist skills arises, usually as an enterprise grows. This invariably means the delegation of duties which the owner-manager did previously and a more consultative approach which some owner-managers find difficult to come to terms with. The idea of a management team, which means that others will have a share in decisions, sometimes seems threatening to the owner-manager's highly valued independence.

This is compounded by the typical specialist's personal commitment pattern. For him, the firm is often just one more step on his career ladder: he has not got his life savings bound up in the enterprise and other jobs in other firms may emerge as more attractive. Equally, the loyal jack of all trades who has frequently been with the firm from its early days, and who did part of the job previously, sometimes feels cheated when a newcomer takes over. All these problems can be minimised by careful planning. If not, they can be an organisational time bomb blowing up just when the firm is vulnerable because it is going through fundamental change.

As firms grow, relationships with the outside world become more complicated. Banks, local authorities, government departments and perhaps trade unions all begin to take more of an interest. Owner-managers often resent this 'interference' but the outside world will not go away. The mark of a successful small enterprise is that its owner-manager recognises that positive strategies are needed to adapt to the outside world rather than simply ignoring it or indulging in an energy-wasting attempt to take all comers on.

One strategy is to find a good accountant – using the resources of the outside world to cope with that same outside world. Good accountants need seeking out. Too many accountants simply do the books every year regarding their main job as minimising the tax bill. They do not offer any useful and needed additional advice for a growing business. 'Management accounting', providing skilled advice and help to augment the firm's in-house planning and controls, is increasingly being recognised as what accountants should be doing. Younger members of the profession are now being trained and are keen to do just this. They become part of the business, albeit part-time – consultants rather than fillers of tax forms.

There are now many advisory schemes aimed at the small business which provide cheap but valuable advice and other resources for the small firm. In fact, it has been said that there are now so many sources that the average small business owner is entitled to be bewildered. Some are government initiatives, such as the Small Firms Service run by the Department of Employment. Others are a mix of public and private enterprise, such as many of the 300 plus local enterprise agencies now up and running in Britain.

College courses abound, often run on a subsidised basis and at times convenient to the busy owner-manager. Small business clubs are also mushrooming, helping to counter the isolation of so many of those who have set up for themselves. The chance to meet others, to talk, learn and exchange ideas, is far from a waste of time. It can prevent the loss of perspective which arises from over-involvement in a single activity like running a business and a break from over-preoccupation with your own problems.

In a small business, more so than in any other, 'management intensity' and overload are likely. Functions merge into one another, tasks are left uncompleted and short-time perspectives dominate. Making room for planning is not a luxury but an essential, if sanity and business are to be preserved. Planning uses time to make more effective use of time and enables the owner-manager to discover how to get more out of life. Running a business should be creative, rewarding and even fun, not a treadmill which deadens the soul and shortens your life.

2.5 Tenants' rights

CLARE DYER

Since the passage of the Landlord and Tenant Act in 1954, more and more protection has been given to the residential tenant, but the businessman's right to carry on trading when his lease or tenancy expires remains hedged about with strict requirements as to notices and time limits. The Act can be a minefield for the unwary tenant who walks in without the benefit of good professional advice.

What types of premises are protected by the Act? Any in which a business is being carried on, and 'business' is widely defined to include not only the usual shops, offices, factories and workshops, but professional offices. It has even been held to include schools and sporting clubs. The Act confers rights on the *occupier* of business premises, so if they are let to a sub-tenant it will be he, rather than the tenant, who will be able to claim the benefit of the protection.

What exactly are these rights? As long as the landlord takes no positive step the tenant is entitled to stay on in the premises even though tenancy has expired, on the same terms and at the same rent as before. The Act also gives him the right to apply to the court for a new tenancy at a fair market rent.

It is up to the landlord to take the first step if he wants to get the property back or to raise the rent to the current market level. He must serve a notice specifying a date, not less than 12 months in the future, for the tenancy to end. The date named can be the date on which the lease or tenancy agreement expires, or any time after its expiry.

The notice must ask the tenant to let the landlord know within two months whether he intends to apply for a new lease. The landlord must indicate in the notice whether he intends to oppose the tenant's application and, if so, on what grounds.

There are seven grounds on which an application can be opposed, but the most important are that the landlord genuinely wants to occupy the premises, or has some definite scheme for redevelopment. Vague plans are not likely to recommend themselves to the court: it will be looking for 'a clear intention, fixed and settled,' as the Court of Appeal put it in one case. Nor is the court likely to refuse a new tenancy if the landlord's plans can be carried out without dislodging the tenant, if, for instance the tenant is willing to allow the landlord's workmen access through his premises.

A landlord who has bought an already tenanted property faces a further restriction: he must have owned it for five years before he can successfully resist a claim for a new tenancy because he wants to occupy it himself.

Most new tenancies are hammered out by agreement between the landlord's and the tenant's advisers. Of 10,000 applications to the court each year, only 500 or so go to a full hearing. But the right will be lost if the tenant does not apply to the court between two and four months after the landlord's notice is served.

There is a danger of being lulled into a false sense of security if negotiations seem to be going reasonably well, but once four months have passed, if the new tenancy hasn't been sewn up and no court application made, the right is irretrievably lost. The time limits in the Act are applied absolutely rigidly by the court, which has no discretion to waive them, however much it may sympathise with the tenant.

In one case, court proceedings were well under way when it was discovered that the landlord had never received the tenant's counter-notice, the statement of his intention to apply for a new tenancy, which must be served within two months of the land-lord's notice. It had been sent by ordinary post, and had never been delivered. Although the court had every sympathy for the tenant, they were unable to give him a new tenancy.

It is a common misconception that the terms of the new lease will be exactly the same as the old, apart from the rent. The landlord and tenant can agree any changes they like, and in default of agreement a judge can put in any clause he thinks reasonable in the circumstances. In practice, though, the terms will be the same unless there is good reason to alter them.

Variations which have been granted by the court include a shorter term where the property was ripe for development, though plans were not sufficiently formulated for the landlord to obtain possession; a rent review clause where there was none before; and a change made to legalise an existing use of the property which contravened the old lease.

Once the terms have been agreed, the most important item – the new rent – has to be negotiated.

Finally, what about the tenant whose lease has expired and whose landlord hasn't taken any steps? If he wants more security before making alterations or putting capital into the business, he is not obliged to sit tight waiting for his landlord to make the first move. The Act allows him to serve a notice on the landlord requesting a new tenancy.

2.6 The need for records

DOUGLAS DONLEAVY

Some recent research into the causes of bankruptcy among small firms shows that, while poor sales, bad initial choice of site, misguided spending and sheer bad luck were all factors that occurred very often in the history of failure, one element dominated all of these – a general absence of reliable records.

One creditor that generally pursues its debtors all the way to bankruptcy is the Inland Revenue, and the major reason why small firms get into trouble with their tax bill is absence of records. Without records, the small businessman has only, at best, a vague idea of his profit. The Inland Revenue presents him with an assessment and he finds himself without the paper evidence necessary to argue against his tax bill. He is saddled with a demand, the basis of which he does not really understand and which he is unable or unwilling to pay. Lack of records also means that he has been unable to plan his cash flow to ensure he has enough saved to meet the tax demand and any other sudden expenditure. As a result, a promising business may be aborted and its owner driven into bankruptcy, all for the lack of a few simple records.

Readers may doubt that records are simple. An illusion often encountered these days is that enterprise is stifled by a bureaucratic government's unappeasable appetite for complicated forms that nobody needs and nobody reads. This has some validity in the case of government statistical forms and VAT returns, but this article is concerned with the firm too small to be involved in either of these. The Inland Revenue forms are not difficult and generally involve no more than the appendage of a set of annual accounts. Annual accounts, however, cannot be prepared without books of account.

It would be understandable for the new businessman to protest that he went into business for himself, not for the taxman, and that he is damned if he is going to spend a couple of hours a week writing up books just to please the Revenue. However, it is failure to keep books that will almost always guarantee a higher tax bill than is really fair to the taxpayer. The Revenue fights with paper, and the taxpayer must do likewise. It is quite futile to hope that you are too small to come to the attention of your tax office and quite hopeless to believe that a nice line in patter and excuses is any substitute for proper records.

It is not only the tax bill that can be controlled by good record keeping. The businessman who wishes to survive, let alone grow, must know how he is doing on a weekly, even a daily, basis. This means he must know two very important things about his business at all times: first, the amount of cash he has to spend, and, second, the true profit or loss he makes from his sales.

It is important to realise that making a profit does not necessarily mean having any spare cash and that having a lot of money in the bank does not mean a big profit has been made. The Inland Revenue is interested in the profit or loss, and the bank in both the profit and the cash, while the businessman is interested in success (a matter of profit) and survival (a matter of cash).

Now to the records themselves. First and foremost is the cash book. On the left-hand pages are written all the cash received in the form of cheques; on the right all payments made by cheque. Every week the receipts are added up and the total weekly payments deducted from them to give a cash at bank balance. This should agree with the bank's records and, if it does not, the reason for the difference has to be found so a correct view can emerge. If the cash book is written in every time a cheque is received or paid out, the effort soon becomes a habit rather than a burden.

Many small businesses deal in notes and coins rather than cheques and for such transactions a petty cash book is necessary. Money in on the left-hand pages; money out on the right. If possible, retain vouchers for every entry in the book to prove the accuracy of each entry if it becomes necessary. At least once a week add up the receipts and payments to obtain a balance of cash in hand and check that it agrees with the actual amount counted from the till or the cash box. This routine will quickly reveal any carelessness with petty cash and provide an early warning system of alien fingers in the till!

If sales and purchases are made on credit, a sales and a purchases ledger will both be necessary. Both of these have one page for each firm with whom credit deals are transacted. In the purchase ledger, suppliers are recorded in alphabetical order of name. Address and phone numbers are written under the name, and on the right-hand side are listed the date, nature and amount of each item bought on credit. On the left-hand side are recorded all the payments made to the supplier for the items on the right.

Every month the left-hand total is deducted from the right to show how much the supplier is owed. If the supplier sends statements, these should agree with the purchase ledger account. In the sales ledger, customers are listed in a similar way to the suppliers in the purchase ledger but sales on credit to them appear on the left while their payments appear on the right.

The above records represent the absolute minimum for any business. In addition, limited companies must keep a record in a capital ledger of any land, buildings, machinery, furniture and vehicles owned (all entered on the left) showing the cost of such items at the time of purchase.

All expenses are posted from the cash books and purchase ledgers to the left-hand side of the nominal ledger. Income from sales, rent, dividends, etc, is posted to the right. There is a separate page in the ledger for each type of expense or income: one for rent, one for wages, one for sales, etc. It is important to keep expenses on the left and income on the right if the books are to balance.

Every month each page in the nominal and capital ledgers is totalled, taking care to keep right-hand totals separate from left-hand ones. The balances in the sales ledger and purchase ledgers are also totalled, as are the totals in the cash books. These are then listed on a sheet of paper called a trial balance whose left-hand totals should add up to the final total of the right-hand totals. If so, the books balance and the businessman can be confident of his records.

A comparison of expenses with sales will show the profit for the month. The cash book totals will show the cash in hand. The sales and purchase ledgers will show how much the business owes and how much it is owed in turn.

A small sacrifice of time and effort in keeping simple books is well worth the return in terms of knowing where the business stands. Additional benefits are: saving the cost of employing a bookkeeper, confidence in facing the Inland Revenue and control of one's own business destiny based on accurate data instead of on some mythical 'flair' or 'gut-feel' that cuts no ice with the official receiver. Indeed, it can be said that no businessman is in control of his business fate unless he is in control of his business records.

2.7 Starting a co-operative

CLIVE WOODCOCK

The idea of the co-operative form of enterprise has been around for a very long time and in a variety of guises. There has, however, been a tremendous growth of interest in recent years as people have looked for new ways of developing their working environment or simply for ways of creating new jobs where old ones have disappeared as conventionally structured companies take unilateral decisions based on their own need to survive.

Some co-operatives have been formed from companies which were in danger of disappearing or were already in liquidation. Though some successful co-operatives have emerged from these situations, it is far from the best starting point for a viable business. But choice is not always in the hands of those who set up a co-operative.

An unfortunate by-product of this type of situation is that such operations tend to attract publicity and their problems are regularly raked over in public. When they fail, the attitude of outside observers is often one of 'I told you so, co-operatives just don't work'. Because of the publicity attached to the failures of co-operatives – especially when they have been backed by government funds – there is a tendency in the public mind to associate the co-operative form of enterprise with failure. This is an unfair and unrealistic attitude and one which will probably only slowly be changed by greater public awareness of the fact that there are many, and a growing number of, successful and viable co-operatives around the country.

There can also, however, be a tendency among those who establish co-operatives to believe that it is an easier way to run a business because there is no 'boss'. But the existence of a co-operative does not necessarily mean that everyone co-operates. As George Jones, director of the Co-operative Development Agency, has said, the co-operative form of organisation is not an easy form of enterprise but it is a better one than those to which people are accustomed. It is actually more demanding on the people who are part of it than conventional forms of business organisation and demands a far higher degree of commitment.

It should also be remembered that co-operatives are operating in an economic system which, if not actually hostile to them, will make no concessions and will compete with the utmost vigour. The co-operative, therefore, has both to be competitive and to retain its soul, its reason for existence.

Most co-operatives tend to produce goods or services of high quality, but are usually weaker in marketing those products and in general management. With a proper recognition of the requirements of management and training in marketing skills there is no reason why a co-operative enterprise cannot be successful, though it probably has to work twice as hard to achieve it.

Co-operatives should strive to be profitable in order to develop, but profit is not the be-all and end-all of their existence. It is an objective which is harnessed to the wider interests of the co-operative itself and the community in which it exists.

Co-operatives enable individuals to counter general economic problems. The development of neighbourhood or community co-operatives, employing a relatively small number of people to provide services within a limited area, is an example of this. These co-operatives provide a variety of services, such as improving the general environment by removing graffiti from walls, window cleaning, gardening and small repairs.

This, of course, is only one form of co-operative and co-operation is a kind of organisation for activity which can take a wide variety of forms. There are even competing organisations proclaiming that their particular form of organisation is the best, often not recognising that all probably have an application, a role to play, depending on the requirements of the particular situation.

A useful place to start in finding out the differences between the various kinds of co-operative is the Co-operative Development Agency, Broadmead House, 21 Panton Street, London SW1Y 4DR (tel: 01-839 2985), which was established by Parliament in 1978 to represent and promote the idea of co-operatives and the growth of the co-operative sector. It is a useful independent body for initial contact, and guides prospective co-operators baffled by the differences between the Co-operative Union, which represents the traditional retail co-operative sector and the producer co-operatives among their membership, the Industrial Common Ownership Movement, and the Job Ownership organisation which promotes a type of co-operative similar to those at Mondragon in Spain.

The CDA has also produced sets of model rules for co-operatives which can assist greatly in easing the registration of new co-ops, though the best-known and most widely used model rules are those produced by the Industrial Common Ownership Movement (ICOM). Use of these model rules can reduce the cost of registration quite substantially and also provide one of the keys to funds available for co-ops from ICOF (see section 4.6).

The CDA will also be able to put the prospective co-operators in touch with any local co-operative development agency in their area. The local CDAs are backed and financed by local authorities and, apart from their general role of job creation, they also try to cope with the problems of inner city areas which have proved intractable by other methods. The local CDAs have no statutory connection with the CDA itself, but the degree of co-operation between them is increasing, and after an initially wary start the links are developing to the benefit not only of the central and local CDAs but to the co-operatives which they are there to help.

Among other oganisations which will provide useful information on forming a co-operative are ICOM, 20 Central Road, Leeds LS1 6DE (tel: 0532 461737), and Job Ownership, 9 Poland Street, London W1V 3DL (tel: 01-437 5511).

While there is a variety of legal forms of co-operative, there are usually four basic elements: management, objectives and assets are controlled by the workforce, usually implying ownership of the enterprise by the workforce, though this is not necessarily so; there is a voting system based on one person one vote; capital is hired by labour and not the other way around, so those who provide capital do so in the form of loans on which an agreed rate of interest is paid and profits are used as the workforce wishes; the enterprise cannot be dissolved or otherwise broken up for the benefit of the workers, and any surplus available when a co-operative comes to an end passes to the local community or a charity. Any group of people which wants to form a co-operative should at least be aware of these four basic principles.

2.8 Telephone for cash

ROBERT BOYD

Cash flow is a major factor in the daily life of every small businessman, and rising bankruptcy and liquidation rates have emphasised its importance. However, ideas for actually speeding up the realisation of money locked up in debts are in relatively short supply. Our technique that can be used with advantage is that of 'telephone cash collection'.

This method involves systematically telephoning for payment instead of sending first and second reminder letters, seven days warnings and so on. It requires a similar skill to telephone selling, the main difference being the attitude that the telephone collection clerk has to the call. He, or more often she, is concluding the business transaction rather than starting it. She is collecting money due and is entitled to speak with authority to anyone at the debtor company to achieve this. Because of this strong position senior staff can be reached more easily and any likely problems in collection discovered early.

The key to effective debt collection by telephone is preparation. Records to be referred to must be clear and accurate. Muddle and delay while on a call is not only costly but spoils a positive first impression. The caller should always try to keep the initiative, but this is impossible if constant requests to 'hang on a minute, will you' are made.

The main information that should be available is how much money is owing in total, how much is being asked for now, and how the latter total is made up in terms of invoices and credit notes. The sales ledger must be right up to date on the cash received side. It is embarrassing to demand a cheque for invoices that were paid a few days before.

The sales ledger is best kept in a form showing all outstanding invoices separately. Any that are missing from the customers' ledger can then be easily identified. Preferably, invoices for each month should be together.

An 'aged' list of unpaid invoices for each customer is the ideal document to work from. If the present sales ledger system does not provide data in this form, an analysis of invoices into one, two and three months old and over can readily be prepared by hand.

Having verified what is due for payment the next important matter is to decide who to talk to. In most cases the customer's purchase ledger clerks will be the first stage. They will be able to say whether the caller's invoices have been passed for payment and if so when the cheque will be paid. Queries will also be identified at this stage. However, the object of the telephone call is to get payment from the debtor earlier than he would normally wish. Real progress will only be made, therefore, if a promise of payment is obtained from someone who can guarantee that a cheque will be drawn, signed, and actually posted as a result of the telephone call.

This person will normally be the accountant, and his name and that of the managing director should be requested in the course of the conversation with the purchase ledger clerk. This has the added benefit of letting the clerk know that the caller means business and that unfulfilled promises will be followed up.

The result of the call should, if possible, be a specific promise to send a cheque on an agreed date. There is little point in making a series of calls to be told each time that 'I will look into it' or 'A cheque will be in the post soon.' Promises received must be followed up if the cheque is not received on or soon after the date promised.

The telephone collection method works best if a careful record of results is made. The main points of a conversation should be compared with the subsequent receipt or otherwise of a cheque. This leads to the early recognition of the main techniques of avoiding payment.

Good relationships built up with the staff of regular but slow payers help towards earlier payment. Evasive answers or broken promises help to identify the major risks quickly. Combined with legal processes and, if applicable, the cutting off of supplies, the telephone collection technique can be very effective.

2.9 Slow payers

ROBERT BOYD

Large companies are being increasingly criticised for their slow payment to small suppliers. Reports on research by, among others, the London Enterprise Agency and the Association of Independent Businesses show there is some justification for the complaint and the chief general manager of the Co-operative Bank has emphasised the interdependence of large and small firms.

A recent check on payments made by a number of well-known companies showed that the average time taken from date of invoice to payment varied from five weeks to more than twelve weeks. Most companies paid after about eight weeks but some invoices took much longer. Even when compelled to give such extended credit it may be impossible for the small business to cut off supplies or go on to a pro forma invoice basis without doing permanent damage to its main markets.

However, whether or not large companies can be convinced that they should do more to help their small relatives, it is often possible for the latter to get cheques sooner by examining the payment process stage by stage.

All companies of any size are handling hundreds, and often thousands, of pieces of paper every day. To control this flood of

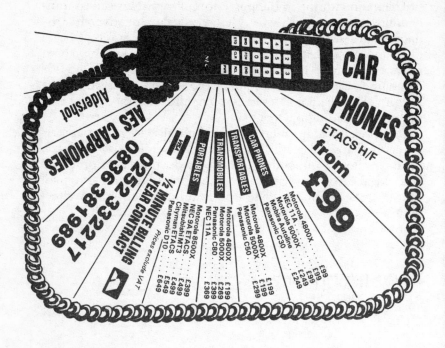

orders, delivery notes, invoices, cheques and other documents they have laid down rigid systems for processing them efficiently.

Their methods of purchasing from and payment to small suppliers are no exception. Once a purchase invoice, for example, has got into the system then its progress is relatively automatic. Whether this movement from input to payment is a matter of weeks or months, the invoices of the small company will not normally be treated any differently from hundreds of others unless they require special attention for some reason. They are in the best position for payment if they pass without delay through each stage from receipt of invoice on to the ledger and finally to payment.

The comparatively unsophisticated organisation of the small firm is competing for payment with the highly organised invoicing and cash collection departments of larger companies.

The latter have examined every link in the chain from sales invoice to payment both in their own organisation and in the customer's. The small supplier must look at this process with equal care if he is to have any chance of receiving payment as soon as his larger competitors.

The main aim is to get the invoice on to the customer's purchase ledger before it closes for that month. Surprisingly, perhaps, many large companies close their ledgers before the end of the month concerned. That is, if it is their policy to pay October invoices in early December, then for their purposes October may only be invoices received up to 25 October or even earlier. Any invoices received after that date are classed as November and paid in early January.

Companies vary so much in their purchase ledger timetables that it is difficult to generalise. What is certain is that a few days' delay in sending off invoices, particularly round about the customer's close off date, can result in those invoices being paid four or five weeks late. The purchase ledger clerk, purchase manager or accountant of each important but slow paying company should, therefore, be asked for details of their timetable.

If it is clearly explained that the reason for the call is to find out how their system works so that your invoices will be paid more quickly, the cause of the delay will soon be found.

It may be that your invoices, though paid late, are not paid any later than other suppliers, but it may be the case that your invoices are getting on to a later payment run than necessary and action can be taken to rectify the situation. The lessons learnt on a few such calls can often be applied generally.

It is obvious that invoices must be raised and despatched promptly. If, because of rising postage rates, a policy has been adopted of holding invoices until several have accumulated it should be reconsidered if it might lead to that customer's ledger being missed for the month. In some cases first class post may be advisable.

All efforts to get invoices to customers quickly are wasted if queries cause them to be treated as exceptions at the receiving end. Needless to say, invoices must be correctly addressed, priced, extended and totalled, but one common cause of delay is order numbers. The need for these varies from the essential to merely desirable.

In the first case an invoice without an order number will be returned. This highlights the matter, which can be noted for future business. In the latter case the invoice will be circulated round the organisation until it reaches the person who ordered or received the goods or services. The invoice is delayed in getting on to the ledger, but to the supplier there is no apparent reason why he gets paid an extra month late.

Customers' staff placing orders, perhaps on the telephone,

do not always tell the supplier he should be given an order number. It may, in any case, have to be obtained from a central purchasing department and arrive after the invoice has been sent. It is, perhaps, best for the supplier to insist that the name and department of the person placing the order is put on the sale invoice when an order number is not received.

The date on the invoice should normally be the date of despatch and not that of invoice preparation if later. This is particularly important if goods are despatched in one month and invoiced, perhaps the next day, in the following month.

The majority of firms close their purchase ledgers three to ten days after the month end and their 'cut off' or finishing date for that month will usually be the last day of the month.

One company, finding a fall in its cash collection rate, discovered that a computer operator had accidentally dated a batch of invoices with the next month instead of the current one. The customers had, therefore, held these invoices back until the following month's ledger.

Some queries on matters such as shortages, returns and price cannot be avoided.

But other errors that could cause a hold-up in payment will be found if all invoices of a significant amount are checked for essential detail before posting.

Examination of one's own and customer's procedures in the way described can pay substantial dividends in speeding cash flow.

2.10 Early payment

ROBERT BOYD

Keeping sales ledger debtors to a minimum is vitally important to the expansion, and sometimes even the survival, of small firms. Streamlining the method of raising invoices will, by itself, often lead to a significant increase in cash flow by getting the invoices on to the customer's sales ledger earlier. It is also helpful to take a close look at how companies, especially the larger ones, organise their monthly payments to suppliers.

The problem for the small company is how to obtain payment earlier, and it should be tackled in the most direct way by asking the customer's accounts staff how it can be achieved. This discussion gives a useful understanding of how their internal systems work, and the importance of computers soon becomes obvious from references to 'next week's computer run' or 'the month end cheque print-out'. The detailed working of every computer system is unique, as sellers of packaged programs soon discover, but certain common methods stand out.

One technique is for the computer to print out a cheque and remittance advice on a certain date or in a certain 'pay week' or 'pay month'. This is entered manually or, alternatively, can be calculated by the computer. Among the factors taken into account when deciding the pay week are the invoice date or company's own month end date, available discounts, terms stated on the purchase order and, most important of all, the number of weeks' credit the company takes as a matter of policy. The credit taken from different suppliers may vary because of pay week decisions made by the purchasing or accounts department. It should be noted, therefore, that invoices can be 'brought forward' for earlier payment by the customer's staff. In this case the original week number is changed by inputting one which causes the cheque to be produced earlier.

If a pay week type of system is not used, cheques and/or remittance advices will be prepared in advance, often at a computer bureau. The flexibility of the pay week system is then obtained in a variety of ways. Cheques may be held for some time before posting and if the dates on cheques are recorded in the sales cash book some interesting patterns can be revealed. On the other hand, cheques may be made out without a date, this being stamped on at the time of despatch. At the extreme, of course, some companies will only post off cheques as final demands and cut-off notices are received.

Larger companies will not normally hold individual cheques in this way or apply onerous terms to particular classes of supplier. The inconvenience is too great and cheques will be released in bulk in some systematic manner. The Ford Motor Company, for example, pays on a four-weekly cycle based on the initial letter of the supplier company name. As long as the information required by Ford is on the invoice this procedure is said to result in payment within normal monthly terms.

Many companies, mainly small to medium ones, will not raise a cheque until a statement has been received and reconciled with their purchase ledger. The statement should, therefore, be sent off within 10 days or so of the month end and show all invoices despatched. Even if these are not all due, a sizeable sum owing on the bottom line can concentrate the customer's mind on paying those that are due. The reconciliation of statements is time-consuming work, however, and many larger companies ignore them altogether, but this cannot be relied upon unless the supplier is specifically asked not to send them.

Attention tends to be concentrated on the slow paying customers when deciding how to improve cash flow from debtors, but it should not be forgotten that an improvement can also be made by speeding up the better payers. As these are usually the more organised companies it is also easier to find out the information they require to get the fastest payment from them. As long as ultimate payment is not really in doubt, the expense of getting a debt paid a few weeks earlier by a slow payer may be uneconomic. The measures taken to reduce outstanding debts should, therefore, involve a review of all customers, with the greatest attention being paid to the larger ones whether they happen to be slow payers or not.

Allocation of cash resources is the function of accounts departments and, if necessary, they should be pressed vigorously for money. Contacts in the operating departments may be helpful and for large amounts an approach should be made early, preferably before the debt is overdue and certainly before it is causing serious difficulties. If delay seems certain and will cause cash flow problems it may be necessary to go above the management level directly concerned with payment. In order not to generate unnecessary ill-will it is important not to actually bypass the accountant or purchasing manager, but whenever a commitment to pay or otherwise solve the problem is broken the next level should be contacted. Time should not be wasted arguing about the broken promise because, as the request for payment gets further up the line of command, it becomes more likely that it will be made a case for special treatment.

2.11 Strategy

CLIVE WOODCOCK

The response of many a small business proprietor to exhortations from a consultant or adviser – especially from the academic world – that the prospects of his or her business could be improved through strategic planning would be to reach for the nearest blunt instrument.

There could be a variety of reasons for such a negative re-action – such as the belief that strategic planning is a luxury for large firms with the money and personnel to carry out the processes, that it is irrelevant to small firms who only have the time to concentrate on survival. Or it could be lack of under-standing of a language in which the concept of strategic manage-ment is described and a consequent fear of that which is not understood.

But strategic planning in business is not necessarily an irrele-vant abstraction, it can have pointed, practical applications for even the smallest firm, especially if a firm is going to grow rather than merely survive. Without the jargon which often sur-rounds the idea, it is even a simple process.

A European Small Business Seminar, held in Austria, and sponsored by the European Foundation for Management Development, in fact took as its theme 'Survival by Strategic Management'. There were critical voices there suggesting that strategic planning in this context was simply another example of academic theorists trying to apply big company concepts to small firms.

But the organisers had anticipated the criticism and – unusually for conferences of this kind – had arranged for a number of small businessmen and women not merely to attend but actually to take an active part in the conference in discuss-ing why and how they had approached strategic planning in their businesses.

Two of the companies were from Austria, one from Denmark, and one from the Republic of Ireland, all from widely differing sectors of industry, from sports goods to concrete pre-casting machinery. The stories of two of them illustrate how strategic management has a meaning for small firms as well as large – and probably also that many firms are already planning strategic-ally without realising that is what it is called.

Grabner Sports of Austria was started in 1975 by Wolfgang Grabner who, while working for an Austrian sports goods com-pany, had seen a number of openings in the market. His com-pany grew quickly, making and selling a number of accessories for different sports.

Turnover and staff increased every year and the company moved into a new factory in 1980. But Mr Grabner began to become concerned about trends in the economy, in particular when he saw well-known and established firms in the sports goods field running into difficulties and going out of business.

He saw the need to develop new strategies in order to continue and build the company's growth in the future and so embarked on a study of the company's strengths and carried out research into likely future trends. He picked up several pointers to likely trends from a study by the Patelle Institute in Frankfurt of potential changes in leisure-time needs up to the end of the century.

With the help of consultants recommended by the chamber of commerce the company drew up a written plan of where it wanted to go. In outline the plan was to create, produce and sell products which people needed in their leisure time, products for 'daring' sports, to be distributed in traditional sports shops and warehouses.

Finally, 'We want to become the number one in number two items,' that is not to make skis or bicycles but to produce appropriate ranges of accessories. As the increase in leisure time would come to a considerable extent from people being out of work rather than from increased wealth they saw that 'the available money for leisure will decrease due to high costs of living and sinking income'.

The products were therefore oriented towards items which would help people keep down the cost of their leisure-time activities.

With the help of the manager of the innovation institute linked to the chamber of commerce a group, including a designer, a sales consultant, champions in various sports, a doctor, a leisure psychologist, and members of the company, was brought together which in regular sessions over two years created and developed a new product line for leisure and spare time.

While the recognition by Mr Grabner of the need for forward planning was important, it is interesting to note the number of times which he mentioned the help from the chamber of commerce, assisting with links to the right kind of advisers in various areas with which Mr Grabner himself, as a small firm proprietor employing about 50 people, was unfamiliar, as an important linking and signposting activity.

'I am now never afraid about the future – on the contrary I am confident and looking forward to the next decades,' says Mr Grabner.

The problems facing Moffett Engineering of Clontibret County Monoghan were quite different but over the last ten years the company has changed from being a low technology, production-oriented, local market company employing three people to one with medium to high technology, employing 38 skilled people, exporting 90 per cent of its output, and with a positive market orientation.

'The key to the progress of our company has been strategic management,' says Carol Moffett, the firm's managing director, who took over the company in 1972 in her early twenties, on the death of her father. At that time three people were employed in servicing the local market, making moulds for the concrete industry, friction saws for cutting steel and also doing some sub-contract work.

They continued as before for about three years but began to realise they were in a declining market with increased competition. They recognised a need to find new products with improved technology, and to improve marketing and the skills of the workforce.

'I didn't understand then that this was a part of the strategic planning process,' says Miss Moffett.

More emphasis was placed on marketing of the products they were already making and sales showed a marked improvement. Profitability increased, giving the firm confidence to recruit more skilled workers.

Participation in a business development programme at the Irish Management Institute in 1978 forced her to make a detailed, written plan for the company's development. She examined the strengths and weaknesses of Moffett Engineering and then first set about putting right the weaknesses.

They examined the environment in which they operated and identified its competitive advantages.

They knew that the way forward in the concrete industry was to mechanise so they began a programme of research and development into a concrete products pre-casting machine, resulting in the Moffett Multicast System launched in 1980. A cash grant of 50 per cent towards direct development costs was received from the Industrial Development Authority. The company now has a continuing research and development programme.

A new purpose-built factory was equipped with modern machinery – with a 50 per cent grant towards capital costs from the IDA and long-term funding from the Irish Development Bank.

with the factory construction a more sophisticated ... was developed and a decision made to concentrate ... itish market because it was big, close, and its concrete ... was under pressure to cut costs.

... company now manufactures a range of eight different ... nines and systems for the concrete industry, exporting 90 per cent of its output, mostly to Britain but also as far as Australia.

'I am convinced that it would not have been possible for us to survive and grow if we had not recognised the need for a strategic plan for our company. We are now fully committed to the whole concept of strategic planning and we are confident that we can continue to grow and prosper in the years ahead,' says Miss Moffett.

The two examples illustrate clearly that there is nothing magical or mystical about strategic planning and that it can be relevant and beneficial to the smaller company. Stripped of the jargon which can so easily surround it, strategic planning is little more than knowing where the company is going and preparing the way to reach that target.

2.12 Making them pay up

LAWRENCE M. LEWIS, FICM
Chief Executive, The Lewis Group Ltd, 102 Bath Street, Glasgow G2 2EW

Three short paragraphs could save small companies and the rest of British industry over £1 billion a year. And there are no costs involved. No expensive computers. No extra staff. Nothing. Just three paragraphs. Around 300 words. It must be the biggest bargain of all time.

Like most of British industry small firms are probably finding it difficult to get the money in and are being stretched to the limit. Probably by companies bigger than themselves. And probably by companies who know the small firm won't squeal until the very last minute because it is frightened of losing their business.

Our research shows that companies are now taking longer and longer to pay their bills. In 1984 accounts were being settled on average 53 days after they were due to be paid. In 1985 they had stretched out to 60 days. With interest charges costing over £400 a day for every £1 million outstanding, it is costing industry an unbelievable and unnecessary amount of money.

And it could all be avoided if companies included a single three-paragraph contractual interest rate clause in their terms of payment. It would save companies the time and effort involved in going to court. It would also speed up payments overall, boost cash flow and reduce interest charges.

This is a widespread practice in the rest of Europe and North America. In Denmark, for example, every invoice has a payment date. If it is not paid by then 2 per cent is added without question and repeated every month automatically until the account is settled. Its absence in Britain may be yet another symptom of the lack of such attributes as confidence in the service provided, thoroughness, pride and professionalism which have for so long characterised our national approach to the market place.

It is all the more surprising since it is not very hard to realise that funding a business from a source other than sales revenue costs money. The cost is illustrated by the following table which charts the cost of £100,000 overdue assuming an interest rate of 15 per cent:

Days overdue	Interest £
1	41.09
7	287.67
30	1,232.87
60	2,465.75
90	3,698.63
120	4,931.51

It is sad to realise that it is no longer sufficient to offer a modest discount to ensure that one's invoices are paid on time.

If we accept that there are unnecessary costs being carried by the firm arising from slow payment of invoices, the next question to be considered is who should foot the bill. Should it be passed on to those consumers who pay on time, thereby making the firm uncompetitive in its pricing? Should it be borne by the firm, thereby making it inefficient in terms of rewards to its shareholders? Or should the culprits pay and realise that they will need to look elsewhere for free unsecured loans in future?

Part of the answer is to incorporate in one's terms and conditions a clause entitling the supplier to an interest rate of, say, 2

47

per cent above MLR until payment has been made in full. To be effective the clause must be incorporated formally in the conditions of sale and must be brought to the attention of the purchaser prior to the goods/services being supplied.

1. Clause one should stress the company's terms of payment are 30 days from date of despatch; that in the case of default they reserve the right to suspend deliveries and take steps to recover the outstanding amount as well as compensation for losses incurred.
2. Clause two should say the seller is entitled to 2 per cent interest above Bank of England minimum lending rate from the date until the account is settled.
3. Clause three should forbid the buyer from withholding payment in whole or in part because of any disputes.

The invoice should state unambiguously the due date and refer to the appropriate clause. There must also be no dispute, ie the debt must be accepted.

It is so simple, I cannot understand why companies don't do it already. Everybody says payment in 30 days. But it's the red lie of the credit industry. Few people stick to it. Maybe less than two in a thousand. So long as people get paid eventually nobody seems to worry. It's absurd.

3
Getting Organised

ROD MARGREE, Manager, Barclays Bank

3.1 'I leave that to my accountant'

Numerous proprietors of small businesses have uttered those immortal words, when asked for an explanation of a particular item that appears in their company's trading and profit and loss account or balance sheet. But are they really just a set of figures produced by the accountant to satisfy the Inland Revenue and the bank manager, and of no real benefit to the proprietor? Or can they be used to analyse the performance of the company or firm and thus act as an aid to decision-making in relation to future trading plans? The use of balance sheets and accounts as a 'tool' of management is of paramount importance to the proprietor, whereas the 'satisfaction' of the bank manager and the tax inspector is, in a sense, purely a by-product. There are, however, certain factors which should be borne in mind when analysing annual accounts:

1. A balance sheet details the asset and liability structure of a business at a given point in time, and the position reflected a day later may be very different.
2. The figures may not reflect the current market valuation of certain items (eg a factory) or may be dependent on subjective judgements. However, consistency of approach will enable reasonable assessments to be made.
3. The effect of inflation on the purchasing power of the pound should be borne in mind when comparing this year's performance with last year's.
4. A balance sheet does not reflect satisfactorily all the strengths and weaknesses of a business. Figures do not appear which effectively value the skills of its managers and other employees or, indeed, its market position.

Various techniques can be used to aid management in the interpretation of annual accounts. The approaches adopted within these techniques can also vary and it is obviously not possible within the confines of this section to produce an exhaustive appraisal. We, therefore, propose to look at various aspects of the technique known as 'ratio analysis' relating it to a hypothetical manufacturing company's accounts for 1983 and 1984 (Tables 3.1 and 3.2).

If the figures in these accounts for 1984 are looked at in isolation they give only a broad indication as to the health of the business. However, when collated with other figures as a ratio, a fuller picture will emerge. Following a comparison with similar figures for 1983 a trend will be reflected which may necessitate corrective action. There are various key ratios which can be used to assess profitability and liquidity, but they should be used with caution, given the limitations of the figures.

The profitability ratios

GROSS PROFIT PERCENTAGE

This is calculated by dividing the gross profit achieved in the period into sales and expressing the factor as a percentage. By relating this ratio to our hypothetical company it can be seen that in 1983 a gross profit percentage of 36 per cent was achieved, whereas in 1984 it declined to 30 per cent. It is important to identify the causes of this decline. By analysing the material content of sales for both periods, using a similar approach to that adopted in calculating the gross profit percentage, it can be seen that this is constant at a figure of 50 per cent. However, the labour content of sales has increased from 14 per cent to 20 per cent. The underlying causes of the fall-off in gross profitability and increase in labour content per pound of sales value can be numerous. The following may be applicable:

1. A decline in productivity.
2. Increases in wage rates not passed on to the customer.
3. A deliberate policy of price cutting to achieve a larger share of the market.
4. Other competitive influences.
5. A change in the product mix.
6. Quantity discounts.

A decline in gross profitability is not necessarily bad. It can result from a change in pricing strategy with a view to expansion or, indeed, to ensure the survival of the company. However, if declining productivity is the cause, corrective action is obviously required if the company is to improve its performance in the future.

KEEP YOUR COMPANY'S BOOKS IN ORDER WITHOUT OVERTAXING YOURSELF

Do you find the rules and the language of bookkeeping a complete mystery?

Or the thought of dealing with VAT alarming?

And have you ever worried about how you're going to keep your invoices and records well-organised?

If so, then you need 'Bookkeeping in Context', a new publication that offers a complete solution to start-up companies.

It breaks bookkeeping down into twelve manageable tasks and guides you through each one, using colour photos to make things clear, and plain English, not jargon, to make things clearer still.

With your copy of 'Bookkeeping in Context' you get the Starter Pack of attractively-designed System Sheets (which will last most new companies a year), and step by step instructions for filling them in. And there are handy pockets for things like invoices and the company cheque book.

So, if you want to be a go-ahead company, go ahead and get yourself a copy.

SPEND TIME ON YOUR BUSINESS, NOT ON YOUR BOOKS

Write to Johnson Hall Publishing, 2 Sekforde Court, 217-219 St John Street, London EC1V 4LY or call us on 01-250-1199 for a copy of our free 8 page colour brochure.

'A' Company Limited

The balance sheets

	1983 (£)	1984 (£)
FIXED ASSETS		
Leasehold property	10,000	9,000
Plant and machinery	25,000	28,000
Fixtures and fittings	3,000	4,000
	38,000	41,000
Add		
CURRENT ASSETS		
Cash	1,000	—
Debtors	52,000	78,000
Stock	62,000	100,000
	115,000	178,000
Total assets	153,000	219,000
Less		
CURRENT LIABILITIES		
Creditors	30,000	50,000
Bank	40,000	71,000
	70,000	121,000
Net assets	83,000	98,000
FINANCED BY		
Share capital	10,000	10,000
Profit and loss reserves	73,000	88,000
	83,000	98,000

Table 3.1   *The accounts*

NET PROFIT PERCENTAGE

The method of calculation is similar to that outlined in the previous section. When applied to the example, a net profit percentage of 10 per cent is reflected in 1983, whereas 1984 shows a decline to 5 per cent. Arguably, it is even more relevant, given that profits are a major source of finance for a company, that

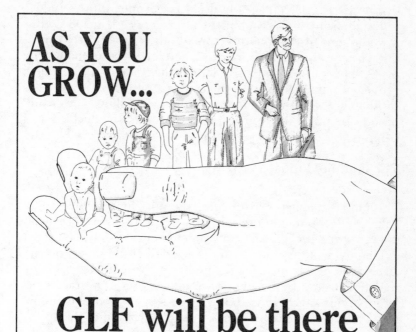

profit in money terms has declined from £25,000 to £15,000, despite an increase in sales of some £50,000. To fully assess the reasons for the fall in net profitability it is necessary to express overheads as a percentage of sales. In fact some improvement is reflected: from 26 per cent in 1983 to 25 per cent in 1984. Thus, it would appear that the directors of our company are controlling costs in this area. It follows, therefore, that the fall in net profitability of the company is largely the result of the decline in gross margins. However, in the converse situation, where gross profitability is constant and net margins are falling, steps would have to be taken to control the escalation of overhead costs if continued growth in net profit terms is to be achieved.

The liquidity ratios

COST OF SALES STOCK

This ratio is calculated by dividing the stock figure shown in the balance sheet into cost of sales. Cost of sales is arrived at by deducting gross profit from the annual sales total. This approach to identifying annual stock turn is generally valid unless there is an element of seasonality in the trading activity. In those circumstances it would be more appropriate to use an average stock figure in this analysis. Assuming that the hypothetical company is not affected by seasonal trends the application of the cost of sales/stock ratio indicates the following annual stock turns: in 1983, 2.58:1, and in 1984, 2.10:1. The investment in stock has also increased by some £38,000 to £100,000. If the stock turn in 1983 had been maintained in 1984, the investment would have increased by some £20,000. The additional investment factor

	1983 (£)	1984 (£)
Sales	25,000	300,000
Less		
Purchases (stock-adjusted)	(125,000)	(150,000)
Direct labour	(35,000)	(60,000)
Gross profit	90,000	90,000
Less		
Overheads	65,000	75,000
Net profit (pre-tax)	25,000	15,000

Table 3.2 *The profit and loss accounts**

* The implications of Corporation Tax have been ignored.

can have major effects on the company in terms of profits (the interest cost) and liquidity. The survival of a company depends upon its ability to generate cash and an over-investment in stock can be a decisive factor in this equation.

SALES/DEBTORS
It is usual to express the debtor figure in terms of a number of days' sales. Thus the ratio is calculated:

$$\frac{\text{Debtors}}{\text{Sales}} \times 365 \text{ days}$$

The seasonality factor mentioned in the previous section must be borne in mind. However, given the assumption made in relation to the example, it can be seen that debtors in 1983 were outstanding on average for 76 days, whereas in 1984 the position worsened to 95 days. This obviously had an effect on cash and, indeed, on profits in terms of the interest cost on the increased investment. An additional factor to be considered is the effectiveness of the debtor control function in the company.

Conclusion
Without going into many complexities, this article has tried to show the way in which balance sheets and accounts can give important information on how a company is performing. The difference between profit and cash should always be borne in mind. A company can be very profitable, but may nevertheless have a liquidity problem: a bulging warehouse does not pay the wages or creditors at the end of the week! In sections 3.5, 3.6, 3.7 and 3.8, we will expand on this aspect, when discussing in more detail the fields of debtor control, stock management, and profit and cash planning.

3.2 Borrowing from a bank: presenting your case

The banks place great store by the banker/customer relationship, and rightly so. However, on occasions, a lack of understanding of each other's problems can arise. This is probably caused partially by a language barrier (ie the use of trade terminology by both bankers and customers), and also as a result of both parties having insufficient knowledge of how each other's business really operates. This situation is unsatisfactory from both the banker's and the small businessman's point of view, as it could result in a bank declining to provide finance for what may be a perfectly reasonable business venture. What can then be done to improve this situation?

The banks are in business primarily to lend money (subject to certain Bank of England constraints) and thus have, in a sense, a commodity 'for sale'. But have we, as bankers, given sufficient guidance to our customers as to how to 'buy' this commodity? This is a question that only our small business customers can objectively answer, but it is probably fair to say that communication in this area can be improved.

As a contribution towards this communication barrier, we attempt within this article to suggest ways in which a small businessman should present his case to his bank manager, with a view to obtaining finance for his business.

A banker, when presented with an application by a customer for finance, asks a few very simple questions:

1. What is the nature of the business?
2. What relationship will the bank's money and other borrowed monies bear to the proprietor's own stake (share capital and reserves) in this business, and how will the bank's money be used?
3. How competent are the people managing the business?
4. What are the plans for repayment and what will be the bank's position if the plans do not come to fruition?

In order that these questions may be answered, the small businessman should be prepared to provide his bank manager with the appropriate information. This falls into three categories, each of which is considered below.

Historical information

Although the future trading potential of the business is the vital factor in determining whether a bank will make a loan, the bank manager will wish to review the past trading record. The information required will include:

1. Details of the history of the company which will cover the areas of activity and trading record.
2. Audited balance sheets and accounts for the past three to five years, which should include the full profit and loss account statement.

3. Details of the borrowing record of the business.

Generally, much of this information will already be available to the bank manager. However, if this were not the case, arrangements should be made to provide it.

The present situation

Within this category, the small businessman should be prepared to provide the bank manager with the following information:

1. The audited, or alternatively the unaudited, accounts for the most recently completed financial year.
2. Details of the company's present ownership and management.
3. Details of the resources of the company in terms of premises, plant and machinery and the labour force.
4. The current nature of the products of the company and details of the marketing strategy which is being applied.
5. Up-to-date management information which will reveal the current levels of profitability, details of the investment in debtors and stock, and liability to creditors.

Future plans

Armed with the information outlined in the two previous sections, the bank manager will have a picture of the business in terms of its past performance and current trading position. To complete this picture, attention must be turned to the most important factor in the equation: the future plans of the business and thus the reasons for bank finance. In order that the plans can be fully assessed, it is usual for these to be quantified in the form of budgets for capital expenditure, sales, profit and cash. The bank manager will, therefore, be assisted in the assessment of the proposition if the following are provided:

1. Budgets for capital expenditure, sales, cost of sales, overheads and profit for, say, the next 12 months.
2. A cash flow forecast which, in effect, interprets the trading and capital expenditure budgets in cash terms and thus helps to identify the projected borrowing requirements.

Conclusion

The presentation of your case in the manner suggested will not necessarily guarantee the bank manager's agreement to the level of lending which is reflected in the cash flow forecast. However, it will ensure that the bank manager has a greater understanding of the business and its needs, and thus will be in a better position to offer constructive advice and assistance, with a view to enabling the fulfilment of the plans of the small businessman.

3.3 Borrowing from a bank: how a bank manager assesses your case

In an attempt to improve the communication between the bank manager and the small businessman, we outlined in section 3.2 the ways that a case for finance for a business should be presented to the bank. Problems arise in this area mainly as a result of both parties having insufficient knowledge of how each other's businesses really operate. If this knowledge or communication gap is to be effectively bridged we should discuss the other factor in the equation: how does the bank manager assess the case for finance presented and what criteria does he apply in this appraisal?

It is difficult to give a definitive answer to these questions as, although the bank manager is concerned with factors (which by definition can only pertain to history), the most important factor to be considered is the future trading potential of the business. The bank manager, therefore, has to test the assumptions made in the compilation of the future trading plans in such areas as the market potential of the products and profitability levels, etc. The conclusions which are drawn will be based on the bank manager's judgement of the probability of the successful fulfilment of the plans. It can be seen, therefore, that the decision to lend or not to lend is not based upon any easy scientific formula. The areas in which judgements are made fall within five main categories, which are outlined below.

Management
This is a vitally important area both in terms of the people and the function. The bank manager will wish to be assured that the management comprises persons of integrity, who are responsive to and aware of the need for change and have the appropriate skills in terms of marketing, production, finance and personnel. In addition, he will assess the quality of the management infor-

mation and control systems. This includes such a
budgeting, cash flow forecasting, profit and loss reporting
chasing, costing and pricing. The bank manager's assessme
this area will be a major influencing factor in his deci..on
whether to lend.

Products

The bank manager will also wish to discuss with the small businessman the nature of the company's products and their position
in the market place generally. The questions which he will ask
include:

(a) Is demand for the products declining, static, or rising?
(b) Are the products competitively priced?
(c) Is the quality of the products appropriate in relation to the
    market that is sought?
(d) What are the implications of any change in product mix on
    volume and profit?
(e) Are the existing and proposed sales levels well spread in
    terms of customer mix?

Prospects

In this category, consideration will be given to the influences of
technological and environmental change which may affect the
future of the business. This will be coupled with an assessment
of the availability of the resources necessary for the successful
fulfilment of the various sales and profit targets of the business.
An appraisal will, therefore, be made of the position regarding
the supply of raw materials and labour, and of the adequacy of
premises, plant and machinery.

The capital base

In general terms the capital base comprises share capital, capital
reserves and revenue reserves (the profit and loss account), less
any intangible assets such as goodwill. In this section, we cannot outline in detail the position regarding deferred taxation,
but, depending upon various factors, this reserve is often included as part of the capital base of the business.

Having ascertained arithmetically the size of the capital base,
a review will then be undertaken of the nature and quality of the
asset structure of the business. This is important, as certain
assets could either be under- or overvalued, and this would obviously affect the size of the capital base. Alternatively, the business may have a relatively high investment in fixed assets which

may affect the working capital position. It is difficult to generalise in the latter area, as any assessment of the asset structure, and indeed of the business itself, must be related to the type of industry in which it operates.

It is usual for bankers to relate the size of the capital base of the business to the level of borrowed money required. This will include both bank facilities and finance available from other sources. This is known as the gearing relationship. As a 'rule of thumb', the bank manager will tend to look for not more than a 1:1 relationship between the capital base and the level of borrowed monies. However, this should not be seen as a definitive guideline, and in some cases he may wish to see the gearing relationship at a lower level than 1:1. Equally, however, where a business has strong management, good products and a growing market, good budgetary control, and above average profitability levels (both historic and projected) giving adequate interest cover, it would not be unusual to see a gearing relationship somewhat in excess of 1:1 being acceptable.

Working capital surplus

The working capital of the business is ascertained by deducting the current liabilities (creditors and bank overdraft, etc) from the current assets (stock and debtors, etc). An assessment of the nature of the working capital surplus is undertaken by using ratio analysis. This will reflect underlying trends in terms of investment in debtors and stock and the bank manager may well wish to review the controls in these areas. For example:

1. Are the debts being collected at a reasonable rate or are there monies outstanding in excess of the normal terms of trade?
2. Is stock turn satisfactory or is a proportion of the stockholding unsaleable?

This is an important area as the continuing circulation of current assets is the life-blood of the business. Any check on the circulation will affect the liquidity of the business and thus its ability to survive.

Conclusion

As a result of making an appraisal of the case presented to him in these five equally important categories, the bank manager will be able to assess the degree of risk that the bank runs in lending money to the business. If the risk is considered reasonable, the bank manager will be prepared to lend, though his assessment in this area may occasionally result in security being requested.

3.4 Is an overdraft always relevant?

In sections 3.2 and 3.3 we discussed the ways in which a case for finance for a small business should be presented to and is assessed by the bank manager. However, we have not yet commented on a key question that should be considered: what type of finance best meets the needs of the business? Many small businessmen, having identified a need for an injection of finance from a bank, tend to ask their bank manager to provide them with an overdraft facility. But is an overdraft always relevant? For example, let us look at a small engineering company, the directors of which have approached their bank for an overdraft facility of £40,000 to finance the acquisition of some new plant and equipment costing £20,000 and the growth in investment in debtors and stock which will occur as a result of their planned expansion programme. We shall assume that the bank has agreed to provide the requested finance at a level of £40,000. Thus the question to be resolved purely relates to the type of finance that is appropriate.

In this hypothetical case there are two distinct purposes for which finance is required: (1) the financing of the acquisition of fixed assets and (2) the financing of an increase in current assets. Overdraft finance is generally of a short-term nature and its primary purpose is to assist in the financing of current assets such as stock and debtors. It follows, therefore, that this type of facility generally does not have a part to play in the financing of long-term or fixed assets. In our example the company wish to acquire items of plant costing £20,000 which will probably have an economic life of, say, six or seven years. It would seem to a bank manager, therefore, that the financing of these assets should be 'matched', thereby linking the payment for the assets to their ability to generate extra profits and cash for the business. In this case, it may well be appropriate for the bank to provide an overdraft facility of £20,000 to finance the anticipated increase in debtors and stock and in addition to make

available a medium-term loan of £20,000 repayable by the company over, say, five years.

We have attempted, by using this example, to emphasise that overdraft facilities are not always appropriate. It is not possible within the limitations of this section to produce a definitive list of the forms of finance that a bank can provide to fit the varying needs of the small corporate customer. However, we will attempt briefly to cover the more common types of finance that are available to small businessmen.

Overdraft

This type of facility is well-known and is commonly made available to assist in the financing of the purchase of raw materials, the manufacture into finished goods and, following sale, the financing of the investment in debtors. Repayment is thus achieved on receipt of funds from debtors. An overdraft is thus in many ways a 'revolving' type of facility forming part of the ever-moving current asset and current liability structure of the business. Facilities of this type are usually reviewable at least once every 12 months. They may be provided on a secured or unsecured basis, depending on the circumstances. The interest rate payable is negotiable and is linked to the bank base rate.

Medium-term facilities

Medium-term credit may be made available for the acquisition of fixed assets such as factories and plant and machinery, for a period of up to 10 years (exceptionally up to 15 years). The finance is generally provided on a secured basis, but it is an extremely flexible form of facility. Drawings and repayments can be tailored to meet individual requirements. For example, a medium-term loan repayable over a five-year period may be provided to acquire an item of plant. However, the increased profits and cash anticipated from this expansion in productive capacity may well not be reflected until two years after acquisition. The bank can gear the repayment programme to the revenue expectancy, ie nominal repayments in years one and two with the major portion of the loan being repaid in years three to five. Finance agreed on a medium-term basis gives the small businessman the assurance of a line of credit which will not be withdrawn unless default occurs. Interest rates which are generally marginally higher than those charged for short-term monies are either linked to base rates or money market rates.

Leasing facilities

These facilities are, in many ways, an alternative to medium-term credit. They can be used in connection with various assets such as machinery, computers, motor vehicles, etc. Leasing facilities are an additional source of funds which do not affect the gearing of the business and do not tie up valuable working capital. The rentals are fixed at the beginning of the leasing period and, thus, are not affected by changes in interest rates. The finance is provided on the whole of the leased asset and the corporation tax implications of the first year's allowances are taken into account when calculating the rental payments, which are in addition fully allowable as a revenue expense. However, the 'lease or buy' decision is one which should not be taken without seeking advice from your accountant and bank manager.

Export Credits Guarantee Department (ECGD) backed finance

There are various types of finance backed by the Export Credits Guarantee Department which the bank will provide. The most common types relevant to the small business are short-term finance for exports on either bills or notes or open account. A bank will purchase, without recourse, accepted bills of exchange or promissory notes, covering exports secured by ECGD Comprehensive Bank Guarantee where goods are shipped with credit of up to two years from the date of shipment. Against similar security a bank will also advance up to 100 per cent of the value of the goods against proof of export on open account. The finance is made available for goods shipped 'cash against documents' or open-account terms up to 180 days. With both types of facility a substantial improvement can be made in the situation of the business as regards working capital. It is also an extremely inexpensive form of finance, the current interest rate being ⅝ per cent over the prevailing base rate – somewhat cheaper than normal overdraft facilities!

3.5 Controlling debtors

In section 3.1, when the use of ratio analysis as a management tool was discussed, the question of investment in debtors was

briefly mentioned. This area is vitally important, as
of any business depends on its ability to generate c
ample, when a sale is made on credit, a profit may
been earned in accounting terms. However, the cash
be received from the debtor for a considerable period.
debtors are not well controlled and are allowed to incre..c at a
disproportionately faster rate than the growth rate in sales, it is
possible that a cash shortage will occur despite evidence of
profitable trading. How can this situation be avoided? The
bank manager may be able to assist by increasing the company's
overdraft facility, but is this the right answer from the small
businessman's point of view? Further finance from the bank
will result in an increase in the overheads of the business and it
is possible that only a temporary solution has been found which
does not resolve the underlying problem – poor debtor control.

How can improvements be effected in this area? It seems that
certain basic questions have to be answered by the small businessman prior to action being taken. What is the size of the
investment in debtors? How is it financed? How can the investment be reduced without harming the firm's ability to meet its
objectives? To aid the small businessman in this assessment
and in taking suitable action we will outline the various aspects
of debtor control that should be examined.

The significance of debtors

The businessman should be aware of the following factors:

1. What is the cost to the business of granting credit? The costs
   involved can include interest charges, administrative overheads, legal costs, etc.
2. What are the true costs of granting discounts for early payment to customers? It may be worth giving discounts if
   liquidity is a problem, but it should be remembered that a
   2.5 per cent discount for payment within 30 days when the
   normal terms of trade are 60 days is equivalent to an annual
   charge of 30 per cent ($2.5 \times 365/30 = 30.4$).
3. What return on sales do you achieve in your business? If, for
   example, a 3 per cent return is achieved, it is evident that a
   £3000 bad debt will nullify the profit on £100,000 of sales.
   On the other hand, if bad debts are not incurred, are business opportunities being missed?
4. How many days on average does it take to collect one day's
   sales? This is a useful ratio and changes over a period will

give an indication as to the effectiveness of the debt collection system.

5. It is a fact that growth in credit sales volume will necessitate an increase in the working capital requirement. Has the amount been assessed?

Recognition of the implications of these questions is vital to the understanding of the significance of the investment. However, to complete the picture, it is equally important that the detailed procedure of day-to-day control of debtors is fully appreciated.

The management of debtors

It is obviously vital that the creditworthiness of all new customers is assessed. The sources of information which can be used include banks, the trade generally, credit registers, etc. However, it is equally important to check periodically on the creditworthiness of your existing customers. A change in their payment pattern may well suggest that inquiries should be made. In this respect it is always useful to give accounts credit limits in order that any change in trading activity can be readily identified.

Assuming that the credit risk is acceptable and that limits have been established for all the customers, it is vital that a good collection system is in operation. The approach which should be adopted in this respect is fairly simple:

1. Send the invoice as soon as possible, and at the very latest at the time of despatch of the goods. Very few customers pay on invoice, and none pay before it!

2. Send the statements appertaining to the previous month's invoices as soon as possible after the month end; at the latest by the third or the fourth of the month following. Statements are often not sent out until the middle of the following month and this generally results in an extension of the time taken to pay by the customer.

3. State clearly the terms of sale, settlement, etc on all statements and invoices as this can avoid 'delaying tactics' by your customers.

4. Ensure that at the end of the month a list of debtors outstanding is produced, aged on a monthly basis. This document will facilitate the identification of overdue debtors and enable appropriate action to be taken, ie telephone calls, letters (a series of three letters should be devised, by which each is progressively tougher). Do not be afraid to chase

overdue debts. Many businessmen consider that to chase debts from important customers will result in a loss of future business. This fear is more imagined than real, and it is probably fair to say that the companies who 'shout the loudest' tend to be paid and respected for it.

5. Ensure that no further goods are despatched to those customers who appear on the 'overdue list'.
6. Consider the possibility of obtaining credit insurance.

When a debt becomes doubtful it is important to ensure that any action taken is cost-effective. If, for example, the debt is £20, it may well be that the administrative and legal costs involved in recovery will be greater than the original debt. However, when larger sums are involved and it has been established that the debtor is worth pursuing, the employment of debt collectors or solicitors should be considered.

These procedures may appear to be time-consuming, but the implementation of such a system of debtor control may well be highly beneficial to the company in terms of reducing the level of investment in debtors and thereby improving liquidity and profitability.

3.6 Managing stockholding

Another major current asset which in most businesses requires similar attention to debtor control is stock. Stockholding in a manufacturing operation generally comprises raw materials, work-in-progress and finished goods, although in certain cases such items as spare parts for machines or tooling are included in the stock figure. The latter items are of a capital nature and care should be taken in instances where they are included, as this will result in misleading information being presented if, say, annual stock-turn is analysed.

Investment in stock can absorb relatively substantial amounts of working capital and it is obviously of paramount importance to the achievement of the twin objectives of most businessmen in terms of profit and cash that stockholding is maintained at an optimum level. Stock management is therefore an important management function. It should not, however, be confused with storekeeping, which is the physical control of stock. Nevertheless effective stock management cannot be undertaken unless adequate controls are exercised in the stockroom and on the factory floor. These controls should include:

1. The checking of deliveries into stock against the original order.
2. The maintenance of records detailing stock movement, stock levels, etc.
3. The issue of raw materials to the factory, the control of work-in-progress and the monitoring of the level of finished goods as compared with the original job card and issue of raw materials or components, etc.
4. Ensuring that all goods despatched are properly invoiced.
5. Stocktaking on a regular basis to ensure that 'actual' stock agrees with the 'book' stock.

It is also important to the effective operation of the stock management function that a satisfactory method of valuation is devised. It should be noted that any inconsistency in the valuation method used from one trading period to another will affect profitability.

Assuming that the business has a satisfactory information base in this area of stockholding, the management of the business will be in a position to make investment decisions in line with their objectives. However, it is not unusual to encounter certain problems when formulating a stock management policy. There is often a conflict between the various aims of managers of different aspects of the business.

1. The sales manager will generally require a relatively high level of stock of finished goods in order that he and his colleagues can meet demand from stock immediately.
2. The production manager will require sufficient stocks of raw materials, components, etc to ensure that production efficiency is maximised, ie minimal levels of idle time, etc.
3. The purchasing manager's aim may be to 'bulk buy' so that maximum discounts can be obtained, or alternatively to buy forward given the expectation that prices of raw materials will rise.
4. The finance manager's aim will generally be to minimise investment in stock in view of the costs involved and to free working capital.

It is the job of the managing director of the business (who in many small companies will perform most, if not all, of the functions outlined) to balance these individual objectives and formulate a policy which, despite the inherent difficulties, will facilitate as far as is humanly possible the achievement of:

1. A first class service to customers.
2. Efficient production.
3. Investment in stock at an optimum level.

The liquidity and profitability factors which are undoubtedly uppermost in the minds of most businessmen are interrelated. Action to improve the liquidity situation will invariably improve the profitability of the business. The costs of holding stock can be high. These may include the costs of damage, theft, deterioration, the rent charge, wages and insurance. In addition, there are two other important costs:

1. The finance cost, which is highly relevant during a period of high interest rates.
2. The opportunity cost: if stocks include substantial amounts of obsolete or slow moving goods, the business may be losing opportunities to sell other lines profitably.

It is important to establish whether the investment in stock is excessive. A useful ratio which can be used here is cost of sales during a period compared to the average stock level. This will give a picture in broad terms but will tend to be misleading if the trading activity is highly seasonal. If this is the case an appropriate adjustment should be made. However, for the purposes of this section, we shall assume that we have a company whose stock-turn ratio suggests that some seven and a half months' stock is in hand, valued at £150,000. The managing director, after further investigation, decides that his target stock level should be five months' stock, an investment of £100,000. Achievement of this target will benefit cash to the extent of £50,000 and if it is assumed that stockholding costs are running at 20 per cent (not unreasonable given high interest rates), the improvement in profits could be in the region of £10,000. It is a salutary thought that if this company was achieving a profitability factor of 5 per cent on sales, the action taken in respect of stockholding could have a similar effect on profits as an increase in sales of £200,000.

Stock management can be highly complex, but in many small businesses it involves making some basic decisions, ie how much, in what quantities and when, to order. This involves in certain cases the establishment of safety stock levels, the analysis of lead times, which will involve the identification of minimum and maximum stock levels in line with usage. It may not be possible to develop this approach across the entire range of stock items in view of the costs involved: the costs should not outweigh the benefits! It may be appropriate, therefore, to single out the most significant items of stockholding, and Pareto's Law can be of assistance in this respect. This is sometimes known as the 80/20 rule; it suggests that 80 per cent of the value of the total holdings is made up by 20 per cent of the items in stock. This is, of course, a generalisation and the percentages may vary. However, it has relevance in most businesses and often strict control over the top 80 per cent in value terms of the stockholding will be highly cost-effective. In addition to the top 80 per cent in value terms, high value/low volume items and any low value items necessary to smooth production should also be strictly controlled.

There are, of course, more sophisticated ways of controlling and managing stock, but an understanding of the various methods outlined in this article, coupled with well-defined objectives and plans for the business, should facilitate the achievement of optimum stock levels.

3.7 The relevance of planning in a small business

'It is impossible to plan in this business' is a cry that one often hears from the small businessman, and yet he will later go on to suggest that he intends to purchase new plant costing, say, £30,000. These two statements are manifestly contradictory. By indicating his intention to purchase new machinery the businessman is, perhaps subconsciously, planning for the future. This is not to imply that the average businessman takes investment decisions lightly, but that on some occasions this type of decision is taken solely to resolve today's problem, without perhaps considering its full implications in the future.

'Planning', as somebody remarked, 'is a hazardous business, especially when it involves the future.' There is no divine right by which a company repeats its successes of yesterday. As major decisions taken today will influence the future success of the business, it is apparent that most small businesses would benefit from a more systematic approach to planning. In the case of the businessman wishing to purchase new plant, he was, despite his protestations to the contrary, planning for the future, so why not do it systematically? Certain assumptions were being made regarding the future pattern of trading, and considerable benefit could be derived from making these assumptions explicit and testing them systematically and continuously against what occurs.

In summary, what is the case for planning in a small business? The pros outweigh the cons, though the doubters would suggest that 'we have managed without planning so far, so why start now?' or alternatively 'the future is uncertain anyway, so why waste time and effort looking ahead?' These arguments are entirely subjective and are outweighed by the positive factors:

1. If a form of unconscious planning is undertaken anyway, why not do it in a formalised manner?
2. We live in a changing world and a company has to react to that change if it is to survive and be successful.
3. The introduction of a planning system can boost the morale of management and staff alike, producing a feeling that 'we know where we are going' and giving the business a renewed sense of direction. As the effectiveness of management and staff are the key to corporate success, this is a vital factor.
4. A planning system can integrate the management effort by defining individual areas of responsibility and functions to be performed towards the achievement of the overall corporate objectives.

If the case for the need for planning in a small business is accepted, an outline of the way in which planning should be introduced into a small business is necessary. Initially, the small businessman must define his (and thus the company's) objectives. Objective setting is the responsibility of top management; it cannot be delegated. It can also be a difficult task and it may be appropriate to attempt to identify the constraints that operate within the business. This inevitably involves an assessment of strengths and weaknesses of the company. As a first step in this analysis, a review of company performance over the past few years should be undertaken, coupled with an assessment of the business's potential, using the existing resources. It would be appropriate to consider such aspects as productive, administrative, management and sales capacities in relation to premises, plant and people. Analysis here tends to give advance warning of the possible need to acquire new premises or plant, recruit further management or labour, etc to facilitate the achievement of the corporate objectives. Moreover, it is necessary to review the market place in which the company operates, bearing in mind the effects of pricing and any technological change which may influence the life of the products.

This approach may seem a little grandiose, but if realistic objectives are to be set it is self-evident that the constraints operating should be clearly identified. For example, there is little point in a businessman deciding that he wishes to increase sales to £750,000 in the next financial year if the constraints operating in terms of premises and plant restrict the productive capacity of the business to £500,000 per annum in sales terms. Similarly, if the market for the company's products is declining, it would seem unlikely that a sales objective could be set to increase volume by 50 per cent during the next trading period unless the initial sales base was insignificant in relation to the size of the market. These two examples are over-simplifications, but they emphasise the need for general planning.

Following this appraisal it should be possible to set realistic, quantified objectives in terms of sales and profit in the short and medium term. As company success in the final analysis is dependent on profitability and liquidity, it would seem relevant for the objectives, as defined, to be formulated into a capital expenditure budget and operating budgets for sales profit and cash for an initial trading period, bearing in mind such factors as productivity and product mix. A further major constraint may be cash, and, if the availability of this vital ingredient is restricted for any reason, it may be necessary to reappraise the targets for sales, profit and capital expenditure in the short term.

Assuming that the appropriate levels of cash are available, the various budgets and forecasts may be evolved into forms of action plan for the individual members of the management team within the business. This ensures a measure of involvement by these managers in the achievement of the overall corporate objectives, coupled with that other vital factor – accountability. It is of paramount importance that company performance is monitored and compared with the various budgets and forecasts in order that variances can be identified, thereby enabling corrective action to be taken, as appropriate. It may be necessary to make mid-course adjustments in the various targets in the light of performance. This suggests a further important factor: that corporate objectives should always be flexible.

3.8 Budgeting for profit

Budgeting is an activity which is undertaken by most people in their private lives, and yet one constantly meets arguments from small businessmen that it is not relevant to the management of their companies. This resistance is difficult to understand. If the technique is relevant to the management of a household, it must surely have even greater significance in the operation of a business. The family budget is easier to plan, as in most cases income is fairly fixed, as are many of the items of expenditure. In a business, many of the overhead costs are fixed (some will vary with sales volume), but income (ie sales revenue) cannot generally be quantified as easily. It is the area of sales forecasting that appears to cause the most difficulty to businessmen and may to some extent explain their reluctance to use budgetary techniques.

The analogy with family budgeting is too simplistic, but the budgetary techniques used in the management of a small business need not be unduly complicated. A budget is in essence a projected profit and loss account for, say, the next six or twelve months' trading activity. It is based on certain assumptions, but reflects the plans of the management for the future of the business following the identification of their objectives, which have been determined after an analysis of the available resources and the constraints which operate.

In most small businesses the budgetary control system would include the following:

1. *An operating budget.* This budget quantifies the planned trading activity in terms of sales, cost of sales, overheads and thus profit (or loss).
2. *A capital expenditure budget.* This is basically a list of the proposed capital expenditure in the budgetary period. Expenditure in this area is financed from profits in the short or medium term and thus is not included in the operating budget. However, acquisition of capital items has an impor-

tant effect on cash flow and expenditure on capital should be included in the cash budget.

3. *A cash budget.* The cash budget or cash flow forecast attempts to identify the implications of the operating and capital expenditure budgets upon the available cash resources of the business. The liquidity of a business is an important area and is given fuller treatment in section 3.9.

4. *Management information.* It is obviously vital to the fulfilment of any plans that the company's performance is regularly measured and compared with the original budget. For example, variances that occur may necessitate a change in policy or activity if the plans are to be fulfilled (see section 3.10).

There are many advantages of introducing this type of approach into the management of a business. Although it will not guarantee the success of the business, it should make failure less likely! Budgetary control aids decision-making and facilitates the control of expenditure. It acts as a motivator to members of the management team, as they see the budget figures as targets to achieve or indeed to exceed. Moreover, budgeting can be used as an important delegatory tool in the armoury of the small businessman. Responsibility can be given to middle management for specific areas of the business activity using the budgetary control system to measure performance. Finally, the budgetary process gives the businessman the bonus of knowing where he is going as well as where he has been.

We may now outline briefly the way in which operating budgets can be prepared. An operating budget is made up of several interrelated budgets and, for the purposes of this chapter, we shall assume that we are dealing with a small manufacturing operation. The various budgets which have to be prepared are now considered.

The sales budget

It would normally be appropriate to forecast sales for, say, six or twelve months ahead on a month-by-month basis. Ideally, the forecast should be made in unit terms and converted into monetary terms at a later stage. However, this is not always possible. Sales forecasting is considered by some businessmen to be a difficult area, but the following can provide a useful base for projections:

1. *Analysis of past trends.* Historic performance is a useful guide as to the future. An analysis of the individual sales perform-

ance of various products may reflect important trends which may affect future sales levels. The seasonality of sales should also be borne in mind.

2. *Trends in the market place.* Is the market expanding or contracting? Is competition increasing? What effect will price increases have upon demand, if any? These are important questions, the answers to which will have an important bearing on the future of the business.

3. *The forward order book.* This can give important information about anticipated sales levels in the short term.

4. *Reports from the sales force.* Salesmen spend their time dealing with customers and should be in a position to make a useful contribution as to future sales levels.

5. *Reports from major customers.* An inquiry to major customers as to their likely future requirements can be rewarding. Indeed, it may facilitate relatively accurate forecasting for the major part of the sales budget.

Cost of sales budget

To establish the monthly cost of materials necessary to support budgeted sales, the number of units to be sold each month should be multiplied by the unit cost. If this is impracticable it would not seem unreasonable to base material costs on the historic material usage relationship allowing for any factors which may cause this relationship to change. Budgeting in this area should take into account such factors as changes in stock levels, manufacturing lead times, etc.

Wages costs pertaining to the manufacturing process should be included in this budget. The projection should take into account planned increases in the wage rate, employers' National Insurance contribution, and productivity factors. In some cases it is appropriate to include certain manufacturing overheads in the compilation of the cost of sales budget.

Overhead budget

Preparation of this budget is generally relatively straightforward. Historic information derived from previous financial accounts can give a useful guide to trends. However, the budget for the next six or twelve months should take into account any known changes in the overhead structure as well as cost escalation resultant from inflation.

Armed with these budgets the small businessman will be able to calculate the level of profit which may be derived in the trad-

ing period, ie sales minus cost of sales plus overheads. It should be remembered, however, that certain components of these budgets are based on assumptions, and thus monitoring of performance is paramount if financial control of the business is to be maintained.

3.9 Budgeting for cash

The concept of cash budgeting, or cash flow forecasting as it is otherwise known, is not new. Many large companies have been using the technique as a tool of management for many years. It is, perhaps, only during the past five or ten years that cash flow forecasting in smaller businesses has gained some momentum. However, there still exists more than a measure of resistance to its use and its validity in the context of operating a small business is often denied. This is unfortunate. Company success and, in some cases, survival are dependent on the achievement of a mix of two main factors, namely profitability and liquidity. Although profitability is obviously a vital ingredient, it is equally important that liquidity is maintained. The most common reason for the demise of a business is that it is unable to meet its commitments as they fall due. Obviously, many factors can contribute to the onset of such a crisis, but liquidation or bankruptcy inevitably follows when the business runs out of cash.

A cash flow forecast is based on a set of well-defined assumptions and inevitably the 'actual' cash flows will not always correlate precisely with the original projection. This discrepancy occurs because the cash plan is developed from the various budgets for sales, cost of sales, overheads and profit, which are themselves based on assumptions and the views of the management as to the future. However, given that a case is made for business planning in order that the corporate objectives can be achieved by maximising the use of the available resources, it follows that the planning process should incorporate the management of cash, arguably the scarcest of resources.

A cash flow forecast should enable the businessman to answer the following questions:

1. Can the plans which I have for my business for, say, the next

six or twelve months, be achieved within the available cash resources?
2. What effect will any planned capital expenditure have on the cash position?
3. At what time will further finance be required from the bank and what type of facilities will be needed?

The technique of cash flow forecasting, used intelligently and updated regularly, can, together with the other planning 'tools', provide information vital to the effective management and control of a business.

The formulation of a cash flow forecast is, for most businesses, a relatively simple operation, provided that adequate base information – the various operating and capital expenditure budgets – is available. Some businessmen attempt to produce cash flow forecasts without preparing these two original budgets, but this method has the inherent risk of inaccuracies. The cash flow forecast is, therefore, a restatement in cash terms of the original budgets, taking into account the timing differences and excluding the non-cash items of revenue and expenditure.

The process of producing a cash flow forecast usually follows the pattern outlined below.

Production of operating and capital expenditure budgets
These budgets will have been produced in monetary terms on a month-by-month basis. For example, sales will have been projected on a monthly basis according to the anticipated timing of invoicing. Similarly, the purchase of raw materials will have been planned to facilitate the achievement of the production cycle and the stockholding policy of the business. Direct labour costs may have varied month-by-month in line with the peaks and troughs in production, but it is quite probable that the overhead budget has been produced on a six-monthly or annual basis. The cash flow forecast will therefore interpret these budgets in terms of the receipts and payments of cash.

Production of the cash flow forecast

SALES
To project the timing of receipt of debtor monies as per a particular month of sales, it is necessary to look historically at the collection times which are being achieved. The implications of VAT must also be considered. For example, if all sales are to the

home market, the budgeted sales figure must be increased by 15 per cent for the purposes of the cash flow forecast.* If these factors are not recognised there will be an in-built inaccuracy in the forecast. Following the review of credit allowed, it should be possible to identify average debt collection times. For example:

1. 50 per cent of debtors collected in the month following invoice – ie 30 days.
2. 25 per cent within 60 days and the remainder within 90 days.

It would perhaps be helpful if we outlined these points by way of a brief example (see Tables 3.3 and 3.4). We shall assume that we are dealing with a small company whose sales are all achieved on the home market. The budget relates to six months' trading.

Month	1	2	3	4	5	6
Sales (000s)	20	25	30	35	20	25
Add VAT at 15% Sales (including VAT)	23	28.75	34.5	40.25	23	28.75

Table 3.3 *Operating budget*

* This does not apply to sales overseas as exports are zero rated.

	50%	25%	25%	Total
Month 4	(3) 17.25	(2) 7.19	(1) 5.75	30.19
Month 5	(4) 20.13	(3) 8.56	(2) 7.19	35.88
Month 6	(5) 11.5	(4) 10.06	(3) 8.63	30.19

Table 3.4 *Making a cash flow forecast*

N.B. The figures in brackets indicate the month in which the sales were invoiced.

The cash flow forecast is for months four to six inclusive and the timing of receipts from debtors is in line with the earlier assumptions.

PURCHASES
A similar approach should be adopted to that described for sales, taking into account the implications of VAT and the average period of credit taken.

DIRECT LABOUR
The costs, including the employer's contribution, should be planned for payment in the month for which they are budgeted in the operating plan. This avoids complications in terms of the forecast, although it is accepted that most companies tend to take a short period of credit from the Inland Revenue.

OVERHEADS
Analysis of the cash book, etc will facilitate identification of the usual payment times for these costs. For example, rent is usually payable quarterly and rates on a half-yearly basis. It should also be remembered that although depreciation is a revenue item it does not affect cash. It should, therefore, be excluded in terms of the cash budget.

CAPITAL AND OTHER EXPENDITURE
If an item of plant or a motor vehicle is being purchased during the period in question, the cash outlay involved should be detailed in the month in which acquisition and payment are planned. In the event that medium-term financing is to be arranged, either from a bank or a finance house, it would be appropriate to enter the cash injection from these sources on the receipts side of the forecast. The appropriate reduction programme in respect of these loans should be inserted thereafter. In terms of capital expenditure, do not forget to budget for payment of corporation tax, etc.

Conclusion
At this stage the businessman will have produced various schedules of cash receipts and payments, which should be compiled into a single document. The monthly cash inflows and outflows should be calculated and related to the cash book balance on a monthly basis. The document thus produced will provide the businessman with a plan of the cash requirement of

the company for the predetermined period which will, if used with the other budgetary systems, greatly aid the planning and control of the business. It should be remembered that, if cash budgeting is to be a useful management tool on a continuing basis, regular monitoring of actual cash flows is necessary. Any discrepancies between forecasts and actual flows should be analysed and remedial action taken to ensure that liquidity and profitability are maintained.

3.10 The relevance of management information systems in a small business

Informed managers are better managers. It is fair to say that we all wish to be better managers, bearing in mind that good management is the key to 'corporate success'. However, one still finds businessmen who attempt to achieve this goal with one hand tied behind their back. In other words, these managers do not have the benefit of regular information on the performance of their businesses. It is often suggested by such managers that as they are involved with the day-to-day running of the business they have their fingers on the pulse and therefore do not need, as they call it, sophisticated accounting systems. Alternatively, or perhaps as well, one hears the view expressed that to produce such information would cost too much. It is difficult to accept either of these arguments. While not decrying for one minute the necessity for a manager to have 'his finger on the pulse', if, in addition, he has relevant information to hand on a regular basis, this would inevitably improve the management of the business. As for cost, the introduction of certain simple management reports does not necessarily involve increased costs, but may require a reassessment being undertaken as to the use that is made of management time.

What then are the basic ingredients of a good management information system? First, the information should be up to date. There is little point in having management information produced today which pertained to company performance of some three or six months previously. The situation may well have changed in the interim and thus current decisions based upon out of date information may be totally inappropriate. Second, the information produced should be simple, easy to read, and highlight the factors relevant to the management of the business concerned. In some companies masses of information is produced for the directors but has not been used as its complexity belies its usefulness. One should not lose sight of the basic purpose of a management information system. Its function is to facilitate the monitoring of business performance, enabling management to review current trading and to aid decision-making. This review should, ideally, incorporate a reassessment of the constraints that operate in the business environment and their effect upon future trading performance, such as availability of labour and cash, and the overall state of the market in which the business operates. This is not an easy task and it is vital, therefore, that the key information factors involved are identified and the appropriate systems introduced to aid management if corporate success is to be achieved and sustained.

Corporate success depends on the achievement of adequate or planned levels of profitability and liquidity, and thus any basic management information system should be designed to monitor performance in the following important areas.

Profitability

The production of a profit and loss report on a regular basis is probably the most important ingredient of any management information system. The degree of regularity required must be decided by individual managers. In some businesses monthly figures are produced, but for many small businesses, quarterly reports are probably appropriate.

The compilation of a profit and loss report is the end result of producing various constituent reports (see Table 3.5).

The task of producing these reports is not difficult, but there are one or two areas which can cause some concern. The first is the question of stock valuation. This is an all-important area. A full stocktake in a business with a substantial number of stock items can be time consuming, and, if undertaken on a regular basis, disruptive, costly and thus counter-productive. In this type of case it may be possible to use an application of the concept of Pareto's Law or the 80/20 rule (see section 3.6). When applied by management accountants in the context of stock valuation, it is suggested that 80 per cent of the value of the total holdings is made up by 20 per cent of the whole, in unit terms. This is obviously a generalisation, but in many cases, by applying a variation of this law, it is possible to produce a sensible stock valuation. To arrive at a stock figure using this method, it is necessary to carry out a physical check of the more expensive items held and to calculate a total value by adding an appropriate percentage for the remainder. Another method which can be used, if this approach or a full stocktake is not considered feasible, is that of calculating closing stock values by use of an historic gross profit percentage. However, this is only suitable in a business which has a fairly constant trading pattern and where there is no marked seasonality or discount structure in the sales activity.

The second area which can produce some difficulty is that of overheads. For example, certain overheads are paid on an annual basis and if the entire cost was charged to a particular quarter's profit and loss account, wide variations in performance could be reflected. Thus, if, for example, the year's insurance cost was paid in the first trading quarter, it would be appropriate to charge only 25 per cent of the cost to profit and

(a) Cost of sales report		(b) Overhead analysis	
Opening stock	£	Rent and rates	£
add purchases	£	Insurance	£
add wages	£	Salaries	£
	£	Insurance	£
less closing stock	£	etc	£
Cost of sales	£	Total overheads	£

(c) Profit and loss report	
Sales	£
less	
Cost of sales	£
Gross profit	£
less	
Overheads	£
Net profit (pre-tax)	£

Table 3.5 *Compiling a profit and loss report*

loss account; the remainder should be charged in equal instalments over the three remaining quarters.

Having overcome these problems it should be possible to compile the various reports outlined previously. Ideally, they should be expanded to include comparison with budget on a periodic and cumulative annual basis to facilitate the analysis of any variances.

Liquidity

The achievement of adequate levels of liquidity is vital to the survival and success of any business, and the businessman has an important responsibility in this area. In the preceding sections we advocated the use of cash flow forecasting techniques and good management of stock and debtors. Whereas the latter are generally matters of day-to-day control, cash flow forecasts (if produced) tend to be put in the drawer and forgotten after presentation to the bank manager. However, if the premise of the importance of profitability and liquidity is accepted, it becomes apparent that the comparison of actual cash flows with the budget can be an extremely relevant management report. Any variances which are identified should be analysed and a revised cash flow forecast produced as part of the constant short-term replanning process that is essential to the well-being of any business.

4
Sources of Finance

CLIVE WOODCOCK

4.1 Introduction

The range of sources of finance for the smaller firm seems to increase every year but in spite of that there is inevitably a chorus of voices from the small business sector that the money is never actually there in reality when it is needed.

One of the reasons for that situation has usually been that the funds talked about were available mainly in large slices which were unsuitable for the small firm. The deficiency tended to be for sums of money of less than £50,000, below which it is not usually economic for conventional sources of capital to operate.

One of the interesting features of the last year or two has been the way in which attempts have been made to fill that gap, attempts which have come from both the private and public sectors.

In the private sector Rank Xerox pension fund, for example, established a link with the London Enterprise Agency and Tyneside Enterprise Agency, Entrust, under which the agencies manage £500,000 from its special investment fund for small companies. Investments made can be up to £50,000 in any one company and are intended for companies at an early stage in their growth. A number of investments have been made and the agencies have been encouraged by the numbers and range of projects offered to them.

The involvement of enterprise agencies in assessment and monitoring is the factor which makes investment on this scale of value to the providers of finance and it is significant that another major company which has long been a strong supporter of the small business sector, Shell UK, has taken this route with its enterprise loan fund.

Shell has provided a total of £500,000 which has been allocated to enterprise agencies in Cardiff, Bolton, Newcastle upon Tyne, Falkirk, Belfast and London, to distribute in loans of up to £5000. The decisions on who gets the money are made by the agencies.

The majority of the Shell funds are intended for young people between 16 and 25 but older people starting up or expanding an existing business are not excluded.

In the public sector the running has been made by local authorities and often the enterprise boards which they have established in setting up loan funds to provide relatively small amounts.

One of the most remarkable features of the small business scene lately has been the explosion of assistance offered by local authorities to entrepreneurs, a growth which is described in more detail in section 4.9.

The government is currently directing more of its attention to improving existing schemes and reducing the bureaucratic burdens on business rather than in devising new schemes.

The venture capital field continued to expand with a sharp rise in the value of investments made by venture capital companies – though many of them are now tending to be rather cautious as they wait to see the performance of their earlier investments.

And it is not only the venture capitalists who are looking at performance; government too is looking for some results from the efforts made in recent years to encourage smaller firms. The banks are also anxious to see an improvement in the performance of the companies receiving finance and are interested in encouraging small business managements to improve their skills, particularly in areas such as financial management, a perennially weak area.

Small business owners do not necessarily want to use the funds available to expand their businesses, as recent research produced for the Small Business Research Trust by a leading academic, Dr James Curran of Kingston Polytechnic, indicates. He found that most small business owners in fact opted for a 'steady state' business 'perhaps only too aware that rapid growth could undermine their independence and autonomy and take them out of their depth managerially'.

The concentration on survival rather than learning and developing the techniques, financial and otherwise, which would help them to grow has also been noted in a very comprehensive survey of manufacturing firms by another academic, Dr Alan Hankinson.

To use the old saying, there may be plenty of water around

but the horse will not necessarily drink it. Finance for a wide variety of purposes is available for the small firm as this special report shows – but the small firm has to be very clear what it wants it for and know how to use it effectively.

4.2 Cash to start

Most people starting a business do so with limited means, and for some raising even the smallest amounts of capital and sustaining themselves through the first year of existence can represent a major problem.

For a large and increasing proportion of people now going into business the way round the problem seems to be the very popular Enterprise Allowance Scheme run by the Department of Employment.

It enables those who are unemployed to obtain an income from the state in the first year of trading, thus softening the blow of the loss of unemployment or supplementary benefit.

Full information about the scheme can be obtained from Jobcentres but basically it provides successful applicants with £40 a week for a year to offset that loss of benefit. Applicants must either be receiving unemployment benefit and have been out of work or under notice of redundancy for eight weeks.

One requirement which sometimes alarms applicants is that they must have at least £1000 to invest in the business, but in fact this does not have to be in cash; it can be in the form of assets or of an overdraft facility at the bank.

In practice this has rarely proved an obstacle and banks have actually been very supportive of the scheme. Midland even offers free business banking services to those taking part.

Accounts, whether in credit or overdrawn, are operated free of charge for all normal banking services during the 52-week period of the scheme. Interest on borrowing or other specific services is charged at normal commercial rates.

The Co-operative Bank also has special facilities and has arranged for new businesses to receive a day's free advice from chartered accountants, Thomson McLintock and Deloitte Haskins and Sells, on setting up a business, preparing a business plan and raising additional finance.

The bank offers commission-free banking for six months to

all new business accounts opened after one or all of these services have been used.

To enter the EAS applicants must be over 18 and under retirement age and propose a business which is suitable for public support, a description which is very wide.

The potential viability of a project is not tested, an omission which has been criticised because it is said that it encourages false hopes and leads unsuitable people into business and on to inevitable failure.

There is, however, counselling advice available from the Small Firms Service for new starters and also from the more than 300 enterprise agencies which exist around the country. Participants can actually have three counselling sessions during the year they are on the scheme.

The allowance is paid every two weeks directly into applicants' business bank accounts. The MSC makes a monitoring visit to all participants three months after joining and half receive a second visit.

Since its inception in 1982 the number of places on the scheme has been steadily increased by the government, which is obviously pleased with the scheme.

The tax treatment of EAS participants is also being improved, as under the scheme previously tax could be paid several times on the allowance payment.

Two major pieces of research have been carried out on the effectiveness of the scheme. The first surveyed a sample of early entrants and showed that 86 per cent of participants who used the full year's allowance were still trading three months after their allowance came to an end.

For every 100 continuing businesses at the 15-month point, 68 additional new jobs had been created of which 24 were full-time and 44 were part-time.

The second major research survey looked at all EAS completers who had entered the pilot scheme and took place three years after they had entered the scheme. This found that just over three out of five who used the full year's allowance were still trading two years after their allowance stopped. For every 100 continuing businesses at the three-year point 99 additional new jobs had been created, of which 50 were full-time and 49 were part-time.

The value of the scheme as a job creation project is also significant as the MSC estimates that while the cost to the exchequer in the first year is £2090, by the third year there is in fact a credit to the exchequer.

About three-quarters of participants are men and one-quarter are under the age of 25. Nearly seven out of ten participants, however, are in the age group 25–54. Nearly two-thirds of the businesses started are in the service sector, 13 per cent in manufacturing and 16 per cent in construction.

Within the service sector 16 per cent of businesses were in retailing with 7 per cent in vehicle repair and other goods and 7 per cent in finance, advertising and other business services.

The Enterprise Allowance Scheme is operated from about 70 Jobcentres around the country where qualified staff are located but information can be obtained from any Jobcentre or by dialling 100 for the operator and asking for Freefone Enterprise.

4.3 Finance for young people

Initiatives aimed at helping young people create their own jobs have increased rapidly recently, and alongside that development has come a growth in the sources of funds available to them.

The amounts available are not huge but are in keeping with the fact that many projects planned by young people only require limited amounts of finance to get them off the ground. Normally, raising even these limited sums would present a problem owing to their lack of both track record and many of the skills potential backers would be demanding.

The sources of funds which have become available are not a soft touch by any means but their aim is to take a different approach from that which would normally be taken by conventional sources. They aim really to provide pump-priming finance which will enable the projects to start and develop to a point where other backers will provide funds needed for further development.

The major organisation involved in providing funds and other assistance for young people wanting to create their own jobs is probably the Prince's Youth Business Trust, which has been formed from a merger of the Youth Business Initiative – which was backed by the Royal Jubilee and Prince's trusts and set up in 1983 – with the Youth Enterprise Scheme and the Fairbridge Society, as a result of which the merged grouping has very considerable assets.

Their activities are aimed at young people under the age of 25 and the range of assistance includes bursaries, loans of up to about £5000, and education and advice for those wishing to start in business. Applicants are expected to produce a business plan and to be prepared to accept continuing advice and support.

Further information can be obtained from the Prince's Youth Business Trust, 8th Floor, Melbury House, Melbury Terrace, London NW1 6LZ (tel: 01-262 1340).

For slightly less young entrepreneurs, Sir Philip Harris, of the Harris Queensway stores group, has started a Young Entrepreneurs Fund, which he has backed with £1 million. The definition of young is usually in the 20–40 age group.

The fund's purpose is to make investments in the range of £50,000 to £100,000 which will help those young people to build and develop successful businesses. A percentage of the fund is, however, being set aside for investment in smaller businesses and start-ups offering good growth and employment potential.

Merchant bankers, Hambros, have also said that they will provide second or third stage finance when this is required and their criteria are met. Any profits from the fund will be reinvested in other young entrepreneurs.

Further information can be obtained from David Wells, executive director, Young Entrepreneurs Fund, Seymour Suite, 65–69 Walton Road, East Molesey, Surrey.

The Northern Youth Venture Fund for projects in northern England is administered by Project North East and recently received a further injection of funds amounting to £60,000 from the government's City Action Team for Newcastle and Gateshead.

The fund has experienced heavy demand and more than £125,000 has been lent to 65 people. Loans are for young businesses, usually at a rate of 5 per cent, up to a maximum of £5000 and over a maximum period of three years.

Further information can be obtained from Project North East, 60 Grainger Street, Newcastle upon Tyne NE1 5JG (tel: 091-261 7856).

Project North East is also one of six enterprise agencies which administer the Shell Enterprise Loan Fund, which also provides loans of up to £5000. These funds are available for small firms just setting up or existing ones which need a little financial help but are particularly oriented towards young people.

The other enterprise agencies involved are London Enterprise Agency (tel: 01-236 3000), Bolton Business Ventures (tel: 0204 391400), Cardiff and Vale Enterprise (tel: 0222 494411), Falkirk Enterprise Action Trust (tel: 0324 665500), and Action Resource Centre (NI), Belfast (tel: 0232 234504).

The Enterprise Allowance Scheme, under which unemployed people above the age of 18 can receive an allowance of £40 a week from the government for a year, is also a source of finance for young people. Information can be obtained from Jobcentres.

There have, however, been criticisms that some young people are encouraged to join the scheme at too early an age, before they have done even basic market research, with the result that their year on the scheme ends by the time they have got the business off the ground and are in need of a boost to cash flow.

There are a number of other schemes in local areas which can be useful to young people starting in business. For example, Birmingham Action Resource Centre's youth enterprise project has linked with three ethnic business groups to operate a loan guarantee scheme, with support from a local charity.

The project does not itself provide funds but guarantees all or part of loans offered by commercial sources to the potential entrepreneur.

Another possible source of funds may be among local charities in an area; they may be able to provide outright grants or soft, unsecured loans. In some areas redundant local educational charities – such as those intended for training young people in obsolete trades – may have funds which can be reallocated.

In Leicester the Thomas White Foundation offers interest-free loans for up to nine years to young people in business. In other areas local authorities are examining ways of reallocating similar funds.

The Scottish Development Agency has also set up a loan fund for young people under 25 and uses local enterprise agencies to run the scheme. In this way the funds and advice under the Enterprise Funds for Youth Scheme are available from one source.

Local authorities may provide funds on their own account to

support young people starting in business. Wandsworth Youth Development, for example, offers grants of up to £500 to young people, helping them to find appropriate advice, information and support, encouraging them to consider what they want to achieve during and beyond their project.

This scheme is not purely for commercial projects; in fact it is aimed at encouraging the self-development of young people and can include drama groups and other community projects.

Some companies also do so; the insurance group, Legal and General, has for some time had a scheme which aims to help young people with soft loans of between £1000 and £2000.

Another potential source of funds for the young entrepreneur is to keep an eye open for local competitions aimed at encouraging the development of small businesses, as often these are aimed at young people.

A scheme which operates at both local and national levels is Livewire; this is not a competition, indeed its prime aim is to encourage the idea of enterprise among young people and to link them with advisers who can help them to develop their ideas into viable propositions. There are, however, awards at both local and national level for the most promising projects.

Livewire is now an annual event with its launch in September. Further information can be obtained from the national director, Livewire, 60 Grainger Street, Newcastle upon Tyne NE1 5JG (tel: 091-261 5584).

4.4 Bank finance

Banks came in for considerable criticism in a recent controversial report on the relationships between banks and their customers, which was hardly surprising given that providers of finance have always been a favourite target for the small business owner. But paradoxically, in spite of their criticisms, the bulk of small firms also said that they were satisfied with the services they received from their banks and had either never changed banks or had no intention of changing.

That complaints arise from time to time, however, is hardly surprising given that banks are by far the largest source of funding for the independent business sector, currently lending it a massive £24 billion, even though only about half of all small businesses borrow at all.

Equally the banks often protest that they do not get credit for the efforts they do make to change what they also admit have not always been 'user friendly' attitudes in the past. A great deal depends on individuals, of course, and one way in which banks are trying to ease this problem is by restructuring networks into business and personal branches, putting people with business understanding in the right places.

Most banks have centralised small business units at head office involved in developing policy towards small business and ever more schemes, but the concentration of expertise on, for example, small business problems in certain branches takes this process a step further.

While banks devote much effort to devising different schemes for providing funds for smaller firms, they are also taking a particular interest in the management skills – or lack of them – present in the business concerned.

National Westminster Bank, for example, recently announced that more than 3000 specially trained small business advisers are to be introduced into branches to help start-ups. They will encourage and help customers with the business plan, cash flow forecast, and operating budgets, and explain the importance of each. They will also help in obtaining specialist advice from other organisations.

Midland Bank has appointed 150 small business development managers located in area offices to provide specialist support and advice and has also expanded its Credo range of business products, originally launched to starter businesses, to cater also for established firms.

One of the facets of Credo is that participating businesses, if they agree to undertake a course of management training, qualify for loans at a rate of 0.5 per cent below their standard small business loan rate. The bank's standard small business loans are available in sums of up to £15,000.

Some schemes have been around for a long time, such as NatWest's business development loan, launched in 1971, which has provided nearly £2 billion up to 150,000 businesses. This scheme provides loans of between £2000 and £250,000 for periods of up to 20 years at rates which vary with the term and security.

New small business customers of Barclays can apply for a business starter loan for working capital and/or asset purchases of up to £15,000 over one to five years at a fixed rate of interest. Lloyds also has a special small business loan scheme for any business purpose in amounts from £1000 to £15,000 at fixed rates of interest for up to five years.

Many bank schemes are similar to one another, such as the links between NatWest, Barclays, Midland, Lloyds and the Co-op and the Rural Development Commission. The Commission's business services division – formerly the Council for Small Industries in Rural Areas – filters applications before they are assessed by the banks. There is also monitoring during the period of the loan but the benefit to the business is that the loans can be on more advantageous terms than otherwise.

The banks also have a number of longer-term schemes for larger sums, such as Midland's business development loan for amounts over £15,000 for periods of up to 30 years at variable or fixed rates, or an option to switch between the two. Lloyds main loan scheme, which provides for any amount from £2000 for periods of up to 30 years, also allows borrowers to switch from a fixed rate to one linked to the bank's rate. Barclays, too, has a flexible loan scheme for amounts or more than £15,000.

The TSB has a variation on this theme with a fixed repayment scheme offering £25,000–£250,000 for up to 20 years. If interest rates generally fall, repayments remain at the agreed level but the term of the loan shortens. If rates rise, the terms is extended at the same repayment level.

A novel scheme has been developed by the Co-operative Bank in joint ventures with local authorities in providing loan guarantees; these are separate from the government's Loan Guarantee Scheme. The Co-op's scheme aims to help businesses in economically hard-hit areas to raise finance which would not otherwise have been available.

All the major banks have special financial packages for franchising proposals, one of the fastest growing areas of enterprise. The Royal Bank of Scotland is providing strong competition in the franchising area for the established leaders. The attraction for the banks in franchising is that returns are usually quicker and the sums involved larger and the failure rate lower than in conventional small businesses.

Some banks are also the main channel for European Community funds directed at small firms, as is the venture capital firm 3i. Typically the kind of funds available from Europe are European Coal and Steel Community loans for coal and steel closure areas, providing funds for up to 50 per cent of the capital investment costs of a project. As with all European schemes it is essential to get approval before starting work, otherwise rejection is virtually certain.

The range of schemes currently available from banks is enormous – and it must not be forgotten that they also provide what is probably the major source of working capital for the smaller firm, overdrafts, though of course interest rates vary and they are repayable on demand.

This is by no means a comprehensive survey of what is on offer but gives an indication of that range and perhaps also some signs that banks are trying to change the perceptions of their independent business customers and improve services.

4.5   Loan guarantee scheme

Much to the surprise of many observers of the small business finance scene, the government's often criticised Loan Guarantee Scheme was given a new lease of life in the 1986 Budget. To many the scheme had seemed to be dead on its feet because of the higher premium, lower guarantee and other restrictions introduced in an attempt to stem the losses, which the government had not expected. It had thought, rather naively, that the scheme would pay for itself.

The businesses which received funds under the scheme were inevitably high risk projects, otherwise they would have been able to obtain finance anyway. One aspect of the scheme was that it gave people who either did not have collateral or were unwilling to provide it a chance of finding capital.

In its peak year of 1982–83 more than 6000 loans were made under the scheme, with the government guaranteeing up to 80 per cent of approved bank loans up to £75,000 in exchange for a 3 per cent premium on the guaranteed part, paid in addition to the bank's own interest rate.

The scale of losses, however, caused the government to cut its guarantee to 70 per cent and raise the premium to 5 per cent in June 1984. This did not reduce the loss rate, however, and further restrictions were introduced later that year. One of the new requirements was that applicants had to provide, where possible, personal security, a requirement which in fact cut right across the basis of the scheme.

Other curbs were more acceptable, including the need for a business plan giving details of management, products, markets. Management accounts also had to be produced to the lending bank every three months. These were necessary in view of the poor financial planning and inadequate monitoring by banks which had been a feature of early failures.

The result of those measures, however, was to reduce loan guarantees to 2000 in 1984–85 and to a mere 550 in 1985–86, as banks were unwilling to market a scheme which many thought the government was preparing to ditch and which potential borrowers found too onerous and too expensive. The rate of loss, unfortunately, did not seem to show any reduction and continued to run at a rate of around two out of five businesses, sharply higher than the generally accepted national average for failures among smaller firms of one in three.

The government clearly saw in the end the advantages of what, at the very least, was a very cheap job creation scheme.

The result was a move in the 1986 Budget to extend the life of the scheme by three years, ending the uncertainty over its future. The premium was halved to 2.5 per cent; if that is spread over the whole of the loan, including the guaranteed part, the cost of the premium comes down to 1.75 per cent.

The original idea was that the premium income should cover the losses but few apart from the government believed that it would. But even so the scheme is a relatively low cost creator of jobs and the Department of Employment estimates that each job supported or created by the scheme costs around £700. That figure compares very favourably with the estimated cost of £5000 to £7000 for each person receiving unemployment benefit for a year.

There does appear to have been a revival of interest in the scheme as a result of the changes.

The Loan Guarantee Scheme has led a rather chequered existence for the past five years, with all but one of the banks opposed to it originally and showing varying degrees of interest afterwards, and the government never really seeming to be quite sure what it had got itself into. Now that it seems to have made up its mind, the scheme could become, especially if all concerned take heed of the experience of its early years, a very valuable source of funding for the smaller firm.

Its critics may well continue to say that the costs, which even now are undoubtedly high, put heavy strains on the cash flow of firms when they are at their weakest, but the fact of the matter is that high risk projects covered by the scheme would probably never have been able to raise the funds on normal commercial terms anyway and the potential wealth and jobs would never have materialised.

4.6   Co-operatives

Raising finance to start or expand a co-operative has never been easy but the number of sources of funding specifically oriented towards co-operatives is slowly beginning to increase and co-ops themselves are finding new ways of tapping financial support.

An example of the latter is the equity participation co-operative which Industrial Common Ownership Finances (ICOF) used last year to raise £500,000 which will enable it to continue its expanding lending programme for the worker co-operative movement. The public subscribed for what were described as 'co-operative shares' in multiples of £250 with a 6 per cent return.

It is often said that investors will not be interested if their share is not full equity capital, gives them no control and does not allow them to have a director on the board. The ICOF initiative showed that this theory does not always apply.

Another illustration of this is the £50,000 of loan stock raised in 1989 by Paperback, a London co-op that supplies recycled paper to the print industry and stationery trade, to finance their rapid expansion.

'We were staggered by what people put in – two people put in £5000 each. It was also individuals, not businesses. We achieved our target in less than four months,' said Frank Broughton of Paperback.

Paperback's turnover has increased so rapidly that it intends to issue extra units of loan stock on the basis of revised projections of income. This way of raising finance has proved equally successful for two other co-ops.

A very useful guide to new types of funding for co-ops has been produced by the Industrial Common Ownership Movement. *The ICOM Finance Pack* by Malcolm Lynch is published by ICOM Publications and is available from Turnaround, 25 Horsell Road, London N5 1XL, price £5.45.

These experiences have shown that there is potentially a considerable pool of people willing to make investments from an ethical viewpoint with limited returns rather than always run for a quick profit from a privatisation issue.

The chances of them losing their money are in fact smaller than investing in conventional small businesses as there is evidence to show that they have a better survival rate. ICOF, the best-known source of funding for co-ops, has an annual write-off rate of only 10 per cent for loans, which compares favourably with commercial bank experience on bad debts with small firms in general.

ICOF has been lending to co-ops for more than 15 years, during which time it has lent more than £1 million to more than 100 co-ops. It also administers funds for regional authorities in West Glamorgan, Northamptonshire and the West Midlands.

ICOF administers a revolving loan fund, recycling its finance within the worker co-operative sector, each pound being used again and again as borrowers repay their loans, with interest. One of the reasons for its success is probably the continuing link between the fund and the borrower during the life of the loan.

Typically ICOF lends between £7500 and £10,000 for periods from six months to six years. Personal security is not required but security is taken over the co-op's business assets in the form of floating and fixed charges.

ICOF also encourages and advises local organisations on setting up and running revolving loan funds, of which there are now several around the country, often run by local authorities or local co-operative development agencies (CDAs).

The local CDAs have an important role in carrying out feasibility studies, drawing up business plans and assisting with finance applications, as well as linking potential sources with potential borrowers and providing the often essential after-care.

Other major contributors to funding facilities for co-operatives are the London Co-operative Development Fund, established by the Greater London Enterprise Board, which has survived all the changes there, the venture capital fund for worker co-operatives in Scotland, Co-operative Venture Capital (Scotland), and West Midlands Co-operative Finance which, with a £1.25 million fund, probably operates the largest single co-op fund.

The aim of the Scottish fund is to help individual members of Scottish co-ops who have difficulty in raising equity capital and it has been a long-term objective of the Scottish Co-operatives Development Committee, which provides the fund's secretariat.

Clearing banks in general are not especially enthusiastic about co-ops as, on conventional banking criteria, co-ops are highly geared but they all say they respond to a visible, well-presented proposition for a co-operative enterprise.

In practice much depends on the attitudes of individual managers, a hazard which faces conventional private businesses equally. Even so a substantial proportion of co-ops formed in recent years have received their funding through the clearing banks.

One clearer which should provide a sympathetic hearing is the Co-operative Bank, part of the consumer co-operative movement. The Co-op Bank also operates a number of special loan guarantee schemes with local authorities, which have strong interests in encouraging co-op projects.

The Co-op Bank also offers worker co-ops with a turnover of up to £250,000 free banking; if the co-op stays within its agreed overdraft limits – not just in credit – the bank gives free banking for six months to start-up and existing co-ops which move their accounts to the bank.

Information about the situation in a particular area can be obtained from local information or economic development offices, who should know whether there is a local co-op development agency or loan fund.

Further information can be obtained from: Industrial Common Ownership Finance Ltd, 4 St Giles Street, Northampton NN1 1AA, 0604 37563; London Co-operative Enterprise Board, 63–67 Newington Causeway, London SE1 6BD, 01–403 0300; Co-operative Development Agency, 21 Panton Street, London SW1Y 4DR, 01–839 2985; West Midlands Co-operative Finance, 31–34 Waterloo Street, Birmingham B2 5TJ, 021–236 8855; Scottish Co-operative Development Committee, Templeton Business Centre, Templeton Street, Bridgeton, Glasgow G40 1DA, 041-554 3797.

4.7   Business Expansion Scheme

Persuading the owner of the smaller business that taking in an outside shareholder could be beneficial to the financial stability of the company has always been difficult, but if the success of the Business Expansion Scheme is anything to go by attitudes are changing.

Since the scheme was launched in its present form – as a successor to the ill-fated and unlamented Business Start-up Scheme – it has not only attracted strong support from investors looking for the tax benefits but also the number of projects seeking finance in this way has been considerable.

One of its aims was to fill the gap believed to exist at the smaller end of the market, for firms looking for equity investment of under £50,000, the relatively small sums which in the distant past came from private sources – the legendary Aunt Agatha.

While the scheme has not entirely succeeded in doing that it has been more successful than had previously been thought as figures from both the Inland Revenue and the Peat Marwick report on the scheme showed.

The government certainly considers that the scheme has been a success. The Inland Revenue statistics show that in the tax year 1983–84 some £105 million was raised and investments were made in 715 companies. More than half of these, 388, received less than £50,000; in fact the average funding was £18,500.

Three-quarters of those companies receiving less than £50,000 were regarded as start-ups, that is, less than five years old. These figures are encouraging to those who believed there was previously a gap at this level but of some concern was the fact that these companies also had a significant failure rate, though there are no overall failure figures.

The most comprehensive report on the scheme so far has been carried out for the government by chartered accountants, Peat Marwick. Their report said that more than 70 per cent of the funds invested could not have been raised as equity if the BES had not existed.

Firms which raised less than £50,000 only accounted for 3 per cent of the total amount invested but they represented more than a third of the 102 firms surveyed, confirming the Inland Revenue's indications that the scheme was benefiting an area of the market which more conventional sources were not interested in because they found it uneconomic.

The scheme has also been a good generator of jobs, with the 715 firms receiving investments in 1983–84 producing 4000 additional jobs and a combined £100 million a year rise in turnover 12 months later.

Later figures on job creation may be somewhat distorted by the explosion of asset-backed schemes which could have drawn funds away from companies which generate jobs. This loophole was closed in a recent Budget, however, and heavily asset-backed projects no longer qualify.

Businesses with more than half their assets in land or buildings do not qualify for BES relief, unless the amount raised is less than £50,000 in any one tax year. Businesses based on items normally collected for investment purposes, such as wine or antiques, are also excluded.

The attractions of the scheme for investors have also been improved. Investors are able to offset investments in the equity of most unquoted companies against their highest rate of tax, up to a maximum of £40,000 a year. The investment must be held for at least five years to qualify for relief.

An investor taxed at the top rate of 40 per cent could, for example, invest £20,000 in a qualifying company at a net cost of only £12,000. It should also be remembered that the minimum amount which can be invested in a company is £500, so the benefits of the scheme are open to the smaller investor as well as the wealthy, provided a home can be found for the investment.

In addition to these incentives for investors, in the 1986 Budget the Chancellor gave a concession under which BES shares can be sold free of capital gains tax – an encouragement to investment in riskier projects.

A chance for the smaller investor to identify possible investment opportunities has over the past year or so materialised in the form of the investment registers, held by enterprise agencies, which provide lists of companies looking for funds and of potential investors.

The 'marriage bureau' idea was initiated by the London Enterprise Agency but variations of it have been developed at other agencies such as those in Manchester, Milton Keynes, and Colchester. In the Manchester Business Venture register, called Business Capital Connection, businesses file detailed business plans with the BCC and prospective investors can examine them. If they find anything of interest a meeting is arranged and the two parties pursue the matter with their professional advisers. Businesses pay nothing for the service but there is a charge to investors. Business Capital Connection is not a fund and no investment advice is given; its role is purely an introductory one.

Another platform of this kind is the investors' clubs which are rapidly springing up in association with enterprise agencies. This again was a London Enterprise Agency idea under which several entrepreneurs give presentations to a group of potential investors, who are then free to approach and question anyone they find interesting.

These are not, however, the main methods of raising finance under the BES. At present the most popular method is to issue shares directly to the public. This can be done through a private placing, arranged by a stockbroker, with a published prospectus or through a direct approach to investors without professional assistance. Attracting funds through a public prospectus is the most expensive way because there are the costs of solicitors, accountants, stockbrokers, and printing to be considered.

A method which avoids this problem is to approach the funds which gather together the money subscribed by individual investors and invest it in business projects which they assess. The funds were originally the most popular method of raising finance through the BES but have since been overtaken by the direct issue route.

Investments from funds are cheaper because they do not involve the prospectus costs. On the other hand, they will require accountants' reports and may well offer management advice or put a non-executive director on the board, as well as taking an option on a percentage of shares which they would probably exercise if the business was a success.

Funds are looking for capital gains and generally envisage realising their investment through a flotation on either the unlisted stock market, the new third market, or the over the counter market.

The regional and local funds which it was hoped would emerge under the scheme have been slow to materialise but they are now beginning to. The enterprise agency, the Community of St Helens Trust on Merseyside, produced the first local scheme and has since run others successfully, with funds going to firms looking for sums of between £20,000 and £50,000.

Much of the publicity given to BES projects is concentrated on the benefits for investors but of more importance is the benefit received by companies in which the funds are invested. Among these are the reduced gearing, as the pressure to pay dividends can be resisted if the money is needed to develop the company, unlike the situation with a loan where interest and capital repayments must be made even when no profits are being made. A firm expanding rapidly and eating up its cash resources quickly, such as on research and development, but which would produce returns at a slower rate, could find the five-year time-scale for BES investments very acceptable.

Many firms could benefit from selling an equity stake in this way, which does not mean giving up control, particularly as they can now buy back their own shares when the time comes for an investor to realise the investment.

4.8   Exporting

The burgeoning balance of payments deficit requires action not only to reduce imports but to increase exports, but real or imagined difficulties in doing business outside Britain often results in potential growth opportunities overseas for expanding companies being missed.

Yet many of the apparent problems and costs can be reduced or eliminated through use of the facilities developed in recent years for the smaller exporter by banks and other organisations.

All banks provide export facilities for their customers, not only those who have developed special schemes, though it is sometimes claimed that interest is limited unless the amount of business is substantial. The purpose of special schemes, however, is to provide easier export finance for businesses with relatively small or infrequent export trade.

One of the earliest special schemes is that run by Midland Bank, whose scheme caters for firms with an export turnover of up to £1 million and individual orders of up to £100,000.

Barclays' smaller export scheme provides 100 per cent loan finance to companies with an annual export turnover of up to £2 million. The Co-operative Bank has also introduced a smaller exporters' scheme which caters for enterprises with export turnover of up to £500,000 and individual orders of up to £50,000.

Lloyds Bank has a slightly different scheme which provides insurance up to 100 per cent and finance up to 85 per cent of invoices or bills of exchange. Their smaller exports scheme is primarily for firms with an export turnover of less than £1 million and is operated through the bank's factoring subsidiaries, International Factors and Alex Lawrie.

The factoring companies take the export book debts as security and repayment of the money advanced is made when the invoice is paid by the overseas customer.

Export factoring is widely available elsewhere, also from factoring companies, many of which are in any case bank subsidiaries.

The Export Credits Guarantee Department (ECGD) is still the country's major export insurer, providing insurance cover for around a quarter of all United Kingdom visible non-oil exports. The needs of smaller exporters, however, are generally met through the banks, who take ECGD credit insurance and handle all paperwork. ЄМЄ → В → ЄССД,

Acceptance of a proposal by banks depends on whether the buyer is creditworthy and the markets to which goods are sold themselves being acceptable. Where banks do not provide full 100 per cent cover the unfinanced portion is paid when payment is received from the customer.

Otherwise the funds are provided without recourse, which means that the bank will not ask the firm for the money back if the buyer fails to pay – though, of course, the selling company must have met its obligations as well.

The cost is usually a charge of a percentage over base rate for the funds and a further charge of 1 or 2 per cent on the amount of the invoice or contract value.

The British Overseas Trade Board is not in itself a source of finance for export trade but it can provide financial and other help for firms wanting to explore the potential of exporting. An example of this is the export marketing research scheme under which the Board makes grants towards the cost of making market research studies in overseas countries outside the European Community. As with many government-backed schemes it is essential to approach the Board at an early stage because contributions are not made towards projects already commissioned, started or completed. The estimated cost must also be agreed with the BOTB before research is started.

A business can receive up to one-third of the cost of buying published market research, up to half the cost of commissioning research overseas and research by the firm's own staff is also supported.

Exporting companies can also raise finance through using the services of companies like Exfinco, which makes what it calls a 'standing offer' to buy from the exporter, at the time of shipment, the full, credit-insured value of the goods. This is generally 90 per cent of the invoice value, less a discount. Exfinco then pays the balance, less the value of credit notes or other adjustments, at a fixed time from the date of invoicing. The selling of the goods and contact with the customer remain with the client. The exporter must, however, have an acceptable short-term credit insurance policy as security in the event of non-payment.

Further information on BOTB schemes can be obtained from the Board at 1 Victoria Street, London SW1H 0ET, or from its regional offices; information on bank schemes from bank branches; and from Exfinco at Exfinco House, Sanford Street, Swindon, Wiltshire, SN1 1QQ.

4.9 Local authority aid

The recent rapid growth of interest in local economic initiatives as a means of generating new jobs has led to a major explosion of assistance for business projects from local authorities at a time when the government has been cutting back on regional aid.

The vast array of help now available has meant that the independent business operator has had almost to acquire the skills of a financial juggler to be able to try to assess the merits of what is being offered.

Help from local authorities can come from almost anywhere, provided the public body can raise the money. A number of methods have been devised, ranging from grants, loans and interest rebates to equity participation.

As far as direct government regional aid is concerned, full details are available from regional offices of the Department of Trade and Industry. Further help with information and probably also with the processing of applications – which can be the biggest problem for the smaller business – can be obtained through the network of enterprise agencies which now covers the country.

A directory of enterprise agencies is published by Business in the Community, 227a City Road, London EC1V 1LX (tel: 01-253 3716). Another source of information should be the government's Small Firms Service, which can be contacted by dialling 100 and asking the operator for Freefone Enterprise.

One of the most interesting aspects of the explosion of aid from the local authorities is that a great deal of their support is being directed at the end of the market which is supposed to be neglected by other sources, namely the projects which require relatively small sums of money.

York City Council, for example, has contributed £250,000 to a fund run by the York Enterprise Agency so that it can provide loans of between £500 and £25,000 with repayment in five years at an interest rate of 3 per cent above base rate.

Milton Keynes Business Venture, the local enterprise agency, manages a seed capital fund financed by Milton Keynes borough council. Applicants have to show that the money could not be raised through normal commercial sources and loans are available in amounts of up to £2500.

Several other schemes are run by enterprise boards, which were set up by the metropolitan authorities, but have survived the demise of those bodies. The West Yorkshire Enterprise Board, for example, has a small firms fund with an upper limit of £15,000 per company, while the Greater Manchester Economic Development Corporation has its Worknorth scheme, started in conjunction with the Co-operative Bank.

The Kent Economic Development Board has also been active in the field of financial provision and can meet the capital needs of companies looking for between £20,000 and £250,000.

In addition to schemes such as these there are, of course, many councils which are prepared to make small loans, interest relief grants or training grants which perhaps enable small firms to take on young people.

The Selby District Council in Yorkshire, because of its concern at the high level of youth unemployment in the area, devised two schemes, one of which provides up to 75 per cent of a young person's wages for one year, 50 per cent in the second year and 25 per cent in the third year.

An unusual feature of Selby's schemes is that they are resident rather than company based which means that if employers in other parts of Yorkshire or Humberside are able to employ young people from Selby they will be eligible for the grants.

Other councils have developed different support schemes, such as Sheffield City Council's product development grant scheme which helps in the development of new products and the improvement of existing ones. This project has had considerable success.

The grant can cover project feasibility studies, material costs, prototype assembly costs, and the cost of equipment used in development and product promotion. In return for the finance the City Council receives a royalty on subsequent sales.

The various types of assistance available from local authorities have not always been as well publicised in the past as they could be but a number of bodies are now remedying this. London, in fact, is well served by the recently published *Guide to Local Authority Assistance* produced by the London Research Centre in collaboration with the London Chamber of Commerce. This booklet, which costs £2.50, contains a wealth of detailed information in its 54 pages on the range of assistance offered by the local authorities in the London area.

Individual authorities have also produced their own directories, a good example being that from Hammersmith and Fulham, a new edition of which was published recently. This borough was also the most recent recruit to a development which has been progressing steadily for a few years – the local authority backed Loan Guarantee Scheme.

These schemes have been developed by the Co-operative Bank in joint ventures with several local authorities. They have no connection with the government's national Loan Guarantee Scheme. The aim is to enable businesses in economically hard hit areas of the country to raise finance which may not otherwise have been available.

It was the Local Authorities (Miscellaneous Provisions) Act 1982, which gave local authorities powers to give guarantees for industrial development.

The bank saw the opportunity to develop this special loan scheme, designed to form an integral part of an overall financial and industrial aid package.

The loans usually have a maximum limit of £50,000 and carry an interest rate of 3 per cent above base rate; the local authority guarantees a proportion of the loan in the event of a failure.

There are probably many business operators who would say that the best financial assistance a local authority can give is to use the money available to reduce the rates, but until the millennium arrives they would probably be well served by a call to their local economic or industrial development officer or enterprise agency to find out what is on offer in other forms.

4.10   Venture Capital

One of the most remarkable features of the venture capital scene in recent years has been the way in which the management buy-out – and now its cousin, the management buy-in – has come to dominate activity in the field. They account for 55 per cent of the £1 billion invested altogether by members of the British Venture Capital Association and for nearly one in five of the total number of financings. Ian Kreiger, partner in charge of management buy-outs at chartered accountants Arthur Andersen, points out that compared with £26 million only nine years ago, £3 billion was invested in buy-outs last year – a figure which is expected to double by the end of the decade.

Over the same period buy-outs by managers of the companies or subsidiaries for which they work have risen six-fold in less than ten years, from 52 in 1979 to 300 in 1988. The average value of buy-outs during the same period has risen from just £500,000 to more than £10 million.

While many buyouts are relatively small the size of some has been huge, the largest being the £718 million purchase of MFI by its management, followed by Reedpack at £618 million.

In the first three quarters of 1989 figures from chartered accountants Peat, Marwick, McLintock show there were worth between £10 million and £25 million compared with 11 in the whole of 1988 and 7 between £25 and £50 million compared with 5 in 1987 as a whole.

Competition in the sector has become enormous but there is little sign of a slowing of interest and in fact in the first nine months of 1989, Peat, Marwick, McLintock estimate that there were 210 buy-outs, worth £2.33 billion.

An indication of this competition is the extent to which managements have been able to dictate terms to venture capitalists, with the result that the proportion of loan finance in the deal is becoming higher and higher and the amount of equity held by the financier smaller and smaller.

While some venture capitalists may prefer income at present to capital gains, in today's uncertain stock markets they are certainly not happy at having their returns squeezed. As a result they are turning increasingly to the management buy-in where they have more control.

The risks may be higher – because the process is that of an

outside management team taking control of a business with which they are not necessarily familiar backed by the providers of finance – but so are the potential rewards.

Furthermore it is frequently the venture capitalist who seeks out the target company, puts together a financial package, and then brings in the managers to run the business.

One of the major operators in the field, Electra Investment Trust, has recently recruited a senior executive from a headhunting firm to lead its 'management resourcing unit', which will identify key managers in business and help them in undertaking buy-ins.

3i, which has financed 55 per cent of all buy-ins so far, set up a dedicated management buy-in unit in the summer of 1989 and was overwhelmed by the interest from managers around the country.

Even so, buy-outs and buy-ins do not represent the whole of the venture capital scene. There is estimated to be a pool of around £4.5 billion of venture capital in the United Kingdom, with new funds being raised all the time, all looking for somewhere to generate profits.

The 90 members of the Britain Venture Capital Association (BVCA) invested £1.03 billion in nearly 1300 companies last year. Of this start-ups and early stage financing accounted for 27 per cent of the number of financings but only 13 per cent of the total amount.

The most important single sector continued to be consumer-related businesses, accounting for 22 per cent of all businesses financed and 28 per cent of the total amount.

The south-east continues to dominate the investment pattern but there has been an increasing movement out to the regions, with Scotland and the East Midlands being the main recipients.

Corporate venturing is another aspect of the venture capital scene which has not so far achieved the prominence in the UK that it has in the United States. This form of investment involves a large company investing in a smaller company, usually by means of an equity stake. For the large business the attraction is the access to new markets, products and technologies.

The idea could be on the point of expanding as the National Economic Development Office (NEDO) has set up a corporate venturing centre to handle large corporate subscribers and a regional network is being formed for smaller companies. In Lancashire, for example, Lancashire Enterprises has been appointed by NEDO as an agent to advise local companies.

Sources of Venture Capital compiled by Chancery Corporate Finance Division

The headings in the table below are fairly self-explanatory but should be taken as guidelines rather than rigid criteria.

The 'stage of investment column' covers seed capital, start-up, early stage, expansion, buy-out or buy-in, secondary purchase, other. Management involvement is shown by a star rating, with * indicating monthly reporting to the investor and *** indicating monthly attendance by investor at board meetings and close involvement on all significant decisions.

\# = Member of the British Venture Capital Association

Investor	Min/Max investment	Stage of investment	Equity stake	Special features	Investment profile	Management involvement
			%			
#Aberdeen Fund Managers Ltd 10 Queen's Terrace Aberdeen AB9 1QJ	£50k–£500k	Expansion, buy-out, development	5–49	Scottish investments	No fixed criteria. No preferences	**
#Abingworth plc 25 St James's Street London SW1A 1HA	£250k–£1m	All stages	10–40	Strong US links	Management of proven ability. New technology, high growth industries and sectors	***
#Advent Ltd 25 Buckingham Gate London SW1E 6LD	£300k–£3m	All stages	10–40 preferred	International venture capital links through Advent International network	No industry or geographical preferences, but specialists in high technology	***

#Alan Patricof Associates Ltd 24 Upper Brook Street London W1Y 1PD	£50k–£5m† †will lead a syndicate for larger sums	Start-up, expansion, buy-out, rescue	10–49	International	No preferences	***
#AIIB Venture Capital Pinners Hall 8–9 Austin Friars London EC2N 2AE	£250k–£2m	Expansion/ development capital, buy-outs, start-up in specific circumstances	10–40	UK/Ireland	No preferences. All sectors considered except property deals	*/**
#Alta Berkeley Associates 25 Berkeley Square London W1X 5HB	£100k– £1.5m	Start-up, early stage, development, buy-out	10–40	Strong US links and European involvement	Healthcare/life sciences, media, information services and electronics	***
#B & C Ventures Ltd 36–37 King Street London EC2V 8BE	£500k– £15m	All stages considered	0–49		No preferences	*
#Barclays Development Capital Ltd Pickfords Wharf Clink Street London SE1 9DG	£150k– £5m	Some expansion but mainly buy-out	10–40		No preferences	*

Investor	Min/Max investment	Stage of investment	Equity stake %	Special features	Investment profile	Management involvement
#Baring Brothers Hambrecht & Quist Ltd 140 Park Lane London W1Y 3AA	£100k-£1m	All stages	10-40	USA/Japan/Europe links	Prefer businesses or start-ups with international potential	***
#Barnes Thomson Management Ltd 65 New Cavendish Street London W1M 7RD	£100k-£500k	Start-up/expansion/buy-out	10-40	Information tech and computer	Strong market position with expectation of profit growth	**
#Biotechnology Investments Ltd advised by N M Rothschild Asset Management Ltd Five Arrows House St Swithin's Lane London EC4N 8NR	$0.5m-$5m	Any: preference early stage	10-25		Biotechnology and medical technology exclusively	***
#Baronsmead Ltd Clerkenwell House 67 Clerkenwell Road London EC1R 5BH	£250k-£1m+	All stages but particularly expansion and smaller management buy-outs/ins	Varies with deal but not more than 49	Provision of finance for reorganisation and management of sole investor funds	High growth potential	**

Company	Amount	Stage	Range	Notes	Criteria	
#Birmingham Technology Venture Capital Ltd Aston Science Park Love Lane Aston Triangle Birmingham B7 4BJ	£20k–£250k plus syndication	Seed capital and start-up	10–49	Located Birmingham	Able to satisfy minimum rate of return. High growth technology	***
#British Linen Fund Managers Ltd 32 Melville Street Edinburgh EH3 7NZ	£100k–£1m	All stages but expansion to buy-out preferred	0–49		Flexible	*
#British Rail Trustee Company Ltd 6th Floor Broad Street House 55 Old Broad Street London EC2M 1RX	£500k–£1m+	Expansion and buy-outs/ins	10–40		Not rescue	*
#British Technology 101 Newington Causeway London SE1 6BU	£50k–£1m	Seed capital/start-up/expansion	10–40		Must involve technological innovation	*
Brown Shipley Development Capital Ltd Founders Court Lothbury EC2R 7HE	£750k–£3m	Development, replacements or buy-outs/ins. Not start-ups or rescue	10–40	Recent new fund	Profitable. Not property	

Investor	Min/Max investment	Stage of investment	Equity stake %	Special features	Investment profile	Management involvement
#Cambridge Capital Management Group Ltd 13 Station Road Cambridge CB1 2JB	£200k– £500k	Expansion, buy-outs, buy-ins and exceptionally replacement	10–40	East Anglian bias	Profitability preferred	***
#Candover Investments plc Cedric House 8–9 East Harding Street London EC4A 3AS	£9m–£50m	Buy-out/in, development capital	10–40		Cash generating, proven management	**
#Capital Partners International Ltd Kingsmead House 250 Kings Road London SW3 5UE	£30k–£300k	All stages	10–40	Very active assistance in overseas marketing and international joint ventures particularly in EC	Flexible With global expansion potential	*
#Capital Ventures Ltd 37 London Road Cheltenham GL52 6HA	£250k– £500k (no limit)	All stages	10–40		Balanced management team with enthusiasm and commitment. All sectors considered.	**

Company	Investment	Stage	% Equity	BES	Conditions/Preferences	Rating
Castleforth Fund Managers Ltd 150 Strand London WC2R 1SP	£250k–£750k	Start-ups unlikely	10–40	Recent BES fund	Prefer profitable	***
#Causeway Capital Ltd 21 Cavendish Place London W1M 9DL	£250k–£2m	Expansion and buy-out	10–40	UK only	Prospect of growth profitable. Any sector. UK only	**
#Centreway Development Capital Ltd 1 Waterloo Street Birmingham B2 5PG	£100k–£250k upwards	Start-up, expansion and buy-out	10–40		No preferences. UK only	**
#Charterhouse Development Capital Ltd 7 Ludgate Broadway London EC4V 6DX	£100k–£25m	Expansion and management buy-outs	10 plus		Good management. Profitable	***
#Charterhouse Venture Fund 10 Hertford Street London W1Y 7DX	£200k–£1m	All stages	10–40		Healthcare, biosciences, environmental management, electronic related	***
#Chartfield & Co Ltd 24–26 Baltic Street London EC1Y 0TB	£50k–£700k	All stages, especially recovery and special situations	Varies		No specific conditions. No preferences. Some excluded areas	***

Investor	Min/Max investment	Stage of investment	Equity stake %	Special features	Investment profile	Management involvement
#CIN Venture Managers Ltd PO Box 10 London SW1X 7AD	£250k–£1m+	Start-up, develop-ment capital, management buy-outs/ins, replace-ment capital	Minority		No set parameters	***
#Citicorp Venture Capital Cottons Centre Hays Lane London SE1 2QT	£250k–£2m	All stages	10–40	International	No preferences	**
#Close Investment 33 Great St Helen's London EC3A 6AP	£500k–£5m	Mainly expansion buy-in/out, and secondary purchase, some early stage	10–40	Recent new fund of £30m	Minimum sales of £2m preferred	*
#Consolidated Credits and Discounts Ltd Chelsea House West Gate London W5 1DR	£50k–£500k	Expansion (flexible)	10–40		Profitable, well-managed companies. Retailing, travel and leisure, low tech, property related	*

Company	Investment range	Type of investment	£m	Notes	Preferences	Rating
#County NatWest Ventures Ltd Drapers Gardens 12 Throgmorton Ave London EC2P 2ES	£250k–no limit (will syndicate if necessary)	Expansion buy-out/ buy-in plus early stage selectively	Varies	Has considerable experience of arranging syndications	Strong management team. Excellent prospects for profitable growth	*/**
Cygnus Venture Partners Wellington House 4 Cowley Road Uxbridge UB8 2XW	£250k–£3m Syndicates up to £15m	Start-ups through to development capital, including management buy-out/in	10–40	Recently closed a new £35m fund	Healthcare, biotech, information technology, communications, service related industries	***
#Dartington & Co Securities Ltd Bush House 72 Prince Street Bristol BS1 4QD	£100k–£250k (Avon Enterprise) £500k–no limit (Capital West)	Start-up, expansion, buy-out	10–40	SW England	No preferences	**
#Development Capital Corporation Ltd 103 Mount Street London W1Y 5HE	£250k–£2.5m	Expansion, replacement, buy-out, buy-in, exceptionally start-up	5–70	UK/Ireland	Profitable, growing companies	***

Investor	Min/Max investment	Stage of investment	Equity stake %	Special features	Investment profile	Management involvement
#Development Capital Group Ltd 44 Baker Street London W1M 1DH	£250k–£1.5m	Start-up, expansion, buy-out, replacement capital	25–49	Active management support given to investee companies through experienced non-executive directors. Wide range of funds available; general, specialist, regional, and BES	Good growth prospects, sound management. All sectors considered	**
#ECI Brettenham House Lancaster Place London WC2E 7EN	£500k–£5m	Expansion, buy-outs, buy-ins	10–40		Management track record. Realisable in 5–7 years. All sectors considered	***
#Electra Investment Trust plc 65 Kingsway London WC2B 6QT	£750k–£10m	All stages	10–40		No preferences	*
#F & C Ventures Ltd 1 Laurence Pountney Hill London EC4R 0BA	£500k–£2m	All stages	10–40	Mainly UK	Preferably post start-up	*

#Fleming Ventures Ltd International House St Catherine's Way London E1 9UN	£500k–£1m	All stages	10/40		High technology, Electronics sector	**
#Fountain Development Capital Fund 100 Wood Street London EC2P 2AJ	£250k–£2m	Expansion, buy-in buy-out, secondary purchase	10–40	UK only	No preferences	**/*** Dependent on nature of investment
#Gartmore Investment Management Ltd Venture Capital Division Gartmore House 16–18 Monument Street London EC3R 8AJ	£250k–£2m	Start-up, expansion, buy-out, buy-in	10–40		No preferences	**
#Globe Management Ltd Electra House Temple Place London WC2R 3HP	£1m–no limit	Selected start-ups, management buy-outs, development capital, property development	1–49		No preferences. All considered	**
#Granville Development Capital 8 Lovat Lane London EC3R BP	£50k+	All stages	10–40	Regional funds	No preferences	**

Investor	Min/Max investment	Stage of investment	Equity stake	Special features	Investment profile	Management involvement
			%			
Greater London Enterprise 63–67 Newington Causeway London SE1 6BD	£40k–£500k	Most stages	10–40	London	Minimum rate of return. Usual commercial considerations, progressive employment policies	***
#Gresham Trust plc Barrington House Gresham Street London EC2V 7HE	£25k–£1m	Start-up, buy-out/in, development capital, share purchase/replacement capital, preparation for flotation	Minority	Venture capital for smaller and medium-sized businesses. Any industrial sector	Quality management and growth prospects	**
#Grosvenor Venture Managers Ltd Commerce House 2–6 Bath Road Slough SL1 3RZ	£200k–£1m	Expansion, replacement capital, buy-outs	10–40	Positive support	Preferably product-based technology £100k	***
#Guinness Mahon Development Capital Ltd 32 St Mary at Hill London EC3P 3AJ	£100k–£1m more with syndication	Expansion, buy-ins/recoveries, early stage only in biosciences and meditech	10–40			***

#Hambros Advanced Technology Trust plc 20–21 Tooks Court Cursitor Street London EC4A 1LB	£100k–£500k	Start-up and expansion	10–40	High technology	***
#Hodgson Martin Ltd 36 George Street Edinburgh EH2 2BD	£100k–£1m	Start-up, expansion, buy-out	No restrictions	Flexible	***
#3i Group plc 91 Waterloo Road London SE1 8XP	N/A	Start-up, expansion, buy-out/in. Expertise in funding and advice to businesses of all sizes through all stages of growth	10–40	Flexible investment packages to suit all situations	**
#Industrial Technology Securities Ltd 54 St James's Street London SW1A 1JT	£150k–£250k	Start-up, expansion	10–40	Good management. High gross margins. Defendable market position	*
#Ivory & Sime Development Capital 1 Charlotte Square Edinburgh EH2 4DZ	£150k–£10m	Mainly development and buy-outs	10–40	No preferences	*

Investor	Min/Max investment	Stage of investment	Equity stake %	Special features	Investment profile	Management involvement
#Kleinwort Benson Development Capital Ltd 20 Fenchurch Street London EC3P 3DB	£300k+	All considered but seed capital unlikely	10–40		Realisable in 4–7 years	**
#Larpent Newton & Co Ltd 4th Floor 24–26 Baltic Street London EC1Y 0TB	c £100k–£1m	Start-up, expansion and buy-out	10–40		Profit potential of at least £750k (at present-day values) in 5–7 years	***
#Legal & General Ventures Ltd Bucklersbury House 3 Queen Victoria Street London EC4N 8EL	£250k+	Expansion, buy-out	5–20		Up to 20% equity stake. Agreed exit strategy	*
#Lloyds Development Capital Ltd 40–66 Queen Victoria Street London EC4P 4EL	£200k+. Larger amounts may be syndicated	Expansion, buy-out	Up to a maximum of 40		Well-managed companies with growth potential. Pre-tax profits in excess of £100k	*
#March Investment Fund 33 King Street Manchester M2 6AA	£250k–£2.5m	Expansion, buy-out, buy-in, secondary purchase, sometimes start-up or early stage	10–40	UK, especially NW and Midlands	Preference given to buy-outs or expansion of existing profitable businesses	***

Company	Investment range	Type of investment	Equity %	Location	Conditions	Rating
#Mercia Venture Capital Ltd, 126 Colmore Row, Birmingham B3 3AP	£50k–£150k	Start-up, expansion, buy-out	10–40	Not SE England	BES qualifying service/manufacturing	**
#Mercury Asset Management, 33 King William Street, London EC4R 9AS	£500k–£1m	Predominantly development capital	10–40		Potential for realisation of investment through sale or flotation within 7 years	*
#Midland Montagu Ventures Ltd, 10 Lower Thames Street, London EC2R 6AE	£500k–£7.5m+	Mostly management buy-outs, buy-ins, share purchases and expansion	10–40		Strong management. Growth prospects	**
#MIM Development Capital Ltd, 11 Devonshire Square, London EC2M 4YR	£250k–£3m	Expansion, buy-outs	10–40		No fixed conditions	*
#MTI Managers Ltd, 70 St Albans Road, Watford WD1 1RP	£200k–750k	Start-up, expansion, buy-out, rescue	20–80		UK-based high technology product companies	***
#Murray Johnstone Ltd, 7 West Nile Street, Glasgow G1 2PX	£100k–£10m+ Syndication on large deals	Development and buy-out/buy-in. Some start-ups	10–40	Aims to encourage synergy and two-way transfer of technology between USA and UK	Management product and markets	

Investor	Min/Max investment	Stage of investment	Equity stake %	Special features	Investment profile	Management involvement
#Newmarket Venture Capital plc 14–20 Chiswell Street London EC1Y 4TY	£250k–£1m	Start-up/early stage, expansion	10–40	Prefer UK/US	Technology companies. Sound business plan which supports ultimate sales and profits	***
#Northern Investors Company Ltd Centro House 3 Cloth Market Newcastle upon Tyne NE1 1EE	£25k–£250k	All stages	10–40	NE and Cumbria	No preferences	**
#Norwich Union Venture Capital Ltd PO Box No 53 Surrey Street Norwich NR1 3TE	£100k–£1m	Preference for development or management buy-out finance but will consider well-researched start-ups	Up to 40		UK registered unquoted companies demonstrating major growth potential. All sectors considered except property development and financial services	**
#Oakland Investment Management Ltd	£300k–£1m	Buy-out/buy-in, expansion	Not restricted.	Flexible funding, mostly equity	Strong growth potential in	***

			Prefer majority			
Ramsbury House High Street Hungerford RG17 0LY					engineering, information technology, leisure distribution, fashion industries	
#Octagon Investment Management Ltd Cambridge Science Park Milton Road Cambridge CB4 4WE	£100k–£500k	Start-up/ expansion capital	10–40	(see also Close Investment)	Strong growth potential. Information industries – computing, telecommunications, broadcasting, advertising	***
#PA Developments Ltd Bowater House East 68 Knightsbridge London SW1X 7LJ	£750k–£2m	Expansion, development, buy-out	25–40		Should be profitable and well managed	*
#Phildrew Ventures Triton Court 14 Finsbury Square London EC2A 1PD	£250k–£20m	Buy-out, buy-in, expansion	0–49	Funds available > £100m. Capable of arranging deals up to £1bn	Not natural resources or property development. Break even or better	**
Piper Retail Fund 182 Campden Hill Road London W8 7AS	£100k–£1m	Start-up, early stage, expansion, buy-out/in	10–60	Retail specialist	Looking for significant growth potential	***
#Prelude Technology Investments Ltd The Innovation Centre Science Park, Milton Road Cambridge CB4 4GF	£20k–£500k	Seed, start-up and early expansion capital	Usually in range 10–40		Investment in emerging technology businesses with the prospect of substantial growth	**

Investor	Min/Max investment	Stage of investment	Equity stake %	Special features	Investment profile	Management involvement
#Prudential Venture Managers Ltd Audrey House Ely Place London EC1N 6SN	£250k–£12m	All stages less seed capital	10–40	Can underwrite large management buy-outs up to £50m	Companies with above average growth potential	**
#Quayle Munro Ltd 42 Charlotte Square Edinburgh EH2 4HQ	£100k–£1.5m	Expansion, buy-outs and buy-ins	10–40		Well established	***
#Rothschild Ventures Ltd New Court St Swithin's Lane London EC4P 4DU	£100k–£2m	Start-up, expansion, management buy-out, management buy-in, turnaround	10–40		No preferences. Not property	*
#Schroder Ventures 20 Southampton Street London WC2E 7QG	£500k–no limit	Start-up, expansion, buy-out	10–85		No preferences. Not property	***
Scimitar Development Capital Ltd Osprey House 78 Wigmore Street London W1H 9DQ	£300k–£2.5m	Expansion, buy-out/in, development	Minority	US interest also	Proven management and track record. Profit > £200k	***

#Scottish Development Agency 120 Bothwell Street Glasgow G2 7JP	£10k–£1m	Pre start-up only rarely. All other stages of funding available.	10–40	Scotland	Committed management team which can exploit niche market opportunities. Commercial rate of return. Priority areas are healthcare, electronics, energy-related service industries, advanced engineering	**
#Security Pacific Hoare Govett Equity Ventures Ltd 4 Broadgate London EC2M 7LE	£500k–£2m	Expansion, buy-out	10–40		No preferences	*
#Security Pacific Venture Capital 130 Jermyn Street London SW1Y 4UJ	non min/ max £600k+ preferred	Start-up, expansion, buy-out	Minority		No preferences	**
#Seed Capital Ltd Boston Road Henley on Thames RG9 1DY	£5k–£25k	Prototype financing pre start-up and seed capital	10–40	Close support	Technology	***
#SUMIT Equity Ventures Ltd Edmund House 12 Newhall Street Birmingham B3 3FR	£300k– £1.25m + syndicate	Expansion, buy-out/in	10–40	UK only	Strong management SUMIT: No sector preference STF: Technology related companies	*

Investor	Min/Max investment	Stage of investment	Equity stake %	Special features	Investment profile	Management involvement
#The St James's Venture Capital Fund Ltd 29 St James's Place London SW1A 1NR	£250k–£750k	All stages	10–40		One year sales history. Technology	**
#Thompson Clive and Partners Ltd 24 Old Bond Street London W1X 3DA	£100k–£2m. More by syndication	All stages	10–40		Systems, electronics, healthcare, bio-technology, service businesses, professional and industrial markets	***
#Transatlantic Capital Ltd 55 Gracechurch Street London EC3V 0BN	£50k–£250k	Seed capital, start-up, expansion, development and buy-out	10–40		Proprietary technology or unique market opportunity. Biosciences	*
#Ulster Development Capital Ltd 10 High Street Belfast BT1 2BA	£50k–£300k	Expansion, buy-out	10–40	N Ireland	Minimum potential profit of £100k in short term	***
#Venture Founders Ltd 50–51 Conduit Street London W1R 9FB	£100k–£600k	Start-up, expansion	10–40	Technology	Developed product or service. All industrial, technological and service sectors	**

Company	Investment	Stage	%	Region/Sector	Preferences	
#Venture Link Investors Ltd 17 Berkeley Street London W1X 5AE	£200k–£400k initially then up to £1.5m+	Start-up, then follow-on finance	Varies	Software and biotechnology specialist	Excellent management team	**
#The Welsh Development Agency (Investment Division) Pearl House Greyfriars Road Cardiff CF1 3XX	£50k–£500k	All stages	10–30	Wales	All potentially viable propositions considered (not media, local retail and agriculture sectors)	**
#The Welsh Development Capital (Management) Ltd Pearl House Greyfriars Road Cardiff CF1 3XX	£100k–£300k	All stages	10–40	Wales	Strong growth potential	***
#West Midlands Enterprise Board Ltd Wellington House 31–34 Waterloo Street Birmingham B2 5TJ	£100k–£750k	Large start-ups/expansions/buy-outs	10–40	West Midlands and Oxfordshire	Minimum potential internal rate of return of 25%	**
#Yorkshire Enterprise Ltd Elizabeth House Queen Street Leeds LS1 2TW	£25k–£2m+	All stages	10–40	Yorkshire and Humberside	No preferences	**

A variation on the corporate venturing theme has been operated for some time by the quoted industrial group, Johnston Group, through its subsidiary, Johnston Development Capital. JDC makes individual investments of between £100,000 and £350,000, relatively small in venture capital terms, and emphasises the value of its background of commercial and industrial experience.

Smaller sums of venture capital have always been difficult to raise – the average of BCVA investments for start-up and early stage financings, for example, is £347,000 – but there have been a number of moves to fill what is called the 'equity gap'. One of the most promising of these is the 'marriage bureau' type of operation, which aims to link those requiring finance with those who have it. The main exponent of this initiative is the Local Investment Networking Company (LINC), a network of 15 enterprise agencies, which grew out of the London Enterprise Agency's 'marriage bureau'.

One aim is to achieve a more even spread of investment around the country, with the entrepreneur who is looking for cash being able to approach an agency in the scheme within easy travelling distance. It is hoped that this will lead to money being channelled from areas where investment is plentiful, such as London and the south-east, to areas where it is needed but not available.

Another source of venture capital in amounts of less than £100,000 is the local funds which are increasingly being developed around the country, such as the Avon Enterprise Fund, set up by the south-west based investment bankers, Dartington. Local decision making is one of the attractions of these funds as well as the relatively small amounts but if more substantial funds are required these are also available, often through regional funds operated by enterprise boards – West Midlands Enterprise Board, for example, operates a number of funds – or regional pension funds.

The venture capital industry is flourishing and awash with funds for investment. What it needs is a fully effective mechanism to bring it together with the viable projects in need of funding. But at least the trends now seem to be moving in the right direction.

4.11 Technology

While it may not be entirely unfair to say that venture capitalists lack enthusiasm when the phrase 'high technology' is mentioned, there are in fact a useful number of providers of funds for technologically oriented projects. It may well be that funds for high technology projects will never be plentiful – there are too many risky ways of making money – but it is probably true that there is no real shortage. On the other hand it should also be remembered that more than a quarter of the £1 billion invested by members of the British Venture Capital Association in 1988 actually went to technology-based projects. Whether they obtain funds also depends on the businesses wanting to start or expand technology-based ventures thinking out and planning thoroughly the business base of the operation and presenting it effectively.

Where they fail to develop a realistic business plan they are unlikely to fare any better than firms in conventional areas of business and allow the venture capitalists to say that there are insufficient viable prospects in which to invest.

One way of making progress is to use some of the facilities available for assessing technology-based projects, that can also provide information on which a proposal and business plan can be built.

Lloyds Bank, for example, has long had a technology appraisal scheme in conjunction with Cranfield Institute of Technology under which customers seeking funds for development or innovative use of new or high technology are provided with a technical assessment by Cranfield. The bank and the Institute then both examine the commercial implications.

National Westminster has its technology advisory points scheme, providing independent appraisal, aimed especially at the smaller and medium-sized business. Half the fees of the adviser are met by NatWest, with expert advice covering such areas as market competitiveness of the product, likelihood of achieving sales forecasts, research and development work undertaken, production techniques and overall feasibility.

Barclays Bank, which has produced an excellent series of booklets aimed at the technology-oriented business, has specialist technology managers in more than 60 branches around the country with experience in making detailed market and technical assessments of business plans.

It also offers specialist services, such as its tandem account system which allows customers to draw funds automatically against their debtor book at the technology branches.

And, of course, the old faithful of the venture capital world, 3i, is actively involved in technology financing through its 3i ventures division, specialising in backing, with money and management support, early stage enterprises in high-growth industry sectors.

One of its initiatives to increase the supply of seed money for significant inventions and technological advances is the 'enterprise cheques' scheme in conjunction with Research Corporation. Under this scheme 'enterprise cheques', typically of £25,000 each, are made available to inventors to support leading edge technological projects with commercial potential. The scheme is intended to appeal to those working in universities and research establishments but there is no bar on applicants working on their own. Once a project reaches a stage where it is ready for commercial exploitation, 3i will help to set up an independent company or provide assistance in patenting and licensing.

A company which has taken a particular interest in the past in technology projects is the Pru through its venture capital arm, Prudential Venture Managers (PVM). One of the Pru's activities was to back the South Bank Technopark in London which provides specialist accommodation for start-up high technology enterprises.

The long-term nature of most high technology projects is what deters many venture capitalists and one indication of the time-scale involved is a PVM investment in 1982, when £250,000 was spent on development of a pyrolysis mass spectrometer. This was backed right from the concept stage but it only reached the stage of commercial manufacture, with its first order, four years later, in 1986.

An indication that the financial world does have an interest in investing in technological development is the formation of specialist vehicles backed by groups of institutional investors, such as Managed Technology Investors (MTI), the three original backers of which were the Pru again, PA Consulting Services, and bankers Morgan Grenfell. The Pru's stake has since been bought out.

MTI not only provides finance of between £250,000 and £750,000 for start-up, small and medium-sized firms in the high technology field but also participates extensively in the management of those enterprises. It expects to be able to realise its investments in three to seven years.

Other venture capitalists in the technology field specialise in particular sectors in which they have expertise, such as Octagon Investment Management, which is specially interested in the information industries, and Alta Berkeley Associates, who as well as information services are interested in healthcare, media and electronics.

Greater London Enterprise is interested, through its research and development fund, in investing in innovative products from new and existing companies which want to explore new markets. A joint venture between Lloyds Bank and Birmingham City Council, called Birmingham Technology, is of special interest because unlike most organisations it is interested in starting to talk about amounts of less than £250,000.

One source which should not be overlooked is the British Technology Group, even though its role has changed and it does not use specific vehicles for investment in small firms. The main criterion for its support is that the proposed project has to be based on a new invention or contain a significant technological innovation. There is no formal minimum or maximum size of investment and the usual method of investment is through joint venture finance specially designed for technology-based projects.

Finally several of the major firms of accountants have their own technology specialists whose advice can cover formulating and developing business plans as well as locating possible sources of finance.

4.12   Factoring

Coping with the twin problems of extracting money due from slow paying customers and generating cash for the expansion of growing enterprises is a major problem facing independent businesses, but increasingly one of the solutions to these difficulties is seen in the practice of factoring.

An indication of the rising demand for this particular form of financial management is given by the growth of 24 per cent in business recorded last year by members of the Association of

British Factors, taking their total business to more than £7.07 billion compared with £5.68 billion in the previous year.

Factoring at its most basic is the selling of trade debts, though it is now a very much more sophisticated service. In its modern form it began to develop about 20 years ago but its initial expansion was held back by a reputation of being a 'last resort' and companies using factors were often thought to be in difficulties.

It took the industry a long time to shake off that image but its real benefits have been understood for some years now. Far from being a last refuge for a shaky business or a means of unloading bad debts it has become a valuable tool of financial management, an essential element in the juggling act of achieving a balanced financial structure.

For an expanding, fast growing business the improvement in cash flow achieved by quick transformation of debts into money in the bank can be a major advantage.

Some extent of the difference can be gauged from the estimate that an average company's trading debts can be as much as 25–30 per cent of sales at any one time. The benefits of releasing those debts is obvious.

Factors provide four main services: the chief form is non-recourse factoring, which means that the factor takes full responsibility for debts and agrees to make no claim on the company if the debtor fails to pay.

Naturally, therefore, the factor chooses very carefully which debtors are taken on to avoid being used as a dumping ground for bad or doubtful customers. Usually up to 80 per cent of the debt is advanced to the client company immediately – or when it is required – with the balance, less charges, being paid either when the debtor pays up or after an agreed period of time.

The second form is recourse factoring where the main difference is the factor does not take on responsibility for the debt. If the debtor fails to pay, the client company has to reimburse the factor.

Recourse factoring is often used by companies with many customers with small debts or firms whose customers are of very sound financial standing. Critics sometimes say that recourse factors are less choosy about the debts they take on because they do not shoulder responsibility for the debts, but this is definitely not the case with reputable companies in the field, such as Kellock, who are not members of the ABF.

The bulk of ABF members' business is in non-recourse, but

in fact their growth in recourse business last year at 32 per cent was much more rapid than non-recourse.

Another fast-growing area is invoice discounting, and Association members increased their business in this area by 31 per cent to £3.06 billion.

This service is cheaper than the full recourse or non-recourse factoring services and advances cash on the debts of selected customers, who are not aware of the involvement of a factor. The client company maintains the sales ledger, collects its own debts, and has no debt cover from the factor.

The fourth major service offered by factors is taking over responsibility for sales ledger administration. The theory is that factors have advanced computer systems and experienced credit control personnel, enabling them to provide services that a growing business may not otherwise be able to afford and at the same time free company staff to concentrate on sales and production.

Assessment of creditworthiness, sending out invoices and reminders, and collecting the cash are also services provided by factors.

Costs for these services are levied on two levels – discounting and service. The discount charge depends on the amount of cash drawn against the total invoiced amount and is usually 2 or 3 per cent above current clearing bank base rate and effectively should not cost much more than bank overdraft charges.

Service charges depend on the work load assigned to the factor by the business but are usually made as a percentage of annual company turnover, ranging from 0.75 per cent to 2.5 per cent.

Factoring is available on export business too, and can be especially valuable to new exporters who may be concerned at potential costs and problems of collection and administration. Factors who specialise in export business maintain overseas links, especially in areas such as creditworthiness assessment and debt collection, which can be very helpful.

Banks have a strong connection with factors; indeed they own many of them, and this has led to special services being developed such as the Lloyds Bank Factoring Guarantee Scheme in which it works with the subsidiaries of Lloyds Bowmaker, Alex Lawrie Factors and International Factors.

Under this scheme the bank's branches introduce customers, in the main small and medium-sized firms, to one of the factors. If the assessment is positive the factor guarantees the firm's bank overdraft up to 65 per cent of approved trade debts.

In addition, the factors themselves may provide a further 15 per cent, giving the opportunity for the enterprise to obtain finance for up to 80 per cent of the debtor book. A major benefit for the business is that the scheme combines the flexibility of a bank overdraft, where interest is calculated on a daily basis and only on the amount outstanding, with the traditional factoring service.

Factoring is not the ultimate solution for all financial problems, indeed it is no substitute for proper financial management. It is not a remedy for short-term cash flow problems nor is it necessarily appropriate for all firms or for business startups – though it is by no means unknown for new firms to benefit from factoring. It is, however, a valuable tool which can bring considerable advantages when properly used.

Further information can be obtained from the Association of British Factors, Hind Court, 147 Fleet Street, London EC4A 2BU.

Recourse factors who are not members of this association are Kellock Factors, Abbey Gardens, 4 Abbey Street, Reading, Berkshire RG1 3BA.

4.13   Leasing

The cheapest way of generating funds for capital investment is from retained profits but for many small businesses this may seem an impossible dream as pressures on profitability squeeze that source.

But one way in which they can get round the problem and obtain the modern equipment they need is through the facility known as leasing. Large companies have long been aware of the advantages of leasing but in recent years private businesses have also become familiar with this method of easing the strain on their resources.

When it leases assets, a business has the use of a piece of equipment immediately but pays for it out of its income. The payments are set against revenue for tax purposes and so help to reduce the company's tax charge.

Existing credit arrangements are not affected and the firm's gearing is not increased because a lease is not considered as borrowing, as would happen if the enterprise had taken on a loan to buy the asset.

Leasing will enable a business to calculate its cash flow more easily because payments have to be made at regular intervals and in known amounts. The leasing company cannot change the amounts – provided the firm pays on time – no matter how economic conditions change during the lease period.

Any business looking for certainty will find a fixed-term contract of this nature attractive, although for anyone who wants it, it is possible to negotiate a wide variety of terms in which rentals vary with such factors as tax changes or money costs.

One reason why a firm might want to negotiate different terms to a lease is that it may be in a business which experiences seasonal variations in cash flow, such as in tourism or farming. Payments can be tailored to fit in with this.

Leasing companies have devised a number of methods to meet different requirements, such as a plan where the amount of the instalment reduces as time passes, perhaps for such purposes as financing the purchase of a commercial truck on which more money has to be spent as it gets older.

Another version of this is the low start lease where instalments are low for the first three, six or nine months of the agreement. This could be useful where the machinery or equipment being installed may not come on stream or start paying for itself for a few weeks or months.

A feature of leasing is that the leasing company obtains the benefit of capital allowances on the equipment, which is reflected in the charges paid, but as well as the instalments being fully set against tax the lessee can reclaim VAT on the rental charges.

Another version of leasing is sometimes called lease purchase under which the firm does have the option to buy the equipment eventually. Under this scheme the firm can claim the full capital allowance itself, reclaim VAT on the purchase price, and set the interest payments against tax.

The reasons for opting for lease purchase rather than leasing itself depend to a large extent on tax implications. If a firm can make full use of the capital allowances available, lease purchase may be the right course, otherwise leasing may be the choice.

Leases usually run for three to five years, depending on the assets being bought – office equipment, for example, would usually be leased for the shorter period.

The theory is that decisions on replacing outdated machinery and equipment can be made more easily because there is no longer a temptation to hold on to a piece of equipment after its real economic life is over because of the impression that it then 'costs nothing' – though in fact there are facilities for low cost extensions to leases.

This does not necessarily mean that everything should be leased. Although payments are being made out of future income, so that real costs are falling over the period, payments are fixed and must be made on the due date.

A company should not commit itself too heavily to leasing any more than to other forms of finance; leasing must always be part of a balanced mix of funding. While capital may not be tied up in fixed assets, careful consideration has to be given to the uses for which equipment is intended and the income it is going to generate.

Costs vary considerably and it is advisable to shop around – remembering, of course, to get quotes which are on a comparable basis. One way of doing this is to ask for quotes of so many pounds per £1000, thus giving a common base.

The different forms of lease available can be confusing – there is finance leasing, operating leasing, and sales aid leasing. There is also contract hire, rental, hiring or plant hire, where the main difference is that leasing companies actually buy the equipment and lend it out from stock for specific periods.

In every case the leasing company retains ownership and the equipment only becomes the property of the firm leasing the equipment if it buys it at the end of the lease term.

With a finance lease the user makes payments over a period to cover the leasing firm's capital outlay, borrowing costs and profit and the equipment is maintained by the firm using it.

Costs are not completely covered under some kinds of lease and the leasing company aims to recover the balance and make a profit by selling the asset or leasing it again once the first lease is completed.

These usually involve goods with a good second-hand market or where there may be rapid changes in technology and the equipment is not needed by a firm for all its working life.

With sales aid leasing there is usually a link between the leasing company and the manufacturer or seller of the goods, with the leasing package being offered as an alternative form of financing a deal or as a sales incentive.

Further information and addresses of leasing companies may

be obtained from the Equipment Leasing Association, 18 Upper Grosvenor Street, London W1X 9PB.

4.14   Help from government bodies

Considerable changes have taken place in government assistance to smaller firms in the past year, though the cynics may say that change is more apparent than real, amounting to more of a repackaging of what was already available than providing anything new.

The Enterprise Initiative is being promoted vigorously by the Department of Trade and Industry – or the Department of Enterprise as the Secretary of State for the Department prefers to call it. Full details of the Initiative can be obtained free by ringing 0800 500 200 and asking for the Enterprise Initiative booklet (the phone call costs nothing either). During 1988–89 more than £50 million will be available for six Enterprise Initiative consultancies – marketing, design, quality, manufacturing systems, business planning, and financial and information systems. This will support 1000 consultancies every month for independent businesses with fewer than 500 employees. By 1991 total spending will be more than £250 million.

There are 10 key elements to the Enterprise Initiative. These are:

Marketing – with consultancy advice on all aspects of a company's business, including exports;

Design – with specialist design aid for new and better products and services to corporate image;

Quality – with expert advice on quality management systems;

Manufacturing systems – to help firms apply modern technology and methods in the right way;

Business planning – where consultants will help businesses develop management skills and plan properly to make it easier to raise funds;

Financial and information systems – experts will help to improve or institute proper budgeting, financial control and information systems;

Regional assistance and advice – which covers selective assistance for investment projects, a higher level of grant for the consultancy schemes and investment and innovation grants for small firms;

Exports – advice to improve planning, research and making contacts in export markets;

Research and technology – help for firms to solve technical problems, to undertake collaborative research and generate links with researchers in universities and colleges;

Business and education – assisting the business world to work more closely with the education system.

Full information can also be obtained from regional offices of the Department of Trade and Industry. Help in deciding what is best for your company can be obtained from the Department of Employment's Small Firms Counselling Service and also from the enterprise agencies which now exist in many towns throughout the country.

Quite apart from the DTI's Enterprise Initiative there are a number of organisations which provide help to independent firms in a variety of ways.

Two organisations which have sprung from the nationalised bodies of British Steel and British Coal – namely BSC (Industry) and British Coal Enterprise – can also be very helpful in advising on the financial assistance available.

BSC (Industry) also has its own small workshop units as well as being able to help with the low interest loans available through the European Coal and Steel Community. In the last resort it also has its own loan facility.

British Coal Enterprise's main activity is in providing funds in the form of loans to individuals, partnerships or companies who want to start, locate or expand in the coalfields. Their loans are for up to five years and in amounts of up to a quarter of the total required or £5000 per job created. They too have small workshops.

Funds for both start-up and development are available from several public bodies set up around the country to promote economic growth, such as the Development Agencies in Scotland and Wales, which both have small business divisions.

They channel aid to smaller firms through loans, grants, and equity participation as well as advance factories and advice in many skills, such as financial management.

In Northern Ireland the organisation responsible for dealing with companies employing up to 50 people is the Local Enterprise Development Unit. The LEDU provides a financial package of grants, loans, and loan guarantees to manufacturing and service firms.

The agency has a wide variety of financial aids for different purposes, such as capital grants of 30 to 50 per cent for new plant, machinery and equipment, or enterprise grants of up to £5000 for individuals with limited capital who want to go into business for the first time, or management salary grants to pay up to 80 per cent of the cost of employing specialist management.

In England's rural areas, the Council for Small Industries in Rural Areas – which has been merged with its parent body, the renamed Rural Development Commission – gives counselling and technical advice. It has funds of its own to finance projects but in general it prefers to assist a business to obtain its own funds from other sources.

One of these is the arrangement it has made with a number of the clearing banks under which it filters projects, thereby reducing the costs to the banks, and helping them to qualify for better rates of interest.

Another popular scheme with which it is involved is the provision of grants in certain areas for converting redundant buildings in country areas into workplaces. The Rural Development Commission is also in a position to help firms which want to develop rural transport operations following deregulation with financial support.

Rural areas of Scotland are served by the Highlands and Islands Development Board which has a wide range of loans, interest relief grants, removal grants, and grants for building and other purposes.

In rural Wales the organisation concerned is Mid Wales Development, which has its own development grant in addition to being able to arrange financial packages and other assistance to create jobs in manufacturing and certain service industries.

Advance factories, grants for the conversion of rural premises, and a full range of advisory services are provided by both HIDB and Mid Wales Development.

5
Marketing

TOM CANNON
Professor of Business Studies, Stirling University

5.1   The small firm's route to profits and performance

Recently, the clarion call has gone out for more aggressive, more rigorous, more sustained, or simply more marketing by Britain's small firms. Improved marketing, particularly by smaller manufacturers, is central to the industrial strategy. The need for small companies to emphasise marketing in developing their business was the cornerstone of the 1978 report on industrial innovation by the government's Advisory Council for Applied Research and Development.

Despite this, many managers of small firms question the relevance of marketing to them, given the severe limits on their resources, particularly of time and money. Large advertising budgets, expensive and time-consuming market research projects and the jargon which marketing appears to involve hold little appeal to the practical small firm manager. Problems in measuring the pay-offs from this effort reinforce the notion that marketing is a luxury, which only large and wealthy firms can afford.

However, many smaller businessmen intuitively apply the marketing concept every day. This is often done in a manner almost impossible for the large firm manager to achieve. It is because, as an approach to business, marketing is both simpler and more subtle than any of the cruder notions of large expenditures in areas such as advertising. It involves seeing the firm's goals in terms of meeting customer needs and wants. It means recognising that the better the firm matches its offering product, process or service to what the customer wants, the higher the value he will place on it. The higher this valuation, the stronger the relationship, with resulting improvements in returns for both the producer and the buyer. It is not a philanthropic gesture by firms, but an approach to improving the

143

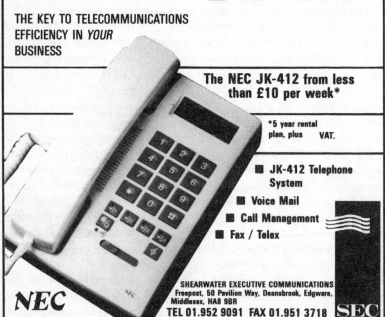

management of the exchanges between producer and buyer with resulting gains in performance.

The closeness that characterises relations between the managers of small enterprises and customers, whether a small plastics processor dealing with industrial buyers or tenant landlord with regulars, provides a powerful basis for the dialogue essential to effective marketing. The initial step involves recognising the importance of looking outside the firm into the market place for leads to further developments.

This was seen by Midland Furnishings. They produce a wide array of furniture, particularly wooden dining and living room furniture. Timber wall units are a major line. They used to produce these in teak and to a height of about five feet six inches. A few years ago the firm made a major effort to introduce their products into Europe. They suffered an early setback, primarily because these styles were not popular in the major European markets, and the wall unit market was dominated by other woods and different sizes. A product-oriented firm would probably have abandoned its efforts to develop these markets. A sales-oriented company might have worked very hard, spending large sums of money to win sales against retailer reservations and customer rejection. The response of this small, owner-managed firm was very different. Lacking the money or resources immediately to introduce new designs for these markets, the lessons from the market were built into long-term design work. In the next major styling exercise conducted by the firm, its offerings incorporated these ideas. The intervening period has been used to explore their thinking with major UK retail buyers who encouraged their developments. In fact, changes in housing design, particularly the popularity of converting traditional domestic storage space to other uses, were creating changed customer needs. These pressures were encouraging sales of larger units in Britain. The rapid growth in demand at home for their units is now preventing a new European initiative.

This contrasts dramatically with the difficulties facing Century Belting, a small producer of transmission belts. Their prosperity had been built over many years through their strong relationships with a number of major manufacturers. An export initiative some time ago had failed because of the highly automated equipment used by European customers. Despite their considerable technical expertise and longer-term potential to adapt, the firm decided to concentrate their resources on satisfying the day-to-day needs of their current domestic customers. However, the progressive growth in inter-European trade has forced their British customers to adapt rapidly to meet European competition. Over the last two years, a number of major accounts have bought new equipment from other suppliers as the company has worked to solve the technical problems associated with the newer systems. A number of competitors have established toeholds with Century Belting's traditional customers.

The adoption of a marketing perspective by Midland Furniture permitted them to steal a march on their competitors. There were no increases in advertising or more conventional marketing costs. They recognised that their prosperity was built on successfully meeting customers' needs both today and as they changed over time. Their networks of relationships and contacts provided their information base. Their technical skills and production capability gave them the opportunity to develop.

Century Belting's difficulties contrast vividly with this. Their primary focus of attention was their current offerings and capabilities. They assumed that they were immune to change. Technical skills, production orientation and dangerous assumptions trapped them into a negative approach to buyer needs. Changes in the market place forced them to invest heavily in price cutting, increased services, advertising and promotion to arrest the tide which their lack of marketing insight had led them to ignore.

It is recognition that successful businesses are based on effectively meeting buyer needs that is the essence of marketing. The different areas of activity – information gathering and organisation, product policy, promotion and selling, pricing and distribution – gain their real value from being built on this and the firm's willingness to implement lessons from the market place. The smaller firm with its stronger, more direct links to the market place, shorter lines of communication, flexibility and ability to act quickly and decisively has the scope to implement the reality rather than the appearance of marketing.

5.2 Information for marketing decisions

Information is the cornerstone of modern marketing. It binds the marketing system together by providing data on the needs of customers as well as building a picture of the external pressures and internal capabilities determining the firm's ability to meet the market requirements profitably over time.

The manager of the smaller firm has greater access to his customers and shorter lines of communication. These give him major advantages over the large corporation executive. He is seldom cut off from customer comments, attitudes and needs. Despite this, his intelligence gathering capability is often not used to the full. This reflects a lack of recognition of the potential value of information and a failure to plan its role in the firm.

The marketing-oriented firm works hard to ensure that the gathering, organisation and use of information from the market place is geared to effective management decisions. The retailer hearing an assistant say, 'You're the sixth person today to ask for that but we don't stock it as there's no demand', and the engineering firm convinced that it is their level of after-sales service that sells their product but 'we still offer the lowest prices in the area' already have some of the data to improve their market position.

Collecting this information and organising it to answer questions, solve problems and meet customer needs is the sphere of marketing research. The array of sources ranges from the firm's own records and staff to government, private and commercial agencies and ultimately to specially commissioned studies. In fact, many managers starting off on the information gathering effort find the sheer volume of data the greatest deterrent to its use. This is why a clear brief which identifies the questions, problems and issues is vital. To specify the data needed and plan its uses effectively, the variables affecting these issues need to be identified. It calls for careful thought before the search starts. But the firm which recognises that there is a problem is halfway to solving it.

The prime source of data for the manager of a small firm is inhouse information. This includes sales records, dispatch figures, stock details, details of inquiries and orders, and the material that can be gathered by salesmen, delivery staff and top management. It appears very easy to collect this information, but it is often so badly organised that the value is lost. Hard thought about what facts are required is necessary. Simplification of the material can provide massive advances in access. This can be as simple as rounding figures to tens, hundreds or even thousands while ensuring that simplification does not lead to distortion. Specific problems can be examined by deeper analysis of company records.

Oceania Motors had always emphasised high service levels and good quality in its new and used car sales. The high costs were paid for by high levels of repeat purchase of replacement vehicles by customers. A progressive deterioration in turnover forced a rethink about the overall approach. Before changing policies, the managing director checked his assumptions about levels of repeat purchase from company sales records. He was shocked to find that, during the 1970s, they had fallen from over 60 per cent of sales to less than 20 per cent. Further data analysis led to other important findings.

The most important of these was the picture from government sources of the changing population profile of the area. It emerged that their home town had changed from being largely self-sufficient in jobs to being increasingly dependent on a major city and several new towns. The middle management groups on which their business has been built increasingly worked for large city-based firms. A research report by their trade organisation pointed out the rapidly growing proportion of managers obtaining company cars. Rival car firms, based in the city, were winning this business. This information was only part of the store collected and disseminated by the government. Any executive who has felt, when filling in government forms, 'how useful it would be to know about my competitors' is most of the way to recognising the value of government information because it is all published somewhere, albeit in a form geared to government requirements while protecting confidence.

This information is supplemented and made more relevant to specific industries by material published by such bodies as trade associations, industry research associations and commercial services. Much of this information can be purchased if firms are not members of their trade associations. Recently, industry research associations have become more marketing oriented. A number of commercial publications now exist providing detailed marketing intelligence.

Much information is available through central, university and polytechnic libraries. They often employ specialist staff to assist inquirers. One Manchester-based electrical equipment manufacturer regularly uses the information gleaned from various publications in the Manchester Central and Manchester Business School Libraries to direct his activities. Some libraries, such as the City Business Library and those of certain chambers of commerce, have outstanding reputations for helping the practical businessman.

Sometimes the need may emerge for a more structured and scientific approach to information gathering. This is the sphere of market research. British firms are fortunate in having access to large numbers of highly skilled and reputable research agencies. These offer systematic and formalised investigations of both general topics and specialised areas. There are costs involved but these should be related to the value of the information and the potential pay-offs. A number of firms have found that, within their limitations, business studies students at colleges and universities have been able to assist with research.

We are now seeing an information and communication revolution. Smaller firms are well placed to take advantage of the opportunities offered to those able to respond quickly, positively and flexibly to market conditions. However, this depends on their willingness to look outside, and build up and use a picture of the market place.

Sources of information

Tupper, E and Wills, G (1975) *Sources of UK Marketing Information* Ernest Benn
Marketfact (weekly) Haymarket Publishing Ltd
Government Statistics: A Brief Guide to Sources HMSO
Trade and Industry (weekly) HMSO: London
Directory of British Associations CBD Research, 15 Wickham Road, Beckenham, Kent BR3 2JS
Retail Business The Economist Intelligence Unit, 40 Duke Street, London W1A 1DW
Mintel Mintel Publications, 7 Arundel Street, London WC2R 3DR
The IPC Consumer and Industrial Marketing Manual IPC Publications, The Market Research Society, 175 Oxford Street, London W1R 1TA (moving in 1990)
The Industrial Market Research Society, 11 Bird Street, Lichfield, Staffs WS13 6PW

Direct access through:
Export Market Information Centre, 1 Victoria Street, London SW1H 0ET; tel: 01-215 5444
or
Central Statistical Office, Great George Street, London SW1P 3AQ

5.3   Products and planning

The firm's product or process lies at the centre of most small firm managers' thinking about their companies. The ability to make some item well, to offer a special service or to meet requests to supply particular components or materials was probably the main reason for starting up the firm.

The commitment, flexibility and creativity applied to the product, service or process has a direct effect on the firm's ability to survive and prosper. In this it is increasingly important to recognise that the company's offering goes far beyond the individual, physical product offered.

The customer will order a particular item of equipment, specific tooling or moulding, a meal or a holiday, but will assume that a host of other things are included. He may expect free installation, regular maintenance of the tools, specific quality levels on the mouldings, quick service with the meal. All these affect his evaluation of the firm's offering, the prices he will willingly pay and the likelihood of repeat business. The close links between supplier and customer in small firms give managers the chance to understand these needs and design offerings capable of meeting them.

The starting point might simply be the division of the firm's customers into groups buying, roughly, the same items but wanting different things associated with them. Moulded Plastics Ltd produce a wide assortment of lines for the building industry ranging from clips and fasteners through to complex, moulded fittings. Some customers such as large builders or local authorities had extensive warehousing, professional buyers, projects under construction and skilled workers. Their need was for large consignments of standardised items at low prices. In contrast the DIY enthusiast needed items for a specific small job, available locally, simple to fit with clear instructions, all far more important than price.

Moulded Plastics eventually subdivided their clients and their needs into five groups or segments: architects, large builders, jobbing builders, local authorities and DIY. The item bought or specified was roughly the same, but there were pronounced differences in requirements for other aspects of the total product. These centred on the product itself: its colours,

quality, robustness and, very important, ease of use. It quickly became apparent that serious attention had to be given to the range of associated items. Contact customers wanted considerable *depth* in product offering with, for example, many different pipe clips.

As the DIY business grew the *width* of their range expanded as wholesalers and end customers called for lines associated with the initial product. Controlling these extensions of the product became more important than spotting new opportunities.

Many firms find that the range of spares, service levels, installation, replacement and warranty policies are more important to some customers than the product. Dividing the market up provides the opportunity for this, as the customer wanting low prices may not want a high service level but others will be willing to pay more for associated services. This lesson came home very clearly to Moulded Plastics with a particular retail line which eventually required expensive packaging and branding to provide the buyer with reassurance about quality and reliability.

Innovation and new product development are increasingly important in ensuring the long-term profitability of smaller firms. Large companies often envy the creativity, speed of response and flexibility that smaller firms can apply to this process.

Successful innovation comes from the combination of a good array of new product opportunities and rigorous selection of a small number of ideas for development. Access to new product opportunities is often easier than expected. Internal sources can be salesmen, production and research and development staff. Other fertile sources are research organisations, government dissemination programmes, new product directories, foreign markets and suppliers. Probably most important is a willingness continually to search outside, perhaps through journals and magazines.

For a country with a long history of innovation we show a surprising reluctance to look outside ourselves for licensing and other forms of technology acquisition. Both Germany and Japan 'buy in' innovation at a far higher rate than the UK. Innovation is often far cheaper than managers expect.

The innovative ideas, new products and developments need to be carefully screened before introduction if they are to avoid joining the large pool of failed products. The first step is to evaluate all the ideas for their practicality and appropriateness to the firm. The market potential of those left can then be evaluated, with only the best progressing. Development of the remainder will probably eliminate others, leaving only a few for tests, perhaps involving selected customers. Full introduction is only worthwhile with those products successfully getting through all these stages.

Many companies embarking on a product management programme find that they are forced to think hard about marketing planning. Unfortunately, the relatively simple process of planning is saddled with an elaborate mythology which deters many firms. A good plan is a simple, practical set of guidelines for the firm's future development based on a proper understanding of its potential.

The main elements are an *audit* of resources and potential and a set of simple, concise and practicable *objectives*, perhaps noting major *alternatives*. Implementation can be seen in terms of a basic *strategy* backed up by specific *tactics*, both judged in terms of their relevance to objectives. *Evaluation* will provide an ongoing basis for learning and modification geared to *control* and *costs*. Medical Engineering Ltd draw up their marketing plan every year under these headings, revising it as necessary throughout the year. Actually writing it down is seen as an important discipline in itself, forcing managers rigorously to appraise their ideas and beliefs about the direction the firm will take.

They are in an area where expenditure and technology are moving at an increasing rate. Their products must compete with larger rivals while remaining competitively priced and efficiently produced. In this, they share the problems of most small firms whose products, the bedrock of their operations, are continually under challenge from changes internally, among customers, among rivals, and in technology. Successful management here is vital to survival.

Sources

NEW PRODUCT IDEAS
British Technology Group
101 Newington Causeway
London SE1 6BU
01–403 6666

International New Product Centre
Newsletter
PO Box 37c
Esher
Surrey KT10 0QN

International New Product Newsletter
PO Box 191
390 Stuart Street
Boston
Massachusetts 02117

MARKETING PLANNING
Winkler, John *Winkler on Marketing Planning* Cassell and Co Ltd

5.4   Sales promotion and advertising

Sales promotion and advertising are the most visible aspects of marketing. They provide the main mechanism for communication between seller and buyer. The representative provides a near ideal basis for the dialogue which helps the company meet customer needs while ensuring that business relationships are developed and orders won. Advertising enables the firm to reach many thousands of prospective customers and project information on and images of the company. Sometimes, such as through mail order, orders can be won directly through advertisements.

In most small firms, the salesman or owner/director actively engaged in selling leads the firm's marketing effort. Among the many facets of their work, the ultimate goal is the construction of a good array of profitable accounts. Partly for this reason sales targets are becoming increasingly important. Originally this involved simply setting targets for volume and perhaps profit contribution. Now targets are being designed to include a proportion of new accounts, direction towards key industries, even a profile of the industries or customers a representative should seek out. Despite some criticism, they provide a spur to action, at least when seen as fair by both salesman and manager. Perhaps surprisingly, the best results are often achieved by the owner/director who, leading the sales effort, sets himself these types of target. A giftware manufacturer in the south-west saw his sales increase over 50 per cent within a year of setting himself targets.

Initiatives here call for careful evaluation of current activities. Customer contact time – the potentially profitable time actually spent in front of the prospect – can easily be swamped by costly time in the car, plane or hotel. In some firms, less than 20 per cent of the salesman's time is spent in front of the prospects.

The calls themselves call for a balance between: (1) *cold canvassing*, sometimes necessary but never to be the norm; (2) *prepared calls* for new and established customers; (3) *repeat visits* with a clear idea of the relationship between customer liaison, business development and order gathering. All need underpinning by effective report back and follow through in the firm.

Too often the sales effort is wasted by inefficient order processing. In fact it has been said that 'in Britain, the problem is buying not selling'. The participants on one sales training course were shocked by the results of a simple exercise involving the attempt to buy, incognito by telephone, a stock item from their firm.

The joint owner and sales director of Hasty Footwear faced his greatest problems when the company grew large enough to employ its first full-time salesman. Recruitment and selection posed problems of job description, finding a sample of good candidates, evaluation and choice. Once the representative was appointed, the almost inevitable problem of the self-motivated entrepreneur in dealing with staff cropped up. He expected the employee's commitment to be as great as his own. In fact, he was forced to introduce a planned process of management, motivation and control, through involving the salesman in planning and setting targets, close liaison, target-related bonuses and detailed evaluation of his work. In Hasty Footwear, the director's gradual change in role led to a greater awareness of other aspects of sales promotion and advertising.

Advertising can be used in a number of ways: *awareness*, to establish *interest*, to stimulate *desire* and prompt *action* by customers to buy the product (AIDA). Specific adverts can be geared to do each of these through a mixture of creative input and the right medium. There is an enormous range of media available to the smaller businessman: from television and newspaper advertisements through to exhibitions, mail shots and brochures. As a result, the scope for achieving different results is enormous. Effective advertising management is built on four elements: clear goals, constant monitoring of performance, evaluation of results and a willingness to learn and adapt.

Most small firm managers handle their own advertising effort but there is a massive body of knowledge of and research into this area which should be tapped wherever possible. Much of this accumulated information is in the hands of the advertising agencies. They vary greatly in size from giants like Ogilvy, Benson and Mather to small local firms. Details can be obtained through the Institute of Practitioners in Advertising.

Much discussion of sales promotion and advertising suggests that they are totally separate spheres of action. In fact, they interact powerfully. The buyer who knows the salesman, his firm, its products, the company's reputation, its other customers and its record will respond to the sales visit. Advertising and other methods of preparing the ground are vital to this.

Public relations can play a major part. Many managers are over-cautious in their media relations. A good relationship with journalists on the local, trade and national media, a system of issuing press releases communicating stories in a simple and pithy form, geared as much as possible to the normal style of the newspaper or magazine, can earn great benefits for any firm. Innovations, major orders and success in any sphere are worth communicating to the media, which will generally handle the topic in a very supportive way.

Sales promotion and advertising provide the firm with the opportunity to direct the process of communication between the firm and its environment. Planning, targets, constant evaluation and updating of knowledge sustained by the vital spark of creativity are the basis of pay-offs here.

5.5   The marketing dimension to price in the small firm

Almost any discussion with managers of smaller firms about buyers, customer relations or any facet of marketing will sooner or later get round to the problem of price. It is at the centre of the relationship between the supplier and his customer. It provides the former with the resources to survive and prosper, while measuring the value the latter places on the goods.

In many smaller firms the price decision has a significance far greater than for larger companies. They may lack the resources to invest in advertising, and to build brand or supplier loyalty to protect them against cut-price rivals. Large numbers of small firms supply industrial and commercial customers on a contract or tender basis. Here specifications might be tightly defined and a number of competitive tenders received. In these circumstances, pricing policies can be a constant battle to keep prices as low as is compatible with holding on to business.

This can lead to a vicious circle in which low prices can produce a steady deterioration in the firm's position as funds are starved from product development, promotion and improving customer relations. The firm can easily become vulnerable on two major fronts: product improvements by rivals meeting customer needs more effectively and price cutting by competitors with lower costs. The marketing approach to price seeks to overcome these problems.

Underlying this is the proposition that pricing is a strategic decision which over time is geared to building a business rather than winning specific orders. To some extent these are inseparable. But, although it is impossible to build a business without winning orders, some orders can contribute towards weakening a firm.

The objectives the firm wishes to achieve through the prices under specific market conditions are particularly important. Understanding these is as important as incorporating operating production and material costs into the price. This calls for systematic information gathering to build up a picture of the likely reactions in the market, among customers and competitors, to price changes.

The close links that top managers of small firms have established with many of their customers can help in this. Industrial buyers can be surprisingly helpful in providing guidance and useful information. The right approach to them, allied to a well-organised system of cross-checking and organising this material, can provide significant insights into the results of changes.

Effective use of the information derives from clearly setting the objectives of the firm's pricing policy. A company seeking increased volume sales will follow a policy totally different from one looking for a particular return per unit or a specific high-quality image for its goods.

A foundry in the Midlands faced a problem common today. Should they increase prices because of an increase in materials costs, and put their prices in line with the rest of the industry? The managing director and his two salesmen raised the issue with a few of the major customers and, perhaps more importantly, some of the firms they part serviced. It soon became clear that the volume would increase so much with prices held that overall operating costs would be dramatically cut.

A furniture company based in West London found a totally different situation. Their customers saw discussions of holding or cutting prices as part of an overall cheapening exercise. For this firm, high prices were a major part of the process of re-assuring customers of the overall quality of its products. Reviewing the alternative pricing policies open to the firm led to a decision to increase prices significantly in the new season, while backing it up with heavy investment in design, development and promotion.

The introduction of a new product, the company start-up or the launch into a new market bring the problems of setting prices into their sharpest focus. Costs can be determined with a fair degree of accuracy for certain volumes. There may be no competition to get clues from. Customers will have no benchmarks by which to judge responses. Here there are two basic strategies: *penetration* prices seeking to win large volume at low prices or *skimming* prices seeking to earn maximum returns from an initial high price. Although specific circumstances are the best guides to action it does appear that it is easier to correct problems caused by high prices. A firm looking to expand will generally find it easier to 'spin down', ie launch lower priced new products, than 'up'.

The decisions the firm makes about its prices affect, and are in turn affected by, all other decisions the firm makes about its offering. At its most basic the income earned will determine the resources for investment in product development, promotion and distribution initiatives. Price is probably the clearest clue the consumer has about quality, and, like all other aspects of the firm's offering, prices have to be designed to make a positive contribution to the firm's performance in the market.

Ultimately, each element in the firm's offering – product, price, promotion and distribution – has to be designed to maximise both their individual and, probably more important, their joint contribution to meeting customer needs more effectively and to building a more profitable business. Small firms, with their shorter lines of communication, clearer decision-making system and greater flexibility, have the potential to exploit fully the marketing concept.

5.6 Exporting by small firms

Some years ago the shock of a £2.4 billion deficit on Britain's balance of trade highlighted the deteriorating trade position of the country's manufacturing industry. By 1982 this deficit had turned into a massive surplus of £4.6 billion – but this dramatic recovery was not the result of a resurgence of manufacturing exports or the pushing back of imports. It was largely attributable to the benefits flowing through from North Sea oil and continued high surpluses on invisibles, such as tourism, finance and insurance. Manufacturing industry has continued to struggle, and although North Sea oil can cushion the blow for the nation as a whole, small firms across the country are feeling the effects of the real crisis in the economy. In key areas of component supply and process industries such as plastics, aluminium and other metal, the underlying weakness of the consumer industries is already affecting business. On the home market future projects are inextricably tied to the fortunes of the car, appliance and other key sectors. The only short- to medium-term opportunity for stability and growth appears to lie in exports or a selective policy of substitutes for imports in certain key areas.

Although there is no shortage of exhortation to action by all manufacturers, including small firms, the degree of real support is small in the light of the potentially crippling effects of deficits in non-oil balances of the type we have seen.

Much of the support that does exist is of only limited value or interest to smaller firms, whose managers do not have the time to cope with the large quantity of bumf that seems to be the inevitable corollary of action here. Even more important, many managers find that export schemes involving two or three weeks overseas are not practical when there are only one or two people running the company. There is an urgent need for export support initiatives geared specifically to the needs of smaller firms. The Market Entry Guarantee Scheme is a limited and tentative step in this direction.

Ultimately, the achievement of significant exports is in the hands of the managers themselves. Government, banks, chambers of commerce and trade associations can only support their action, not be a substitute for them. The scope for effective export business development is often greater and easier to achieve than many managers believe. It is based on four elements: resource mobilisation, market selection, efficient service and organisation.

Resource mobilisation calls for the bringing together of the variety of elements that make up the firm, from its management skills through to its design and development capabilities. The most important single factor is the determination of top management to devote time and resources to building up export business. In this process the inherent flexibility and adaptability of the smaller firm provides a real advantage over larger competitors.

These resources provide the key to the next stage in the export effort – market selection. There are no good or bad markets; there are only those right or wrong for the firm given its resources, skills and knowledge. There has recently emerged a surprising degree of consensus on one issue in this area: whatever you do *concentrate*. British exporters, particularly small firms, tend to spread their export efforts over a very wide array of markets. This can undermine one of their greatest strengths, the network of contacts in the market providing insights into needs and developments to which they can respond more quickly and more appropriately than their competitors. This can be done in one, two or three markets but not in fifty.

Concentration can be a vital aid to the establishment of the right kind of service and marketing relationship with the market. This goes far beyond merely appointing an agent. For some firms in certain markets this may be neither necessary nor appropriate. A giftware manufacturer in Yorkshire decided not to bother with an agent in Holland when he found that he could visit the British Overseas Trade Board in Leeds, sail from Hull and visit 15 prospective retailers in Holland and an exhibition in Utrecht on a drive of less than 400 miles. At the centre of any attempt to establish an effective level of service in any market is the recognition that there is no reason to expect the foreign buyer to expect worse service than UK customers. The overall produce, price, distribution, sales and advertising effort should be designed to meet his market conditions rather than the pattern in Britain. This can only be realistically applied in a number of key markets in which the firm is determined to succeed.

Long-term success requires a well thought out export organisation. This will create a commitment to success throughout the firm ensuring that sales won in fierce competition overseas are not lost in the packing department, on the delivery bay or in the design office.

Britain's smaller firms already play a major part in exporting. There is enormous potential for further growth if real determination in the firm is matched by effective marketing and by the right type of support from government, other institutions and the head offices of those small firms which are part of larger groups.

5.7 Marketing and selling for the start-up firm

The most fundamental questions for the person starting up a new venture are: who is going to buy from it and why? It is seldom sufficient to comment that 'everyone will buy it' and 'because it is better'. The confidence implicit in these statements is probably necessary to persuade the entrepreneur to take the risks involved in starting his own business. To minimise the inevitable risks involved in this step these assumptions have to be examined in a disciplined way. The questioning involved in this ought to be directed towards two basic propositions:

1. Why should anyone buy this product or service from me?
2. If it's such a good opportunity why is someone not already doing it?

These two things – a real need among buyers and the firm's ability to meet it better than anyone else – will probably go a long way to determining the success or failure of the venture. Here, it is not enough to think solely in terms of the customers. Intermediaries, agents, distributors, wholesalers and retailers can have a major impact on this.

Asking the questions is not enough. They must be posed in the right quarters. This calls for some decisions on precisely who the product or service is catering for. No firm and virtually no product or offering appeals to everyone. Their appeal is selective. In fact, it is the ability of smaller firms to be adaptable and flexible enough to cater for the complex and varied needs of their customers that is often their greatest strength.

Once the decisions about who the customers are going to be

161

are made, the detailed specification of the product, service or other offering can be made. The person considering starting up probably has the broad outline of what he wants to do mapped out. He will be seeking to blend this with his increasing knowledge of the target market. His firm's future will be determined in the market place; in judging its prospects or seeking ways to reduce his risks the market provides the most important clues.

Decisions should be made in the light of real knowledge, not on the basis of hopes or wishful thinking. Prospective customers are often willing to invest surprisingly large amounts of time and effort in helping the new firm. The man who has done his homework on the market, perhaps using government or other publications in the commercial department of his nearest central library, will generally discover a real desire to assist him with up-to-date or more detailed information among buyers, whether government, large or small firms or the man in the street.

These groups will ultimately determine the success of his venture. They should be approached, talked to, involved for as long as possible before big risks are taken and large expenditures made. This direct access by the top man to customers will gradually become one of the firm's greatest assets. In some instances, entrepreneurs hold back because of fears about their ideas being stolen or copied. Although this does happen, the overall standards of business ethics in the UK are very high. These dangers are normally far less than those resulting from not having early access to prospects.

The target customers can only say what they might do under certain circumstances. The onus lies on the firm to meet their needs. These go far beyond the physical product itself. The buyer wants a specific item at a particular price with a certain level of service. One customer might want a more robust product and be willing to pay more for it. Or may be less concerned about immediate delivery of the equipment than the provision of a rapid maintenance and repair service. Another might be buying the same basic equipment but want a totally different mix. The notion that it is the combination of product, prices, distribution and service levels, advertising and sales promotion that determines the satisfaction of different types of customers is being recognised increasingly by successful entrepreneurs.

Sometimes the right mix will come intuitively; on other occasions arriving at it will involve hard work, difficult decisions and errors. For the engineer or the craftsman the problems involved in taking this approach can be severe. These and others are so involved in their product that they lose sight of the rest of the forces affecting success. Gaining some direct sales experience and accepting that a great deal of time must be spent on the road are important steps for this type of entrepreneur.

Talk of customers can create the impression that selling and marketing involve a single set of direct contacts. Often the situation is far more complex than that. The farmer or mine owner sells to the processor, such as British Steel. Their output passes in turn to manufacturers such as Metal Box whose customers, like Heinz, will eventually sell to retailers or wholesalers before the product reaches the consumer. All those involved in this chain depend to some extent on the others.

The new firm may have a product with real customer appeal, but if it runs contrary to the intermediary's interest or if the customer's market is hostile or simply depressed, the venture's prospects are bleak.

At the same time, these depressed circumstances may create their own opportunities. Established suppliers may be less able to cope with shorter production runs, low levels of customer stockholding, etc than the new firm. In general, the companies already in a market start with real advantages: better contacts and information besides their capital and equipment investment. It is the gaps that they have left in the market that can provide the most lucrative opportunities.

In some industries, such as rubber processing, industrial brushes, components and many others, long production runs have become the norm. This opens up opportunities for the firm geared to short runs and special products. The circumstances creating the gaps should be closely studied. A hole may exist in the market because no one wants to be there because it is so unprofitable. A site for a shop may be available simply because others have failed on that site. Specific engineered units may not be produced because the trouble involved and the wastage rates destroy profits.

Equally, the opportunity may exist because no one else has noticed or has been capable of satisfying it. Once into a market competition is likely to emerge. Holding on to a market is as important as winning it initially and probably far more difficult. It calls for some kind of plan defining how the market will be developed over time. The twin themes of meeting customer needs better while keeping ahead of the competition are at the centre of this.

This may call for the introduction of new services linked to the existing product. A hotelier might introduce a babysitting facility for guests. A component manufacturer may start factoring certain lines. It may involve new products. In New Technology Based Firms (NTBFs) this is to some extent critical to their very existence. In some new firms the commitment to opening up new markets provides the spur to growth.

It is the scope for this type of development which provides the spur to individuals to take the enormous steps involved in setting up their own firms. Failure by new firms is often at least in part attributable to neglect of the marketing and selling dimension to their activities. They should look to answer these basic questions:

- ☐ Who are my potential customers?
- ☐ How many of them are there and what is their potential demand?
- ☐ Can I reach all of them with my existing or planned resources?
- ☐ Who are the major intermediaries between me and the end users?
- ☐ Will they stock my offering?
- ☐ Will they give it support and display space and hold sufficient stocks for it to be viable?
- ☐ Who are the competitors?
- ☐ What are their competitive offerings?
- ☐ If there are no competitors, what is the reason?
- ☐ What am I offering that is in the customer's eyes sufficient inducement to buy?
- ☐ What is the mix of product, price, distribution and advertising that I am offering to my customers and what is its appeal to them?

5.8   Distribution and the small firm

In no area of marketing are the potential strengths of the small firm more clearly seen than in the use of distribution as a marketing tool. Managers of small firms frequently come back from foreign visits angry at the comments about the 'English disease' of poor delivery and service. Many have records of performance in these areas that their overseas rivals would envy. Jim Duffield of Springfield Furnishings found the prevalence of this belief an eye opener on his first foreign sales trip. In Britain the firm had used its delivery performance as a central plank of its marketing strategy.

The role of distribution in the firm's marketing effort involves many things beyond price. It is useful to subdivide the area into two spheres of action: physical distribution and channel management. Both cover major aspects of the firm's attempts to manage its relations with the market.

It is in physical distribution management – the combination of inventory, delivery, transport, warehousing and location policies – that recent evidence has suggested that smaller firms have assets that large companies need to spend a great deal of time and effort to achieve. Increasing numbers of firms, large and small, are finding it valuable to look afresh at physical distribution.

The sheet size of their investment in this area has forced some companies to review their policies. In some firms stocks (pre-production plus finished goods), vehicles, warehousing and delivery itself can account for over 40 per cent of working capital. The scale of this may not come to light because of the tendency of firms as they grow larger to fragment responsibilities and budgets in this area.

A warehouse or stores manager might be appointed; later a traffic manager and then a purchasing manager will be given responsibility for stocks. Each will try to make his area perform as effectively as possible. Unfortunately, the efforts of each will have a direct impact on the performance of the other areas. All affect in different ways the overall level of customer service.

The stores manager's decision to run down stocks might make his budgets look better. But it could mean that purchasing will be buying in smaller, less economical lots. It might involve the traffic manager in increased costs as he makes multiple deliveries to customers to fill their orders. Perhaps most important it may mean that purchasing waiting time increases with some lost sales.

The overstocked firm might be able to achieve these reductions with none of these losses. Generally there is a price to be paid in other areas for savings in one department. The company might be willing to face these costs but major marketing decisions are involved. Policy formulation and implementation call for top management involvement and need to be seen in terms of costs to the total physical distribution system.

In-depth knowledge of the different areas and of their impact gives the manager of the smaller firm insights not usually open to his rival in the larger organisation. It is a potential advantage which should be matched with a disciplined and structured approach to the pay-offs between service level, transport, stocks, location and packaging.

The same combination of individualism and discipline probably provides the key to the successful marketing of the company's products or services to its distribution channels – the network of intermediaries betweeen the product and his market. It is useful to view the construction of a network of middlemen or industrial users in terms of an interacting marketing chain. The firm is generally dealing with independent concerns with considerable discretion in buying.

Effectively moving the product through the channels is a combination of the producer's push and the customer's pull. Discounts, special deals or packings, longer credit, etc help to push the buyer into purchasing. But it is his customer's demand which will persuade him to rebuy. Improved deliveries, special features and other advantages welcomed by the buyer's customers or giving him the chance to satisfy customer pull have a particular appeal.

It is often said that small firms have special problems in these areas. Some retailers are reluctant to deal with small suppliers, others demand a high level of advertising support, and increasing numbers insist on their own name appearing on the product. When other manufacturers are the main channel members they may expect support in specific areas such as technical development or customer service. In these cases it may be useful to construct a picture of the channel right down to the final user of the product no matter how remote. This can provide management with a clear indication of the different points at which they can influence demand besides giving clues to future prospects and opportunities.

The ability of management to take this broader view but build into it speed of reaction and flexibility is the key to the effective use of distribution as a marketing tool. The enormous costs involved, allied to the continuing pressures for faster service and smaller unit deliveries, are posing major threats to the viability of some concerns. Nevertheless, it represents an area in which effective action can lead to major benefits. The importance of the area has been recognised by the British Institute of Management (BIM) in the establishment of the Centre for Physical Distribution Management.

Useful address
Centre for Physical Distribution Management
Management House
Cottingham Road
Corby
NN17 1TT

5.9 Marketing and the smaller service firm

The growth of the service sector is probably one of the most striking features of modern commercial life. It is now estimated that over 60 per cent of the UK workforce is employed in services. Far more small firms are involved in services than in manufacture. The generally greater ease of entry and widening opportunities here will probably mean that the numbers in services will grow faster than in manufacture. It is arguable that the special strengths of small firms, particularly the intimate involvement of top management in all aspects of the firm's operation, are a great advantage in the service sector.

Despite this growth and the opportunities here, many attitudes to services are marked by a peculiar ambivalence. The impression is sometimes given that service companies are not as important or as acceptable as manufacturers. Government support schemes frequently ignore services. Interest in the special needs of the service sector is negligible. This can be seen in the way the marketing of services is neglected and ill understood.

People are far more important in service marketing than in manufacturing. Individually they play a far more important role in designing and determining the nature of the offering itself. This is partly because services are generally designed around the needs of a specific customer, often on the spot, by the supplier. The travel agent will help the customer to choose his holiday on the basis of his understanding of the buyer's needs, comments and financial resources. He will need to consider all these factors.

The difficulties of the service firm are made even greater in this situation by the intangible nature of their offering. The holiday is not a fixed commodity capable of being measured and judged on objective grounds. The motor trade suffers particularly from this. There can be an enormous gulf of understanding between the supplier, the garage and the customer on as basic a level as the meeting of the 'service' to the car being repaired. Faults or breakdowns totally unrelated to the original problem occurring some time after repair are put down to poor garage service.

Overcoming these problems is critical to ensuring good, repeat business. It is essential to recognise the importance of handling customers carefully, of probing to establish their real as opposed to their stated requirements and of explaining differences of understanding. Here the manager should recognise that the extent of access to staff is generally far greater in services than in manufacture. In many garages the mechanic is spoken to by clients as often as the receptionist.

The degree of contact with customers is a significant difference between most service firms and manufacturers. A small tobacconist has far more frequent direct personal contact with individual smokers than the giant Imperial Group. This can lead to negative, even hostile, attitudes towards the public or specific sectors. In some recent research among 12 to 16 year old children the scale of hostility they felt retailers had towards them was remarkable. A service firm cannot afford the luxury of these sentiments if it wants repeat custom. Its actions determine its offering. There is not the compensation of other aspects of the product.

At the same time sectors of service industry do fail fully to capitalise on their opportunities. A classic example of this is the tendency of retail salesmen to spend all their time selling the product and virtually no time selling their own firm. The top manager should make it clear to his staff that their job is to promote their own company at least as much as their supplier.

This involvement of people creates massive problems of standardisation, and partly explains the high failure rate among rapidly growing service firms. Once the owner's direct control is lost, quality can slump. Before this occurs, the basic appeal and offering has to be identified and isolated. The manager is responsible for closely monitoring and responding to customer needs. Within this framework routes to standardisation can be sought. Individuality and flexibility have a role, but within the framework of objectives and controls set out by managers. Franchising has emerged as one of the best ways of maintaining quality in growth oriented services.

The perishable character of most services places a special onus on management accurately to forecast and sustain an even level of demand. Hotel rooms left vacant and unoccupied tables in restaurants are complete waste. Despite that, many small service companies make little systematic effort to estimate forthcoming demand. Even less effort is put into differential prices and advertising, modifying the offering to even out peaks and troughs in demand.

The close direct personal contact between the small service firm and its client provides an invaluable opportunity for systematic information gathering. This might simply involve giving customers a reply paid questionnaire card or getting all those involved in customer contact to review and explore customer action. A determination to use the firm's intimacy with the customer characterises the market oriented service firm.

The adoption of this approach will do much to influence the service firm's prosperity. The opportunities exist in services. We can reasonably expect the growth of the last 20 years to continue. Three things will dominate the development of services: the use of marketing, people and productivity. The last of these is particularly important. Seeking out innovative ways of resolving productivity problems in established services and using this to open them up to new markets has been the foundation of growth from Butlins to McDonalds. Ultimately, however, the small firm with its closeness of personal control has enormous advantages in an area whose marketing is so dependent on people.

6
Planning the Office

ROGER HENDERSON
Managing Director, Space Planning Services, Hillingdon

6.1   The organised office

In the eyes of many small business owners, office planning is regarded as a subject to which only companies large enough to warrant employing their own office manager could afford to give more than passing consideration. Managers of new ventures in the first throes of development are much more likely to be caught up in the excitement of generating new leads and keeping existing clients or customers happy, and there is a strong tendency to adopt an attitude of *laissez-faire* when it comes to even the most basic principles of the organised office environment. However, no business is so small that it can afford to ignore the benefits of efficiently planned accommodation.

Although there is a great deal of satisfaction to be derived from a close personal involvement in a small but growing concern, any business in such a situation will inevitably be generating more and more paperwork, will need to recruit more personnel and be making large investments in furniture and equipment. One filing cabinet, two telephones and a pocket calculator may have been sufficient to cope with requirements in the early days, but it is a situation which is likely to become increasingly strained as the two-man band develops into a 10 or 20 piece orchestra.

First, considerable thought should be given to a few basic principles of office planning, particularly in the light of a decision to acquire more space. This is probably one of the most important and significant first steps in the life of a small company and one which represents a major investment. Miscalculations or lack of thought can, and commonly do, lead to extremely expensive mistakes which can affect the rate of development for years to come. For example, a decision to acquire accommodation based simply on average space per head and cost per square foot calculation can go badly adrift. The square footage quoted by estate agents often includes some degree of unusable space, so what initially looks like a very favourable rent may not be so attractive once this factor is taken into consideration. A brief layout or plan of the actual floor area offered is essential to ensure that there is enough space for staff and equipment.

The tendency is to take just enough space to suit the company's current requirements, but the importance of developing a plan to cope with future short- and long-term needs when more staff will be taken on cannot be underestimated. This could, for example, involve the acquisition of more space than is needed and organising a sensible sub-let which provides for an option to take over the additional space after a period of time. One way or another, it is essential to allow for growth and expansion to protect the firm against the unsettling and disruptive process of moving more frequently than is necessary.

The next consideration, once premises have been found, must be their layout, fitting out and furnishing. It is again worth assessing the working needs of the staff, in terms of equipment and their interrelationship with each other, and planning accordingly. To take a simple example, it is distracting for someone involved in the preparation of detailed figure work or reports to share a small office with a heavy telephone user; the efficiency of both is likely to be impaired. The location and siting of furniture and equipment should be given at least as much thought as most people devote to planning a new kitchen. The furniture selected should be carefully chosen to meet the needs of the user in terms of his or her job function and not just because it looks good and doesn't cost too much.

Few small businesses can afford the luxury, in terms of space or manning power, of a full reception area, but an assessment of the number and nature of callers received is still a worthwhile exercise. A suitably furnished waiting area to create the right first impression is necessary if visitors consist of clients and customers to whom a certain image is to be conveyed. On the other hand, that image may be tarnished if the waiting visitor is able to overhear irate telephone conversations with recalcitrant suppliers.

The choice of the right storage equipment will also make an important contribution to the smooth running of the business, and help to prevent that 'drowning in paper' feeling from which many small operations (and some larger companies) suffer. A simple inhouse survey of the type of material which needs to be stored, from correspondence, order forms and invoices to ledgers and reference books, wil provide a specification for an appropriate system. Once the analysis has been made, advice from one or two office equipment sales people should be helpful in providing information on a simple yet flexible system to meet your needs. It is only too easy to fall back on traditional box files which are comparatively expensive, wasteful in terms of space, and rapidly become a general dumping ground for irrelevant material.

There is also a tendency for small businesses to overlook the recent advances in office automation, or to dismiss the more sophisticated equipment because of cost. No office nowadays would be without a calculator, which has become smaller and more powerful than ever before, and is now within the reach of everyone's pocket. Yet this advancement has, in fact, been mirrored in many other fields of office technology.

Electronic typewriters, the simplest form of word processors, have become much less expensive, and at around £1000 equate with the financial outlay necessary for two ordinary electric typewriters. Even a microcomputer is now within the reach of many small firms. A computer terminal with telephone link to a bureau has, in fact, been installed in our own offices (where we have a staff of 30), for the purposes of cost control, manpower planning and project programming. The use of a computer to carry out these functions would have been beyond the wildest dreams of most companies of our size even five years ago.

There is one further aspect relating to the organised office, of which every business should be aware. The terms of the Health and Safety at Work Act affect all employers, and potential sources of accidents, such as trailing telephone or electrical wires or a blocked fire exit, could attract an enforcement notice, the execution of which could prove expensive.

Taken step by step, the road to a properly planned office is within the reach of any business, whatever its size. The following sections, looking in detail at the general points made here, attempt to signpost this road.

6.2 Office accommodation

Whether you need 500 or 5000 square feet of office space, the problems remain virtually the same, and the choice of the right kind of accommodation is as important to small businesses as it is to larger concerns. Office space is expensive to acquire and maintain and should be considered as much a part of the company's assets and resources as personnel or capital equipment. A successful company, whatever its size, will expect to grow and it will certainly change as it reacts to market forces and develops new ideas and methods. Unless you give as careful consideration to planning your accommodation needs as you would to marketing and sales strategy, you could find your business in a straitjacket which will inhibit its development and growth as effectively as a badly planned costing system. Shortage of space presents a barrier to recruitment when you most need more staff; overcrowding exacerbates problems of noise, leads to poor ventilation and reduces efficiency.

The short-term expediency of 'squeezing people in' may work wonderfully well if the motivation is there, as it often is with the first flush of success, and if it really is a short-term measure. However, the dynamic hub of your enterprise may quickly degenerate into a sweat-shop atmosphere with disgruntled staff spending their lunchtime scanning the small ads. There are too many office 'slums' around, both large and small, which effectively demonstrate this point.

The search for space
The first consideration is the amount of space you actually require. The legal minimum is 40 square feet per head (or 400 cubic feet where ceilings are less than 10 feet high). However, in practical terms, this is too small an allocation and is certainly not an appropriate figure on which to base your calculations.

A more realistic figure is 60 square feet for clerical workers, but this does not take into consideration space for filing and office equipment which should be added in separately. Other elements for which you should allow space include circulation and corridors, and any supporting facilities such as meeting rooms, coffee machines, library, stationery store, telephone equipment and so on.

Once you have made this kind of assessment, you should

then plan your search for office space systematically, or you will waste time which is likely to be in as short supply as money when you are starting up. Whether you take on the search yourself or instruct an estate agent to act on your behalf, the first essential is to prepare a brief in writing. Your requirement is not just 'a small office suite in West London'; it is important to be as specific as you can or want to be on the following points:

- ☐ Location
- ☐ Usable area: minimum and maximum
- ☐ How it is divided: open space or divided into rooms?
- ☐ Type of office: self-contained suite or multi-tenanted block?
- ☐ Standard: prestige building in prime location or a room over a butcher's shop?
- ☐ Furnished or unfurnished?
- ☐ Ready for occupation? If not, are you prepared to spend money on fitting the space out for your own purposes?
- ☐ Total cost target: rent, rates, service charge, amortisation of any premium payable.

The process of setting down this type of information will help to clarify your thoughts. If you use it as a brief to instruct a good estate agent, he will be able to provide a more informed service and he will not deluge you with details of unsuitable properties.

Assessing the space on offer

With your carefully prepared brief, you will be able to appraise the alternatives and check off the points that have been met satisfactorily. When it comes to the size of space in question, do not take paper figures quoted in the property details at their face value: floor areas measured from plans are notoriously inaccurate and, even more importantly, figures often include space which, in effect, is unusable. It is quite common, for example, for measurements of the so-called carpeted area in an office block to run under the 12 inch deep heating units at the perimeter, into cleaning and electrical riser cupboards, and to include all the corridor space. By taking careful on-site measurements of the areas which are truly usable, we have on many occasions been able to negotiate substantial reductions in the total rent payable on behalf of our clients, when this has been quoted at the outset on a price per square foot or square metre basis.

It is also important to analyse the way you work and what your requirements are in terms of open areas and individual rooms, and recognise that the building will exert constraints on what you can do within it. These will affect the size and shape of single offices, the acoustics, the physical environment and how services such as power and telephone can be provided where they are needed.

In fact there are many factors which may prevent you from providing the size of rooms you had originally planned. Oversized offices, access corridors, dead areas without ventilation, heating or natural light, for example, may all eat into the available space and result in cramped or badly organised accommodation. Draw up a rough layout of the available space ensuring that the constraints the building and its services might impose are not overlooked, and this will help you determine what can and cannot be achieved within the given area. Check your plan on site to make sure that what you have in mind is feasible.

Coping with expansion

There are a number of ways in which you can allow for future development and growth in terms of your accommodation without taking on more space than you can cope with financially, or finding yourself in a situation where you have to seek new premises every two or three years.

The first essential is to maintain contact with the right firm of agents and instruct them to send you information until you tell them to stop (in the spirit of James Bond with vodka martinis). Resist the temptation to shelve the search until a move is crucial; you may then be forced to take the first vaguely acceptable alternative that turns up.

You should also consider properties which offer more space than you appear to need. Take on the excess and organise a sublet on short leases. Small packages of offices are in very short supply, so you should not encounter any problems in finding a tenant. At the end of the first term you can either renew the lease or repossess the area for your own occupation; your legal position is secure in the latter case.

Or you could consider taking on the additional space and simply leaving it empty. This will depend on the total rent you pay for the use of given space, but located almost anywhere outside Central London, it will still represent a small proportion of your total operational overheads. Do not overlook the derating factor on empty space, and the possibility that no heating, lighting or cleaning costs will be incurred.

Consideration could also be given to using the extra space as meeting or conference rooms, or as a staff recreation area or restaurant. This facility could then be rented out or the costs shared with neighbouring tenants.

Then there is the cuckoo-in-the-nest syndrome to consider. If you move into a multi-tenanted building, a close ear to the ground will often secure first option on additional space as it becomes available.

A strategy to provide additional occupation in 'steps' might also be appropriate. Assess your liability to meet the business plan within a given space. If, say, 40 per cent of your staff are out of the office at any one time, they will probably accept a squeeze in order to accommodate extra people. You need then take over extra space only when you have reached a certain target level of recruitment.

Conclusion
The management of office space, or indeed of any space for commercial or industrial use, is as important as any other aspect of management. Tackled in a thoughtful and logical way, it will undoubtedly contribute towards the overall effectiveness of your operation.

6.3 Legal requirements

It is often said that ignorance is no excuse at law, yet the rules and regulations that control our use of office space are so numerous, so complex and so phrased in legalistic jargon that even experienced administrators may find them difficult to understand. Because of their complexity they were often ignored by many small businesses who had no inclination to waste time on anything seemingly so unproductive.

With this in mind and faced with the increasing tide of accidents at work, the Health and Safety at Work Act was introduced in 1974. Its purpose was threefold: to put greater legal emphasis on accident prevention; to define accurately the onus of responsibility; and to simplify previous legislation by bringing under one authority a wide range of rules and regulations introduced over many decades.

So far, because of other priorities, little in the field of simplification and standardisation has been achieved. We are still faced with all the old rules and regulations in all their complexity.

So what action should the small businessman take to ensure his business conforms to the law? He could rely solely on outside advice. Just as his lawyer and accountant give advice on their specialist disciplines, so similarly his estate agent or building surveyor will advise on requirements of the Offices, Shops and Railway Premises Act. His architect or interior designer will be able to advise him on how to meet the conditions laid down by Building Regulations or London Building Acts and the Fire Precautions Act, and his insurance broker will arrange the necessary cover to be provided under the Employers' Liability Act and the Occupiers' Liability Act.

However, this is probably not sufficient. Small businesses grow fast, demand more staff, more space, more facilities, and the investment in these is substantial. It should not be jeopardised by plans based on ignorance of statutory requirements.

The small business owner should also bear in mind that the responsibility for the health, safety and welfare of all employees is his and his alone. He cannot blame bad advice if accidents occur. The wise businessman will therefore balance outside advice with his own efforts to keep up to date on the broad outline, purpose and intent of legislation. He can then assess the effects not only on his current situation but also of the impact of rules and regulations on his future expansion plans.

What in fact are his responsibilities? The legislation states: 'He must ensure as far as is reasonably practical the health, safety and welfare of all his employees' and this is defined under five headings:

☐ Safety with office equipment and plant
☐ Safety in handling or storage of materials
☐ Provision of instruction and training
☐ Maintenance of a safe building
☐ Provision of a safe working environment within the building.

These rules are applied to every building, irrespective of location and size, where the prime use is as an office. Numbers of staff are irrelevant provided they work more than 21 hours per week. Where doubt exists, compliance in terms of reasonable practicality is seen as adhering to and following accepted national and industry based codes of practice.

So much for the spirit and intent. What is the scope of the legislation? The main points have already been referred to. Their impact on everyday office life is discussed by category below.

Administration
Paperwork and form filling is an integral part of all legislation. The Offices, Shops and Railway Premises Act details what is required. It relates to the registration of office premises, reporting of accidents, application for fire certificate and the display of an abstract of the Act itself.

Insurance
The Employers' Liability Act and the Occupiers' Liability Act detail the insurance cover that must be provided for both staff and visitors while on your premises.

Working conditions
The Offices, Shops and Railway Premises Act details quite comprehensively the minimum standards which determine density of occupation, natural light, ventilation and heating. The Act also specifies standards of welfare and amenities in terms of numbers of toilets, the provision of washing facilities, drinking water, coat storage, and the availability of first aid.

Safety and fire precautions
The Offices, Shops and Railway Premises Act and the Fire Precautions Act deal with this aspect. This legislation covers the provision and testing of fire alarms, the need for fire drills and the maintenance of and access to escape routes. The Health and Safety Act has established rules governing the fencing and guarding of machinery and requires all users to be instructed on the dangers and the precautions to be taken. Heavy work is also banned without the proper equipment.

Constructional maintenance
The majority of the rules and regulations which govern methods of construction, the choice and use of materials and the standards of workmanship required, come within the scope of Building Regulations (or, within the Greater London area, the London Building Acts). This subject is so complex and so detailed, there is little purpose in attempting any summary. Suffice it to say that they are in force to provide minimum standards of safety in design and construction, to safeguard the

health and security of the public and to prevent or mitigate the incidence of fire. Their interpretation and application is thereafter best left to your consultants or to an experienced design team.

Alterations and improvements

Most alterations or additions that involve significant structural works will be carried out under the supervision of an architect or other competent specialist. Nevertheless, it is important to remember that all alterations and additions, even of a minor nature, such as changes to partitions, extra lighting runs etc, not only require local authority approval but also can bring existing circumstances and conditions within the scope of regulations retrospectively.

This means that new regulations introduced do not normally have retrospective implications on buildings or surfaces already in existence. However, once you start to alter, modify or improve such buildings you can become liable to bring old work up to certain standards which are now mandatory. This is often very costly, as the type of works most often required to be updated relate to stairs, toilets and perhaps even the reinforcement of structural elements.

Conclusion

Many small businessmen may consider all this to be yet more bureaucratic interference, another administrative millstone which diverts their energies into unprofitable and often frustrating fields. They may feel that, if the information they provide is limited, so too will be the level of such interference. To do this is to misread the spirit and intent of the law and to allow its inadequacies of form and language to cloud judgement. It is a mistake which can lead to prosecution and is one which many have regretted. Consultation and negotiations with both local authorities and specialist consultants will actually speed up the whole process of design, approval and implementation, and could well save time and money. It will certainly help in the successful development and expansion of the business by providing a pleasant, safe working environment.

6.4   Fitting out office space

For the small business, taking on new office premises and fitting them out can be a daunting undertaking when it has to be done in addition to keeping things running without interruption. In considering the problem, it is difficult to generalise about a subject which, in practice, varies so much with the nature of accommodation which is to be fitted out. However, in principle, there are far more opportunities to create an interesting, even unusual, interior office environment where a small organisation is concerned; the scope for imaginative schemes does not exist to nearly such a degree with anonymous 1960s style slab buildings in which many large companies are installed.

Even if you have taken the time and trouble to find accommodation which most closely suits your needs, it will still want some adaptation to get the right space configuration to meet your organisational requirements. The temptation to make do, and bend the structure of the company to fit the accommodation available is great, but the danger of short-term expediency is that more problems will occur in the long term. Shortage of space, overcrowding in shared offices and poor communications will all lead to a deteriorating physical environment which will become more apparent as the firm expands.

A common problem is that very often premises are taken on a short lease, making more than the minimum expenditure inappropriate. There is normally no spare capital for ambitious alterations and improvements. The furniture and equipment may, in some cases, have been begged, borrowed and bought secondhand; however much you improve its setting, it will never work as well for you as furniture selected with a specific job function in mind.

This may not apply to the same extent where the company 'image' is important. Where potential or existing clients visit the offices frequently, expenditure on such items assumes a greater importance. It is undoubtedly true that staff working for a small business often have a high degree of motivation and involvement in what they are doing. However, this should not be traded on to the extent of assuming that their working environment is of no importance. There is no doubt that given good management motivation, a well-designed environment can do nothing but improve performance.

The small organisation should have a number of advantages which it can exploit. For example, in small premises with short leases, you can afford to experiment with more adventurous colour schemes which would otherwise be inadvisable. In the same way, materials can be used which would be inappropriate where a longer life was required. This can add up to having more 'fun' with design, something that can be a disastrous failure where large numbers in more permanent situations are involved.

A tight budget should not be viewed as too great a constraint to improvement; it can almost be turned to your advantage. Designing to a price is a very good discipline, which in the past has produced ingenious *ad hoc* solutions to problems to produce a strikingly original and economical result. One such example is the use of self-coiling conduit lines, or floor to ceiling aluminium poles, to lead power and telephone wires to work stations, thus avoiding expensive and disruptive floor grid modification.

In terms of specific aspects of the design and fitting out process, there are other ways in which the small company enjoys certain advantages. Large offices need an even distribution of light and fluorescent fittings are the norm.

Smaller offices, composed of individual rooms, could make use of tungsten (ie the domestic type of lighting) instead, which gives a more pleasant effect and a greater feeling of warmth. The penalties of greater heat output and power consumption have little significance on a small scale.

In the same way acoustics are less of a problem. Individual offices should ideally be soundproof, particularly if they are used for interviewing, and this often occurs automatically where the premises are converted from residential accommodation with solid walls. Where small numbers of staff are grouped together in a room it will not be possible to provide them with the aural privacy that one might try to achieve in a larger open office, and there will probably be little point in putting up an expensive acoustic ceiling in this size of office.

When it comes to decoration, you will probably only be able to justify the cost of paint rather than, for instance, the use of a harder wearing and relatively expensive vinyl wallcovering. This is where lack of inhibition with regard to colour can apply. With awkwardly shaped rooms, colour can play an important role in offsetting odd visual aspects, and ugly ducts and pipework evident in older, industrial buildings could be painted effectively in contrasting colours rather than attempting to camouflage them.

181

It is not uncommon for office accommodation in the size range we are considering to be offered without any form of heating. In such a case careful thought should be given to the choice of a heating system. In many cases traditional central heating, while probably providing minimum running costs, will be eliminated on the basis of capital cost, disruption to the building, or physical constraints such as lack of gas or space for fuel storage. This leaves electricity as the most obvious answer. Sophisticated controls for storage heaters are now available which reduce the problems of inflexibility and running costs, although the units do take up valuable floor space.

In selecting appropriate floor covering many of the points made previously apply. There are a number of relatively inexpensive floor coverings on the market specifically designed for office use. Heavy duty carpet or carpet tiles are easy to clean, absorb sound and in the long term can be cheaper than, say, vinyl tiles.

It is a commonly held view that it is not economical to enlist professional help for the smaller office project. This is not necessarily true. An ingenious and inventive designer who is capable of working to a strict budget may go a long way to off-setting the cost of his fee by means of savings and short-cuts of which he will have professional experience. If the impact your office premises make on your clients is important, few people should have sufficient confidence in their creative powers to eschew outside help.

Should you decide to 'go it alone' you will have to face the problems of choosing and controlling a contractor. Be wary of using any small jobbing builder unless he is highly recommended and you can see one of his completed jobs. You should prepare a written specification against which he can quote and try to avoid changing your mind or adding in extras once the builder has started; they have a habit of costing more than the whole job put together.

Thought given and care taken during the fitting out process will repay dividends in the long run. Any business must be worth these considerations, whatever its size.

7
Franchising

JOHN STANWORTH AND JAMES CURRAN

Professor John Stanworth, Director of the Future of Work Research Group at
the London Management Centre, Polytechnic of Central London; Professor
James Curran, Midland Bank Professor of Small Business Studies at Kingston
Polytechnic

7.1   Introduction

Franchising is now a widely known, if still not always
understood, business activity in Britain which has become an
important part of the enterprise scene. A special day in the franchising calendar was 1 December 1987 since it was the tenth
anniversary of the launching of the British Franchise Association
(BFA). The decade since its formation has witnessed a meta-
morphosis in the scale and fortunes of franchising in Britain.

One indication of the increase in respectability that has occurred is the way in which the main clearing banks and firms of
accountants have set up franchise sections to assist those wanting to go into franchising as well as those already there. Yet
franchising is still often misunderstood and its importance
underestimated.

The franchise relationship can take various forms and is often
seen as having much in common with licensing. Typically, the
relationship involves satellite enterprises (run by franchisees)
operating under the trade name and business format of a larger
organisation (the franchisor) in exchange for a continuing service fee. The relationship is an ongoing one, with the franchisor
supporting the franchisee in various ways – supplying materials,
management support, marketing services, etc.

The main advantage of this relationship to the franchisor is
achieving national coverage for his product or service more
quickly than through conventional expansion, with most of the
capital put up by the franchisees. Increasingly, established
companies are also franchising part of their activities to get
around problems of operating small isolated outlets efficiently.

In either case, the reasoning is the same – franchisees, being self-employed, are usually motivated to work hard in building up their businesses which, at the same time, ensures success for the franchisor.

The franchisee, on the other hand, has the chance to run his or her own business, training, use of an established trade name, prime or even exclusive rights to a particular territory where appropriate, head-office advice and administrative back-up, plus the benefits of continuous market research and product or service development. While this neat balance of benefits does not always hold in practice, the growth of franchising over the last 10 years in Britain suggests that it happens often enough to spell success for this business form.

Franchising is frequently seen as a relatively recent concept imported from the United States, and texts on franchising published outside Britain usually do little to dispel this idea. However, the real pioneers of franchising were almost certainly the British brewers in the late eighteenth and early nineteenth centuries who created a system of tied house agreements with

their publicans to ensure their outlets, and this remains widespread today.

It is true, on the other hand, that franchising is economically more important in the USA than the UK. Franchise activities in the USA account for around 34 per cent of all retail sales and 10 per cent of gross national product. It is estimated that in the States there are around 480,000 franchise outlets (including around 90,000 franchisor owned) with a combined turnover of $576 billion.

Since franchises can differ so greatly, it is useful to categorise them:

☐ There are the *manufacturer-retailer* franchises where the manufacturer is the franchisor and the franchisee sells directly to the public. Car/truck dealerships and petrol service stations are examples, and these account for 36 per cent of all franchise outlets and 72 per cent of all franchise sales in the USA.

☐ There is the *manufacturer-wholesaler* franchise. The outstanding example is the soft drinks industry dominated by firms such as Coca-Cola, Pepsi-Cola and Seven-Up,

AMBERCHEM

Manufacturers, Exporters & Distributors of Chemicals for Building and Civil Works.

7, WAYMILLS INDUSTRIAL ESTATE, WHITCHURCH, SHROPSHIRE SY13 1RT
TEL: 0948-6234   FAX: 0948-6124

SALES DISTRIBUTION FRANCHISE

If you are highly motivated
Seek high rewards
This could be your chance to start
your own business

You start your business with:

■ **Comprehensive training**
■ **Sales management and technical support**
■ **Your own fully protected area**
■ **Regular monthly payments**

£3,500 cash investment required

Act now-rare opportunity-area strictly limited

who franchise to independent bottlers who, in turn, distribute to retail outlets.

☐ There is the *wholesaler-retailer* franchise, the best known example being the voluntary groups which operate in the field of grocery retailing where the wholesaler (the franchisor) supplies the retailer (the franchisee) who is signed up on a voluntary basis. Well-known names here are Spar, Mace, VG, Londis, etc and similar operations exist in other fields such as photographic retailing.

☐ Finally, we have the *trade-name* franchise which is the form that has grown so rapidly in recent times and which is still developing on an international scale. The franchisor, who may not be a manufacturer, has a product or service to be marketed under a common trade name by standardised outlets. This group approximates to what are often known as the 'business format' franchises which at least implies the idea of a self-assembly kit-form business. The best known examples of business format franchises are probably those in the fast food industry such as Wimpy and Kentucky Fried Chicken. This form of franchise now turns up in an almost endless array of forms from car servicing to central heating installation and, of course, in the high street instant print shops such as Prontaprint.

As yet in Britain there exists no official statistical intelligence-gathering machinery to match that in the USA. However, adopting the broad definition of franchising commonly used in the USA, it has been estimated that there are around 80,000 franchise outlets in the UK which, taking into account the population differential, makes franchising in the UK less underdeveloped compared with the USA than it might appear. This estimate includes petrol service outlets franchised to independent owners, franchised car distribution outlets, voluntary group wholesale-retail franchises and tenanted public houses.

Another recent estimate of franchise industry size in this country, restricting itself essentially to 'business format' franchises, estimates that there are around 250 franchises with 15,000 outlets, employing 145,000 people and turning over £3.1 billion a year. Only around 50 of these franchises were in existence at the beginning of the last decade.

A number of factors appear to be strongly favouring the continued growth of franchising. First is the shift from manufactur-

ing activities to services which has already led to a massive restructuring of the economy. Services offer more favourable conditions for franchising. Second, large companies are divesting themselves of many peripheral activities. Subcontracting and franchising are ways of doing this and, because of greater concentration in Britain's economy compared with our competitors, there is more room for this to occur here. Third, the emphasis on self-employment and starting up on your own is producing an increasing stream of people looking for business opportunities. The franchised small enterprise represents precisely that.

7.2   Setting up a franchise

Setting up a franchise needs not only the same planning and attention to detail as any new business venture, but has important additional elements since, in effect, not one but two business ideas are on trial.

First is the basic business idea for providing a product or service which has to be market tested. In addition, there is the development of a format for 'cloning' the business through a host of independently owned franchised outlets.

There are three principal ways a new franchise can start. First, there are imported franchises, often from the USA, which have usually been very successful there. Well-known examples are the fast food franchises such as Kentucky Fried Chicken, Pizza Hut and Burger King. Other franchises, such as TNT and the recently arrived Jenny Craig Weight Loss Centre franchise from Australia, show that the USA does not have a total monopoly here.

Of course, just because a franchise was successful elsewhere does not guarantee success in Britain, as the imported US ice cream franchises of a few years back showed.

Second, there are the large company divestment franchises where established companies decide to franchise a part of their activities. Good examples here are Holland and Barrett, Sketchley, Sperrings, and the Co-operative Wholesale Society's Late Late Supershops. The Abbey National Building Society has plans to franchise its Cornerstone estate agency chain.

Perhaps the most exciting and challenging source of new franchises is what may be called the entrepreneurial franchise. Here an individual with a franchise idea starts from scratch, attempting to develop the original notion into a full-blown franchise chain.

It starts usually as a small business itself, testing and developing the product/service, and is built into a franchise package to sell to others. These are the most risky franchises usually, and failure may result because of the omission of certain steps in developing the franchise soundly.

Step one is obviously to have the basic product or service itself fully tested, marketed and competitively priced. Then comes the development of the back-up services needed for a franchise – the lines of supply and delivery, the administrative support and financial control systems for a multi-outlet business.

At this pilot stage, several key questions have to be settled. For instance, what kind of sites are needed? Does it need high street visibility, or can it flourish in secondary sites or, alternatively, could it be run from home or a mobile outlet? A franchise, in other words, needs to be fully proved before rushing out and recruiting franchisees.

Entrepreneurs are renowned for their hearty dislike of paper work but a franchise needs pinning down on paper. Careful paper work systems are an essential part of the package for franchisees. They have to reproduce the business in all its essential details if they are to succeed.

Getting the first outlet up and running does not prove the franchise adequately. A franchise runs on multiple outlets in different locations and under varying conditions with different staff.

A second outlet and preferably several further outlets set up in different geographical locations enable other key problems to be solved. Local property markets, for instance, can vary enormously. Staff recruitment and training have to be standardised.

In short, the budding franchisor has to test whether the business can be run at a distance without the direct supervision of the originating entrepreneur.

Methods and techniques evolved in the early outlets have to be passed on to franchisees later. This requires expertise, and a wise franchisor seeks help. The British Franchise Association, for example, offers help and associate membership to developing franchises. Later, full membership can be a useful source of contacts in the industry and may increase credibility when recruiting franchisees.

Marketing is important in franchising. Customer recognition and visibility are crucial. A well designed, distinctive and original logo and livery, which describe the business and give it a highly positive, instantly recognisable image, are crucial.

A scale of fees needs to be developed for purposes of franchise flotation. These include a once-and-for-all licence fee for use of the trade name, an ongoing service fee related to levels of sales turnover plus, possibly, a mark-up on any supplies.

The cost of business premises, fitting-out, equipment, vehicles, working capital, etc all need to be calculated so that potential franchisees know the financial requirements of buying into the franchise.

More than 50 per cent of new franchisees borrow money from the clearing banks, and established franchise companies can often negotiate franchise packages with the banks, resulting in higher levels of loan funding than would normally be the case, plus more modest levels of interest. However, such packages take time to negotiate and approaches should be made in good time.

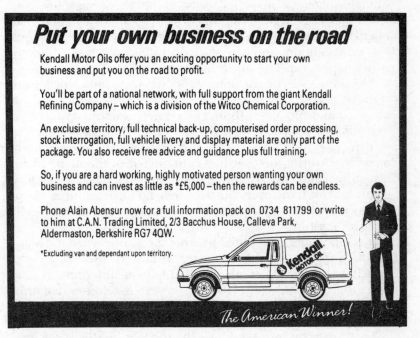

Last, but not least, franchisees need to be recruited. Experience suggests that prior experience in the operational line of the franchise is not necessary for success. What is needed is commitment, hard work and initiative.

The ability to deal with customers and be strongly market-oriented have been found to be particularly important. Not everyone will make a good franchisee – normally less than 1 in 20 initial inquiries produce an effective franchisee.

Franchising is a partnership, and treating franchisees as partners is important. A franchise's major asset, once established, is its franchisees. They need to be sensitively handled and supported wholeheartedly if everyone, and especially the franchisor, is to continue to reap the very real benefits and advantages of this special business form.

7.3   The franchise relationship

Franchising at its most effective combines the strengths of both small and large scale. The franchisee, usually being small, can offer clients a personal service, has a thorough knowledge of local market conditions and can make decisions quickly, so as to ensure a rapid response to problems and opportunities.

The franchisor, on the other hand, has the contrasting advantages of size – bulk buying power, national marketing and advertising and ongoing product or service development.

It might be thought that the franchisor-franchisee relationship is inherently fragile. The franchisor has an overriding interest in ensuring that business conducted in the name of his franchise conforms to certain laid-down practices and procedures. The franchisee, on the other hand, is running his or her own business, which is not only self-funded but is a legally separate entity.

It is sometimes questioned whether the franchisee is, in reality, anything more than a manager firmly controlled by the franchisor, and whether talk of self-employment represents little more than a pipe-dream. However, research indicates that most franchisees feel their needs for independence and autonomy to be largely met.

These may be somewhat less than would be the case with a

conventional small business but, in reality, franchisees exchange a degree of independence for security and know-how.

Also, it should not be forgotten that conventional small business owners, in practice, tend to find their independence whittled away by various external constraints to a fraction of what it might nominally be.

Our research shows that, in order to understand the franchisor-franchisee relationship properly, it is necessary to go beyond an examination of the formal contract, which is the document binding the parties legally.

Franchise contracts are frequently long and detailed and often appear to specify in detail how almost every facet of the operation should be conducted.

However, if we shift the analysis to the operational day-to-day level, an altogether different picture emerges. The contract, though central in the legal sense to franchisor-franchisee relations, does not occupy a similarly prominent position in day-to-day reality. In short, the franchisee's scope for independent decision-making is much greater than an examination of the formal contract would imply.

In certain areas of operational day-to-day decision-making, both parties are usually agreed that decision-making is largely at the discretion of the franchisee.

This is true when considering, for instance, hours of operation, employment of staff, wage levels and bookkeeping procedures. In other areas, such as product/service mix and pricing levels, the responsibility rests largely with the franchisor.

There are other areas, however, where both parties may claim responsibility, such as local advertising and standards of customer service. But these differences seem to result not so much from confusion or disagreement as from genuine differences in views. For instance, franchisors usually claim that customer service standards are fully prescribed in the contract and monitored by field supervisors, the use of 'dummy' customers and/or invitations on promotional literature or invoices to contact the franchisor direct.

Franchisees, on the other hand, often tend to feel that these arm's-length quality control methods are only likely to identify customer dissatisfaction when it has reached crisis proportions. For maintaining good customer relations day-to-day, franchisees usually feel they are the prime initiators.

On local advertising, the franchisor may feel he has responsibility since he may give guidance on content and have final powers of veto over what is published. Franchisees, on the other hand, usually pay for the advertisements, decide the media and, indeed, often decide on the sheer volume of local advertising.

Perhaps a very good indicator of the nature of the relationship between franchisor and franchisee is the frequency and nature of contact between them. Around one-third of franchisees in our research reported contact with the franchisor as occurring at least once a week. The remainder reported contact occurring about once a month.

But most of these contacts were initiated by the franchisees treating their franchisors as a resource for solving operational problems. Franchisors typically visited franchisees every one to two months, though there were wide variations. New franchisees expected to be visited much more frequently to help them become fully established, while some established franchisees claimed to be very rarely visited.

Only 5 per cent of franchisees in our research felt themselves to be 'over-supervised' while 12 per cent would have liked more supervision. The great majority – around 80 per cent – felt the existing level of supervision to be about right.

197

Methods of ongoing franchisor-franchisee communication include joint consultative committees, annual conferences, newsletters, bulletins, competitions and special award schemes. Joint consultative committees, as in other sectors of the economy, tend to serve as tension-management devices. Franchisees feel that they (or their representatives) have the ear of the franchisor while the franchisor has the ear of franchisee opinion-leaders.

At times, such a platform for consultations can fail to satisfy franchisees who may then form an independent franchisee association. This can have something of a trade union character about it. The formation of such associations often coincides with the franchisor seeking to impose far-reaching changes upon franchisees.

Franchising, as a business format, offers a viable alternative to conventionally operated businesses in many increasingly important areas of economic activity. At the same time, it produces its own distinct patterns of personal relations, calling for particular skills on the part of the franchisor.

7.4 Tips for potential franchisees

Franchisees come from a wide variety of backgrounds and range from university graduates to those who left school at the earliest opportunity. What unites them is the idea of running a business of their own with the safety net of a larger company's know-how and resources.

Perhaps somewhat surprisingly, research shows that, in many ways, the typical franchisee is rather similar to the conventional independent small business owner. For instance, around a half of all franchisees have either had previous first-hand experience of self-employment or, alternatively, had parents who were self-employed.

There are fewer women in franchising than among the conventionally self-employed and this is somewhat surprising, since franchising seems an ideal way for women to increase their share of self-employment opportunities.

One reason many opt for the franchise route to working for themselves is that previous employment did not prepare them for self-employment. For example, working for a large company tends to produce fewer who end up working for themselves perhaps because large firm specialisation does not give the all-round experience which lends itself to running a small business.

A franchise substitutes for this lack of experience by offering a proven business package with continuing support. It does much the same for those who have business skills but lack a business idea.

It should be understood by potential franchisees that no business is totally risk free. Although compared with the conventional independent small business the survival rate of franchises is superior, failures do still occur.

The Entré Computer Centres franchise is one recent example, despite the fact that it enjoyed considerable success in the USA earlier in the 1980s. Another is the La Mama franchise, retailing fashions for expectant mothers, even though it was set up by an experienced franchisor.

Besides the benefits of a tried and tested business package, there are other reasons why the small franchised enterprise should be less failure prone. For instance, many conventional small businesses go to the wall because they are hopelessly undercapitalised. In a reputable franchise this should not happen because the franchisor knows the likely costs and can often secure better loan facilities from banks.

Also, many small businesses fail simply because they have no proper financial and management control systems. Their pricing and overhead apportionment, for instance, is often based on guesswork. With a franchise, such systems should be part of the basic business format.

Just as franchisors vet applicants carefully, individuals thinking about this form of self-employment ought to ask themselves if they really are personally well suited. It may be a protected form of business but it requires just as much hard work, long hours and get-up-and-go as any other small business. It also requires someone who can work for himself and yet work harmoniously also with another, host business.

Some franchises have fairly steep entry costs which rule them out for many people contemplating a small business. For instance, Wimpy now ask for a minimum investment of £450,000 but there are others on offer for under £10,000. Anyone deciding which franchise to go for should ask some basic questions to reduce the chances of making a serious mistake at this stage:

☐ Is the franchise company a member of the British Franchise Association? This franchise industry trade association closely vets companies before admitting them to membership. Obviously, some very good companies, for their own good reasons, prefer not to join but, none the less, membership can be generally counted in a company's favour.

☐ Are other franchisees successful using the format that you are considering? Potential investors should visit at least two existing outlets, preferably without the franchisor present, to talk to existing franchisees. These outlets should be freely selected from a complete list of existing outlets and should not be selected by the franchisor.

☐ Is the franchisor's long-term success dependent upon the success of franchisees? An ethical franchisor should be willing to take an income related to the franchisee's own success rather than demanding a fixed royalty or service fee.

☐ Is the franchisor selective in picking franchisees? Any shady operator interested only in short-term gain is likely to accept almost anyone willing to part with money.

☐ What would you get back if you decided to terminate your contract or in the event of your death? In a good franchise operation, an outlet that has been developed into a flourishing small business can be sold as a going concern or inherited by descendants subject only to a minimum of conditions which protect the franchisor's legitimate interests in the transaction.

☐ Is the figure you are told you will need to invest the total figure required to get you started or a *minimum* figure? Sometimes sizeable amounts of loan capital and equipment rentals may also have to be found, putting a heavy repayment burden on the new franchisee. Also, a franchisor who does not readily give clear investment information from the outset may not be an ideal partner for the continuing business relationship that lies at the heart of a franchise.

☐ What is your estimate of the future potential of the franchise? Is demand for the product or service offered likely to be maintained or, it is to be hoped, increased? Some franchises that have been offered attempt to exploit a fad or fashion, but public taste has switched to something else, leaving franchisees with a worthless business.

☐ Do the prospects for success appear just 'too good to be true'? If so, they almost certainly are. Promises of 'success beyond your wildest dreams' are invariably just that – dreams.

Most bogus or unethical franchises in the past have not been difficult to spot. Having said that, they have often not experienced too much difficulty in getting at least a number of people to part with their life savings. If you have substantial doubts, back off and find another franchise. After all, there are now around 250 from which to choose, many of which could provide an exciting and rewarding path to working for yourself.

7.5 Franchising for the future

The launch of the British Franchise Association (BFA) was the single most important event in the history of franchising in this country. Despite relatively modest resources, the BFA has steadily emerged as a powerful and respected mouthpiece and given the franchise industry a sense of identity.

It may seem rather odd that a range of companies, involved in such a diverse mixture of activities, should see themselves as being in the same 'industry'. However, this merely underlines the fact that their similarities outweigh their differences, their principal point of similarity being their distribution format.

The franchise industry, more than almost any other, still appears astonishingly vulnerable to isolated misfortune. A single failure is capable of shaking the public image and composure of the entire industry. The shock collapse of the Young's Franchise Group, since re-formed, (previously one of the darlings of the industry) and the bad publicity attracted by its La Mama operation, cast a cloud over the industry which has only recently been replaced by the atmosphere of self-confidence due to an industry of its size and importance.

But even bad news can have positive spin-offs. One of the key driving forces behind the BFA's initial formation was the goal of self-regulation rather than political intervention and stifling legislation. Bad publicity and the renewed threat of legislation, put the BFA on its mettle. The result was an updated and extended Code of Ethics.

203

This embraces a new arbitration service for the resolution of franchisor-franchisee disagreements, new disclosure obligations laid upon franchisors for the benefit of prospective franchisees, plus new guidelines concerning the interests of franchisees in the event of breach of contract or death. Termination of BFA membership is a sanction held over companies for serious transgressions of the new code.

Figures issued recently by the BFA indicate a slight fall in the number of franchises in Britain during the last few months of 1987 but this appears to be nothing more than a temporary consolidation. The actual number of operating outlets grew by 20 per cent during this period and turnover by 40 per cent to £3.1 billion. The industry now claims the equivalent of 145,000 full-time jobs.

In addition, franchising, so long concentrated in the south-east, is now breaking out and becoming more strongly represented in other parts of Britain. Business services, leisure and home fixture franchises appear to be setting the pace here. Areas tipped for rapid expansion generally are services to business, fast food, health and beauty products/services, plus leisure related activities.

One recurring question never far from the agenda of any discussion of franchising is survival rates. Is running a franchise outlet safer than running a conventional small business? The answer is that franchising *should* be safer and *usually* is. Thereafter, the situation is not totally clear but a picture is at last beginning to emerge.

First, the percentage failure rate among franchisees can be expected to be generally lower than among franchisors. This is because the franchise systems at greatest risk are those at an embryonic stage of development with few franchisees. Those least likely to fail are the larger established systems with most franchisees.

Second, it is still not possible to state a once-and-for-all failure rate for the industry as a whole. What we have is a range of risk profiles for different parts of the industry, ranging from low among the franchising 'establishment' (which is where much of the clearing banks' money is invested) to high around the industry periphery. Using a very general definition of franchising yields a total of around 400 franchises with an annual systems failure rate of around 12 to 14 per cent. A more exclusive definition brings the population of franchises down to around 250 and the failure rate to 4 to 7 per cent.

Making sense of the situation on franchisee failures is even more difficult since American experience suggests that individual failures are often disguised by outlets changing hands. However, an educated estimate, based on the statistics currently available, would put the annual failure rate in the region of 5 to 7 per cent, again based on a franchise population figure of 250.

The growth in franchising, between now and the end of the century, is likely to be parallelled by a growing professionalism within the industry. The BFA, for its part, has come of age and now possesses the credibility and stature to plot the future course of the industry, set guidelines, and police them. It is also becoming increasingly aware of the importance of public relations and political connections.

The growing sphere of influence of the franchise industry is also evident from the 'affiliate listing' in the BFA's membership documentation. It currently includes (in addition to over 100 full members and associates), eight clearing banks, nine leading firms of accountants and 10 firms of solicitors. In addition, there is now a Franchise Consultants Association, set up, among other things, to weed out people taking commissions simply on the sale of franchises to prospective franchisees. British franchising now appears set to make a substantial impact on the British economy in the years up to the end of this century and beyond.

Sources of information
British Franchise Association
Thames View
Newtown Road
Henley-on-Thames
Oxon RG9 1HQ
0491 578049

The Good Franchise Guide, 2nd edn, by Tony Attwood and Len Hough, Kogan Page, 1989
Taking Up a Franchise, 6th edn, by Colin Barrow and Godfrey Golzen, Kogan Page, 1989

8
Employing People

SHELAGH SWEENEY
Senior Employment Law Editor, Croner Publications

8.1   Helping the smaller business

The government has made much of the help it has given to
small businesses, not least in the area of employment law. Two
of the most significant changes here concern the obligation to
hold open the jobs of women for up to nine months while they
take maternity leave, and unfair dismissal rights of employees
in companies with fewer than 20 workers. These areas will be
examined later in this chapter, but, helpful as these changes are
to small companies, there are two changes that could be made,
with little if any impact on employees, that would go a long way
towards simplifying life for the smaller business.

The first point concerns the status of those carrying out work
for companies. Many smaller businesses prefer to use self-
employed workers, so that they do not have to pay secondary
National Insurance contributions and will not have problems
with redundancy or unfair dismissal claims when the job ends
or if the person proves to be unsatisfactory. The problem,
though, lies in determining whether the law will agree that a
person is truly working on his own account, rather than being
an employee. There is no simple test that can be used, and even
an agreement between the person and the company will be disregarded by the courts in almost all cases.

To give an example: a man was offered a job and given the
choice of being self-employed or being an employee. He opted
for self-employed status and this was accepted by the
authorities for both tax and National Insurance purposes.
However, when his job came to an end, he made an unfair dismissal application, claiming that he was after all an employee.
His claim was upheld by the Employment Appeal Tribunal
(partly because he worked alongside employees of the company, doing the same work). Though not of much consolation

to the company, which had to pay him compensation, it was a Pyrrhic victory for the employee: the tribunal appeared to dislike people trying to have their cake and eat it, and made it clear that they would be sending a copy of their decision to the Inland Revenue, having calculated that, as an employee, he now owed rather more in tax than he had won as compensation for his dismissal.

The test used by the courts is a four-part one:

1. Does the person concerned work as part of the employer's organisation? Does he use the employer's premises and equipment? Does he have regular working times? Is he paid weekly or monthly? If the answer to these is yes, it would suggest he is an employee.
2. What degree of control – in terms of method of working, quality control, output, priorities – is exercised over his work by the employer?
3. What are the contractual terms, including the method of paying tax, PAYE or Schedule E, and National Insurance contributions, Class 1 or Classes 2 and 4?
4. Is there a mutual obligation on the employer to provide work and on the employee to carry out the work?

None of these factors, individually, will give the answer; it is a question of whether, taken together, they point strongly one way or the other. However, given that the courts often come up with different answers to apparently similar questions, it is almost impossible for small companies to know whether they are acting within the law, or merely lulling themselves into a dangerously false sense of security.

This point also has strong implications for businesses which employ homeworkers. The main reason for putting work out in this way is to cope with the peaks and troughs that most businesses experience, but in some cases the courts have decided that homeworkers are employees and so enjoy all statutory rights, including protection against unfair dismissal.

The second point that urgently needs clarification – the calculation of continuous service – is more esoteric but still very important for companies. Most rights given by law to employees depend on their having a specified amount of continuous service. The rules on calculating this (which are set out in Schedule 13 of the 1978 Employment Protection (Consolidation) Act) are extremely complex but, with one exception, are precise. It is this exception that causes the difficulty.

The law states that if an employee leaves a company because of a shortage of work and subsequently returns to his old job at some time in the future, his service may be counted as being continuous from the time he first joined the company. The practical implications of this are that if an employee is made redundant after, say, 18 months' service and, because work picks up again, is taken back after six months, he will have, on the first day of his renewed employment, two years' qualifying service. In the case of a woman, therefore, she could immediately claim maternity rights. Similarly, a person employed on a casual basis, who was told at the end of each spell to 'come back in two months' time and we will take you on again', could claim his service was continuous.

The implications are obvious, but there is no formula to determine whether the service is continuous. It can only be decided in retrospect and that is not very helpful to the small businessman who thinks it may be sensible to take on 'the devil he knows' in preference to a totally new employee.

It should not be beyond the wit of government to devise precise formulae to cover both of these situations so that companies at least know what the law is, and how it applies to them.

8.2   Unfair dismissal

The most contentious area of law as far as small businesses are concerned is perhaps the requirement that employees should not be unfairly dismissed. Stories abound which purport to show that no one can be dismissed without employers paying a stiff penalty. For instance, opponents of the law cite one case in which it was decided that a night-shift worker was unfairly sacked, even though he had been found asleep during his shift. However, closer inspection of the facts of that particular incident shows that, in this case at least, the law was not such an ass as it might have seemed. It transpired that the workers on nights, once their work was complete, were allowed to occupy themselves in almost any way they chose – as long as they kept out of trouble and did not leave the premises – and it had long been the custom for some workers to sleep once their work was done. It was for this reason that the dismissal was unfair.

Later articles look at the recommended procedures which have merged over the years, as a result of appeal court decisions, for dealing with various types of dismissal. But first it is worth examining what the unfair dismissal law says, to whom it applies, and who judges the fairness or otherwise of dismissals.

The first important point is the definition of dismissal. In law, if the contract ends in any one of the three following ways, the employee has been dismissed:

1. The contract of employment is terminated by the employer, with or without notice.
2. A fixed-term contract expires and is not renewed.
3. The employee terminates the contract, with or without notice, in circumstances such that he is entitled to terminate it without notice because of the employer's conduct.

As far as (2) is concerned, the employer may include a clause in the contract, provided it is for a fixed term of at least one year, to the effect that the employee waives his right to claim unfair dismissal if his contract expires and is not renewed. If the dismissal falls under (3), it is known as constructive dismissal and this will be dealt with in section 8.3.

If there is a dismissal under any of these categories, the law imposes two requirements. First, there must be a fair reason for the dismissal: capability, including health; misconduct; redundancy; the fact that continued employment would mean breaking the law; or some other substantial reason. Second, having regard to the size and administrative resources of the firm, the employer must have acted reasonably in treating that reason as sufficient to warrant dismissal. The provision about size and administrative resources was inserted into the legislation in 1980 as part of a deliberate policy of easing the burden of unfair dismissal law on small companies. It is, though, questionable whether it has really made any difference in practice. Before 1980 the fairness of a dismissal was always judged according to the circumstances of each particular case. This would, of course, include taking account of the size of the company and whether it could be expected to operate sophisticated rules and procedures which would be appropriate for a large organisation.

The right not to be unfairly dismissed does not apply to all employees. The most notable exception relates to continuous service. The basic rule is that employees must have been employed for at least one year (two years if their employment commenced on or after 1 June 1985), during which time they must have worked for at least 16 hours a week, but there are two variations to this rule. Employees who work in companies which, throughout the whole of their employment, have employed no more than 20 people, need two years' service (regardless of their starting date) before they qualify, and employees who work for less than 16 but more than eight hours a week do not gain protection against being unfairly dismissed until they have been employed for five years.

Other groups who are excluded from the right include: employees who usually work outside Great Britain; registered dock workers; the police; and people who, when they are dismissed, are over their company's normal retirement age or, if there is no such age, are over state pension age.

If an employee is dismissed, and does not fall into one of the excluded groups, who judges his case? His application in the first case is heard by an industrial tribunal which is composed of three members: a legally qualified chairman and two lay members, one nominated by the Confederation of British Industry and the other by the Trades Union Congress. The main difference between tribunals and ordinary courts is that in a tribunal the case will not just be judged on the evidence given by witnesses as a result of questions put by employer and employee (or their representatives). The tribunal will try to establish what really happened and, to this end, will help both sides to put over their case if necessary, thus enabling people to represent themselves and so avoid legal costs.

8.3   Constructive dismissal

The definition of dismissal includes the situation in which an employee is entitled to walk out of his job, without giving notice (whether or not he actually gives notice), because of his employer's conduct. This is known as constructive dismissal, and entitles the employee to claim that he has been unfairly dismissed.

The history of this type of dismissal has had a fairly chequered career in the courts over the last 10 years. Initially, tribunals were inclined to think that an employee had been constructively dismissed if his employer had behaved unreasonably, but in a landmark case (*Western Excavating (ECC)* v *Sharp* (1978)) it was decided that constructive dismissal could only occur when an employer was in breach of an important term of an employee's contract.

It is, then, fairly obvious that, if an employer decides to reduce wages, change the hours of work or change an employee's job, the employee has the right to leave and claim constructive (unfair) dismissal. Even if a written contract of employment does not exist, employers will still know the main terms and conditions of the employment, and can avoid falling into the trap of discovering that, in law, they have dismissed someone without any intention of doing so.

However, the situation is not as clear as it may seem. Since the Western Excavating decision in 1978, industrial tribunals and the appeal courts have gone some way towards reintroducing the 'reasonable' test, by saying that it does not have to be a breach of one of the express – and obvious – terms of the contract to justify a constructive dismissal claim. Common law, which is judge-made and, in general, predates the introduction of statute law, implies various terms in employment contracts. These include:

1. A duty to maintain the contract, which means that employers must not act in such a way as to destroy the 'mutual trust and confidence' which must exist between employer and employee.
2. A duty of care, so that they must not disregard the health, safety and welfare at work of their employees.
3. The duty to provide work: even when an employer has a contractual right to lay off his workforce when there is a shortage of work, a lay-off which goes on for too long can result in a successful constructive dismissal claim.

Examples of such cases include: the employee who was told '. . . off, you can't do the b . . . job anyway'; the employee who could not get anyone in her company to take notice of her claim that she could not wear the safety goggles provided; employees who have been told they will be sacked if they don't resign; and a low-paid worker who was kept on unpaid lay-off for over four weeks. There are, of course, many other cases of constructive dismissal which can arise when the employer is only trying to protect his own interests: the employee is not capable of doing his job properly and so has some of his duties taken away, or whose status is reduced although his pay is unchanged, and so on.

It is, however, useful to remember that an express term in a contract (in essence, a term contained in a written statement given to an employee at the outset of his employment) cannot normally be overridden by an implied term. For instance, an employee without any written contract and whose terms of employment have always been vague, cannot suddenly be expected to uproot himself from Scotland and move to the West Country. However, if he had been given a written statement of the terms and conditions of his employment when he first started, which included the requirement that he work in any part of Great Britain, he could not claim that he had been constructively dismissed when such a move was necessary, no matter how difficult that move may be for him. His employer would merely be expecting him to work in accordance with the contract of employment.

This point serves to emphasise the fact that it is in the employer's interest to set out conditions of employment in writing and to ensure that a copy is sent to new recruits along with the job offer. There can then be no disagreement in the future as to what conditions the employee is accepting.

If an employee does leave and makes a constructive dismissal claim, the procedure at the industrial tribunal is somewhat different from that in the ordinary unfair dismissal cases. The first point that has to be considered by the tribunal is whether or not there has been a dismissal, and there the burden of proof lies on the employee. However, even if he does convince the tribunal that his employer's behaviour amounted to constructive dismissal, all is not necessarily lost: it is still open to the employer to show that the dismissal was fair.

In order to take advantage of this second chance, though, it is essential to go through the correct motions in the early stages of the employee's claim. When the employee has sent in his complaint to a tribunal, a copy of his form is sent to the employer, together with a form for him to complete (an IT3). One of the questions on this form asks whether the employee was dismissed. In a constructive dismissal claim, this question should always be answered in the following terms: 'No – however, if in law there was a dismissal it was fair because . . .'

This means that if the employer had good reason for his actions and went through a fair procedure (for example, consulted with the employee about the change and took account of the employee's views before making his decision, and had good grounds for making the change), the dismissal may well be fair.

After all, employees only win about one-third of all unfair dismissal cases, so, provided employers are aware of the potential pitfalls, they do have a two-to-one chance of winning!

8.4   Capability dismissal

Employees do not have protection against being unfairly dismissed (other than on grounds of race or sex discrimination and trade union membership and activities) until they have been employed for a year or, in the case of companies employing no more than 20 people or people who began work on or after 1 June 1985, for two years.

This provision is of particular importance if a company is thinking of dismissing someone because he is not able to do his job properly. While 'capability' is one of the five reasons for dismissal accepted as being fair by the law, an industrial tribunal would naturally want to know why it had taken the employer so long to discover that the employee was not up to standard.

This time limit means that companies should have adequate opportunity to judge whether or not new employees are capable of carrying out their job to the required standard well before the rights under the unfair dismissal law arise. Larger companies often carry out sophisticated systems of staff appraisal to measure new employees, but this is usually neither practicable nor necessary in small businesses. A more sensible approach is to establish a system to ensure that a positive decision is made at the right time: make a note in the diary three months before the employee is due to acquire his rights to remind you to consider the employee's overall progress.

No matter how good a system is established, however, there will always be cases where the work of an employee gradually deteriorates, or higher standards become necessary. Before an employee is dismissed for such a reason an industrial tribunal would look to see whether:

1. The employer had talked to the employee to try to discover the cause of the poor work (particularly in the case of a previously satisfactory employee).
2. The employee had been told in what way his work was below

standard and, where appropriate, had been offered help or training.
3. The employee was given a reasonable amount of time to improve.

The absence of any of these factors will, in most cases, lead to an unfair dismissal finding. More positively, failure to follow this procedure makes no commercial sense: it can be time-consuming and expensive to recruit a new employee to replace the sacked person, and there are no guarantees that the replacement will prove to be any better.

Another type of dismissal which falls under the 'capability' umbrella is on grounds of ill-health. One of the most widespread myths about unfair dismissal law is that employees cannot be sacked when they are ill. While this is quite untrue, employers do need to ensure that they follow fair procedures before taking action against an absent employee.

In cases of long-term sickness absence, where there are difficulties in covering the job, the normal procedure to be adopted is:

1. Contact the employee to ask whether he knows when he is likely to be fit to return or, if this is practicable, whether he might be able to return to a different job, or on a part-time basis.
2. If the employee does not know when he will be able to return, ask for his written permission to contact his doctor.
3. Write to the doctor, attaching the employee's letter of consent, outline the nature of the employee's job and the length of time he has been absent, and ask if the doctor can estimate his likely date of return to work. Armed with this information, a decision can then be made as to whether the job can be held open until then.

If the doctor refuses to reply, make arrangements for a medical examination to be carried out privately. If the employee refuses to attend such a medical, he can be warned that his job is in jeopardy unless he co-operates with the company in trying to establish when he will be fit to return.

This type of procedure, though, is not relevant in cases of repeated short absences from work, unless there is one underlying ailment causing the absences. A medical examination would be a waste of time for an employee who was off work with 'flu one week, with backache a few weeks later, migraine the next time, and so on. Doctors are not fortune tellers and would not be able to predict the likelihood of future unrelated illnesses.

The sort of approach that is most likely to satisfy a tribunal is to carry out a fair review of the absence record, to ensure that it is significantly higher than that of other employees (or in relation to the demands of the job), and then tell the employee that unless his health improves he will have to be dismissed. This may then give him the incentive to see his doctor, take a tonic, or whatever, so that his attendance improves.

If the employer believes that the absences are not caused by illness at all, for example if they always seem to occur when the local football team is playing away, then the employee should be given a formal written warning that he will be dismissed if the absences continue.

Whether or not the illnesses are genuine, the law does accept that employers and particularly small businesses, which have difficulty in covering absence, are acting fairly if they have to dismiss an employee who is frequently away from work, in order to ensure that the job can be carried out properly in the future.

8.5   Misconduct dismissals

The law on unfair dismissal specifies that misconduct is a potentially fair reason for dismissal, but gives little or no guidance on the sort of behaviour that may warrant dismissal or on the procedure that employers should follow beforehand. The Advisory, Conciliation and Arbitration Service (ACAS), however, has issued a Code of Practice on disciplinary practice and procedures giving useful guidelines on such matters, and this can be readily adapted to suit small businesses. This code, together with case law that has emerged from industrial tribunals and their appeal courts over the last 10 years, provides a good yardstick as to the fairness of misconduct dismissals.

The main points are that employees should not be dismissed for a first offence, except in rare circumstances when the misconduct is treated as gross misconduct; that they should have the chance to give their side of the story before any action is taken against them; and that they should be given the opportunity to improve before being dismissed. These are all the rules of natural justice, particularly since an employee cannot claim that he has been unfairly dismissed until he had been employed for at least a year (two years in companies with fewer than 20 employees).

When a disciplinary matter arises, the initial step should be to investigate the facts promptly, before memories fade and stories get distorted. In some circumstances it may be necessary to get the employee off the premises while the investigation takes place. In such a case, the employee should be suspended on full pay, for a day or two. To suspend without pay would strongly suggest that the issue had been prejudged and the employee deemed to be guilty, and could result in him leaving and claiming that he had been constructively (unfairly) dismissed.

Unfair dismissal law demands a quite different standard of proof from that which is necessary in criminal cases. It is not necessary to *prove* that an employee has committed an act of misconduct: the employer only has to show that he had *good reason to believe* (not just to suspect) that the employee had 'done the deed', and that it was reasonable for him to hold that belief. In order to satisfy that test, therefore, there has to be investigation; without it, the unfair dismissal claim is sure to succeed. Once the investigation is complete, the employee should, in the presence of a witness if he wishes, be told the allegations against him and allowed to put his story before disciplinary action is decided upon.

Many disciplinary matters are fairly minor and can most sensibly be dealt with by an informal warning: 'pull your socks up' or 'start getting up on time in the morning or else'. In more serious cases, or when minor offences are persistently committed, and more formal action is necessary, the ACAS Code of Practice recommends the following procedure:

1. In the case of minor offences the employee should be given a formal oral warning or, if the issue is more serious, there should be a written warning setting out the nature of the offence and the likely consequences of further offences. In either case the employee should be advised that the warning constitutes the first formal stage of the procedure.
2. Further misconduct might warrant a final written warning which should contain a statement that any recurrence will lead to dismissal or some other appropriate penalty.
3. The final step might be disciplinary transfer or suspension

without pay (but only if these are allowed for by the contract of employment) or dismissal, depending on the nature of the misconduct.

The code goes on to recommend that in all but minor cases, where only an oral warning is given, details of the disciplinary action should be given to the employee and he should be advised if he has the right of appeal. The code does say that employees should always have the right to appeal to a manager at one level above the person who took the disciplinary action against him but, in small businesses, this is not usually feasible. Instead the employer has three options: the right of appeal would be dispensed with; the appeal could be made to the person who took the disciplinary action, or an independent arbitrator could hear the appeal (ACAS keeps a list of people who can be called on for this purpose). The latter course, though, does mean that the outcome of the appeal is outside the company's control, and should be used with caution.

It is up to the employer to define what sort of behaviour will justify taking disciplinary action. All the law requires is that companies do not impose rules which are unreasonable in their particular circumstances. So, for instance, it is quite reasonable to insist on a reasonable standard of dress for employees who come into contact with customers, or to prohibit smoking in a company manufacturing flammable goods. It is, though, essential that employees should know of any rules that apply to them and it makes sense to put them in writing. Their prime purpose is, after all, to ensure that the company can operate effectively: keeping on the right side of the unfair dismissal laws is not the only consideration.

Finally, it also makes sense to keep records of disciplinary action taken, the reason for it and any further developments. These records, which obviously must be kept in confidence, are essential in defending subsequent unfair dismissal claims, and are also very useful in ensuring that employees are treated consistently and that a decision to dismiss an employee is made on a rational basis.

8.6 Laying off workers

From time to time employers may face the need to lay off all or some of their employees, perhaps because there is a temporary shortage of orders or because strike action elsewhere has prevented the delivery of essential supplies. Charting the legal complexities of this course of action, however, is far from straightforward, as there are four aspects of employment law and the ordinary law of contract to be negotiated if industrial tribunal or county court claims are to be avoided.

Under contract law, unless employees' contracts of employment allow them to be laid off without pay, the employer will be in breach of contract and the employees affected could go to the county court to recover damages (ie a sum of money equal to the wages that should have been paid for the workless days), or, more seriously, they could leave and claim that they had been constructively dismissed, thus allowing them to make unfair dismissal applications.

A lay-off term can be incorporated into employment contracts in three ways: (a) by being expressly written in; (b) by being implied into the contract by custom and practice in the company or industry concerned; or (c) by the employer reaching agreement with the employees concerned (not as difficult as it might appear when the alternative to lay-off is redundancy).

If there is no express or implied term entitling the employer to lay workers off without pay, and they refuse to agree to a variation of their contracts, county court claims can be avoided by giving employees notice of the change, the length of notice being that which would be required to bring their employment to an end. By doing this, the employer is ending one contract and offering a new one which gives him the express right to lay off his employees without pay.

This procedure would not, however, prevent the employees leaving and claiming constructive (unfair) dismissal. Such claims could only be defeated if the employer was able to show that the lay-offs were commercially *necessary* (convenience or expediency are not sufficient justification), and that they were implemented reasonably (the employer should, for example, consult the workers affected and listen to any counter-proposals they may make before effecting the lay-offs).

To complicate matters further, employers may still face constructive dismissal claims even if they have a contractual right to lay off their employees. The courts have held that any lay-offs must, by definition, be temporary and so, in the absence of an express term in the contract as to how long employees may be laid off for, employees can still claim that they have been constructively dismissed if the lay-off is prolonged for an 'unreasonable' time.

There are few guidelines on what is 'reasonable' in this context, but in one case it was held that four weeks was the maximum period for which workers in the rag trade could be laid off, since they are not highly paid and could not be expected to have sufficient savings to carry them through a longer period.

Even if these hurdles of contract and employment law can be overcome, there are further problems. The 1978 Employment Protection (Consolidation) Act provides that employees who are laid off work (or kept on short-time working to the extent that they earn less than half a normal week's pay) for four consecutive weeks or for a series of six or more weeks in a 13-week period are entitled to give a week's notice to terminate the employment and to claim a redundancy payment from their employer. The employer can only defeat the claim if, at the time the employees notify their intention of claiming the payment, there is a reasonable expectation of normal work resuming within four weeks and continuing for at least 13 weeks.

Finally, the Employment Protection (Consolidation) Act also requires that employees who are laid off because of a shortage of work of the kind that they are employed to do, or any other occurrence affecting the normal working of the business (except strike action by employees of that employer or an associated employer), must be paid a 'guarantee payment' for the first five days' lay-off in any three-month period. The amount of the guarantee payment is £11.30 per day (or the normal rate of pay if that is less), and it is subject to the following restrictions:

1. The employee must have been employed for at least four weeks by the end of the week preceding the lay-off.
2. He must be laid off for the whole of a day on which he would normally be required to work.
3. The employee must not refuse to do suitable alternative work as an alternative to being laid off.
4. He must comply with any reasonable requirements imposed by his employer to ensure that his services are available; for example, he might be instructed to telephone the company each morning to check whether he has to return to work.

8.7 Maternity rights

When a female employee becomes pregnant, who is left 'holding the baby'? The small business pressure groups would no doubt say, because of the rights for expectant mothers contained in the Employment Protection (Consolidation) Act 1978, that the employer is the one to suffer, but there is some evidence to dispute this claim. There has been a radical change in the law on maternity rights over the past decade, and there are now four main rights given to pregnant employees.

First, all expectant mothers have the right to take reasonable time off work, with pay, to receive ante-natal care on the advice of a doctor, midwife or health visitor. This provision seems to have caused few problems since it was introduced, with perhaps one exception. There is no definition to 'ante-natal care' in the legislation, so it is debatable whether attendance at relaxation classes would qualify for paid time off.

The second and third rights, which are the most contentious, apply only to women who, by the beginning of the eleventh week before the expected date of confinement, have been employed for two years, working for at least 16 hours a week (or for five years if they work less than 16 but at least eight hours a week). These are the rights to be paid maternity pay and to come back to their old job after the baby is born.

The provisions on maternity pay are that women with the necessary qualifying service who remain employees up to the beginning of that eleventh week and give three weeks' notice of the date they intend to stop work (in writing if their employer wants) should be paid six weeks' maternity pay, which is nine-tenths of their normal week's pay less the standard rate of maternity allowance (currently £33.20 a week).

As the whole amount of the maternity pay, plus the employer's National Insurance contributions, can be reclaimed from the government simply by completing form MP1 and sending it, together with a receipt signed by the employee (on form MP1(R)) to the Department of Employment, this right is not too onerous, even for smaller companies. It is, though, the right to maternity leave which can be most traumatic. Provided the woman gives at least three weeks' notice in writing of the date she intends to stop working and of the fact that she intends to exercise her right to return to work (and has the necessary qualifying service), she can leave at any time from the beginning of the eleventh week before the expected date of confinement. She has the right to return to work at any time up to 29 weeks after the date of confinement (or the expected date if the actual date of birth is not known), provided she gives at least 21 days' notice of the date on which she intends to resume.

The problems of keeping a job open for up to 40 weeks are obviously legion, but two changes were introduced in the 1980 Employment Act to mitigate these difficulties. The first is that, no earlier than seven weeks after the date of confinement, the employer can write to the woman asking if she still intends to return. If she does not reply within 14 days, or says she no longer wants to come back, she loses the right to return (but the letter must include a statement to this effect). This is a useful measure as many women reserve the right to return purely as a precautionary measure and, once they give birth, decide that they do not wish to resume work.

The second measure was designed specifically to help small firms, and provides that if there are no more than five people employed immediately before the woman begins her maternity leave, the right to come back to her old job only applies if it is 'reasonably practicable' for her employer to give her original job back to her or to offer her suitable alternative work. 'Reasonably practicable' is probable when the expense and inconvenience caused to the employer in holding the job open is not unduly onerous. This is not a particularly helpful definition, but to date there has been no reported case law on this point, although it has been law for some years – perhaps an indication of its usefulness!

The final right given to expectant mothers is that it is automatically unfair to dismiss them on grounds related to their pregnancy unless it makes them incapable of carrying out their work adequately or, because of the pregnancy, their continued employment would be in contravention of a legal requirement (usually under health and safety law when substances used at work might damage the foetus). While this provision applies only to those women with the necessary qualifying service to claim unfair dismissal, it is possible that a tribunal would view dismissal on grounds of pregnancy as sex discrimination, and no qualifying service is necessary before a claim of this type is made to an industrial tribunal.

To what extent do small businesses suffer from the maternity provisions? The only published research relating specifically to small companies on this point was commissioned by the Department of Employment and published by the Policy Studies Institute in 1980. It showed that only 6 per cent of small firms employing fewer than 50 people, in the first three years of operation of maternity rights, reported experiencing any problems with the rights to pay and leave. As far as maternity pay is concerned, the research showed that a significant number of women working in small companies failed to receive the pay to which they were entitled.

On maternity leave, reasons given by employers for the lack of difficulty were threefold: staff turnover, the infrequency of notifications to return, and the fact that many employers were actively keen for their employees to return to work.

8.8   Statutory sick pay

Since 6 April 1983 all employers have had to pay statutory sick pay to their employees for the first eight weeks' absence each year. Since April 1986, this period has been extended to 28 weeks. In principle, the scheme does not seem too disastrous. The payments during illness – one of three flat rates depending on income, not family circumstances – will be made by the employer instead of by the Department of Social Security, but the employer can reclaim the sums paid out. The small businessman might initially see the scheme as giving him more unnecessary work – irksome, but no more.

It is, though, when the scheme is studied in detail that the problems become apparent. Payments can only be reclaimed from the government if they have been properly made, so all companies need to become thoroughly familiar with the scheme. In essence, the payments apply only to *periods of incapacity* (periods of illness lasting at least four days), and these periods themselves must form *periods of entitlement* – periods which begin on the first day of incapacity and end when the employee resumes work, leaves the company, becomes excluded from the right to receive statutory sick pay, or at the end of the tax year.

There are also *waiting days*: payment is not made for the first three days of absence except when two periods of absence are separated by no more than two weeks. In such cases the periods are linked and the waiting days rule applies only to the first absence. The absences can, though, only be linked if they both qualify as 'periods of absence', ie if they each last for at least four days.

Finally, when it has been established that there is a period of entitlement, payment must only be made for *qualifying days*. These are days which have to be agreed between employer and employees as reflecting the days on which employees normally work. No problems occur if employees only work from Monday to Friday each week, but when employees work on shifts or their days change from week to week, difficulties will obviously arise in deciding which days should be chosen, as this will affect the amount of pay employees are entitled to receive – and so the amount employers can reclaim from the government – during periods of illness.

There are still further complications: employees are excluded from receiving statutory sick pay when they have exhausted their entitlement in any year; if they are over state pension age; if their earnings are less than the National Insurance lower earnings limit (£43.00 in the year 1989–90); and if the illness falls during the period of up to 11 weeks before a woman's expected date of confinement to six weeks after that date.

In most of these situations, the employer will have to complete a form and send it to the employee, who may then be able to claim National Insurance sickness benefit. Once an employee has claimed benefit from the state, he is automatically excluded from the right to statutory sick pay for 57 days beginning with the last day of sickness and so, if he falls ill during this period, he must go back to the DSS for sickness benefit and begin a further 57-day exclusion period.

The statutory sick pay scheme applies to all employees under pension age who earn more than £43.00 a week, so groups such as married women who pay the small stamp and are currently excluded from the right to receive state sickness benefit are also covered. This, together with self-certification, which means that employees can take a week's sick leave without having to see their doctor, will probably account for any significant increase in absenteeism.

The scheme may have involved bigger companies taking on new employees just to cope with the requirements of the scheme. Indeed, this scheme could well turn into one of the more successful job creation schemes! For the smaller company, though, already under economic pressure the answer may well seem to lie in dismissing employees who go ill. The government, however, has contingency plans for dealing with such a response: the DSS has powers to make regulations which would require employers to continue to pay statutory sick pay for up to the full eight-week period to employees sacked to avoid liability for payment.

So what can companies do about the costs involved? As regards the record keeping necessary to check whether absences qualify for payment, there is little that can be done other than devising a simple record form. (The government has issued a record form which may be used by small companies – it is available from the DSS.) So far as controlling absence is concerned, the self-certification procedure enables employers to challenge employees' sickness claims when 'the nature of the circumstances, the time of the absence and the general character of the person concerned' give cause for doubt. The employer could then refuse to make the sickness payment. The employee, though, would then have the right to appeal against this decision to a DSS inspector. It is likely that small companies will opt to pay up rather than risk getting entangled with National Insurance officers and tribunals.

9
Choosing a Computer

9.1 Introduction

CLIVE WOODCOCK

'This is Marlboro country. There are so many cowboys around, it isn't true.' Buying a computer for the first time can be a traumatic experience for the smaller firm and the comment of one small businessman on sellers of computers succinctly sums up the hazards. In fact 'beware of salesmen' comes high on the list of points of advice to small firms considering their first small computer in a report prepared by the marketing department of the University of Lancaster and aimed at helping such buyers avoid the pitfalls that others have encountered.*

The list was drawn up on the basis of responses from 100 directors, partners and managers of small companies throughout the UK about their experiences with micro- and minicomputers. The companies ranged in size from one-man businesses to those employing 200, and covered manufacturing, distribution and retail services, and professional practices. Companies were chosen which had recently installed computer systems costing less than £30,000.

The main conclusion was that computerisation was successful for those companies, but that it was not easy or free from problems. The firms themselves were not easy to locate as it was discovered that there were fewer small companies with small computer systems than is commonly supposed. For most of them it was their first system. The people most likely to initiate consideration of buying a computer were directors or partners in a firm, but a few companies responded to outside pressure, though not from salesmen.

Small Computers in Small Companies: available from Marketing Consultancy Research Services, Department of Marketing, University of Lancaster, Lancaster LA1 4YX (price £25).

226

■White

ANOTHER BRILLIANT IDEA FROM ZENITH.

You're looking at the screen on one of the world's most powerful laptops. The Zenith TurbosPORT 386.

Notice the glorious black and white.

The TurbosPORT 386 is equipped with the unique high contrast Page White display.

Why is it called Page White? Because, unlike most portable screens, it's crisp, clear and as easy to read as the page of a book.

It's kind to the eyes over long periods. And retains perfect visibility in any light condition.

The processor is every bit as impressive as the screen. You'll find the TurbosPORT is fast, powerful and gives you true 386 performance when you're on the move. It will also run entirely on batteries.

Can any other manufacturer claim as much?

And, when you need it, the TurbosPORT plugs into your office network in seconds.

The Zenith TurbosPORT 386 laptop.

You won't believe it until you see it in black and white.

ZENITH | data systems

THE QUALITY GOES IN BEFORE THE NAME GOES ON®

FOR MORE INFORMATION ON THE WHOLE
RANGE OF ZENITH LAPTOPS CALL 0800 525156.

There were various reasons for thinking about a computer: improved information and data processing were most often quoted, and other reasons included better planning and control, replacement of alternatives and improvement of working conditions. Nearly one in five of the companies did not look for information about computers on a systematic basis before they bought. The most popular information sources were dealers and other computer users, followed by magazines, exhibitions, consultants and advertising.

Less than two out of five carried out a formal feasibility study, and almost three out of five bought without seeing the system demonstrated.

Decisions on the make and model of computer bought were again usually made by directors or partners, though consultants were influential in about 15 per cent of cases. Choice was mostly on the grounds of features of the systems and supplier relationships and reputations. Only one in four companies mentioned price as being a factor. Yet companies which had the most difficulties had bought the cheapest machines and were more often than not pressurised into buying.

A quarter of those surveyed experienced installation problems and nearly three out of five had problems with either software or hardware during the first six months. Most companies received some form of training, of varying quality, with training periods ranging from one day to six weeks. Most often it was included as part of the package bought, and the majority of the companies considered training to be adequate.

Three-quarters of the systems, a typical cost of which was £15,000, had broken down at some time. The main culprits were output units, mainly printers, followed by backing store and then central processors. More than 80 per cent of the systems were covered by some form of guaranteed servicing and very few companies complained about the service they received. An average service contract cost about 10 per cent of the system's total cost a year.

While most companies were satisfied with their hardware, software was a very different story. More than three out of five had had some software problems, and only half would agree that their software was an unqualified success. Most applications were accounting-based, such as nominal purchase and sales ledger work. The range of uses was very wide, from bookmaking to acoustic engineering calculations. Software was

229

split half and half between tailored software and off-the-shelf packages.

Most users were happy with their computers, this being particularly true of experienced users who tailored their own software and used the system for management accountancy or professional or special service applications. The main advantages of a computer were considered to be improved information processing, planning and control, and better working procedures and conditions.

There were worries about the vulnerability and inflexibility of their systems, but there were surprisingly few staff problems or fears among employees that their jobs would be affected. Only 7 per cent of those surveyed reported a continuing difficulty with staff.

More than one in 10 users felt they had not realised how quickly they would outgrow their existing systems and suggested that the ability to upgrade a system was much more important than they had originally realised. In the long run it was clearly cheaper to buy big, as it was a much simpler process to add new applications to an existing machine than to buy a whole new system.

In spite of all the drawbacks encountered, half the companies interviewed were planning to upgrade their hardware and three out of five were considering new software applications.

Finally, in addition to the advice to be wary of salesmen, those interviewed felt that those considering buying a computer for the first time should obtain background information about computers in general and seek impartial advice, making sure that consultants were genuinely independent. It was also important to understand and analyse those systems at present in operation before deciding to install a computer.

9.2 Buying a micro

CLIVE WOODCOCK

Potential buyers of microcomputers are frequently urged to obtain independent advice and develop their knowledge before committing themselves to a particular system, but the problem then is knowing just where that vital information can be found.

In order to overcome that difficulty the government, as part

of its efforts to encourage and support the growth of information technology, is backing the establishment of a Federation of Microsystems Centres throughout the UK. The purpose is to provide help for users and intending users of business microcomputers, especially for those in the small business sector.

The centres are supported by the Department of Trade and Industry and, as a federation, are co-ordinated by the National Computing Centre, which is based in Manchester. Each centre operates under a common code of practice which ensures that a range of services is offered and that these services are impartial.

A feature of the centres is an open house workshop under the guidance of the centre staff, where visitors can have direct contact and involvement with the microsystems, away from any commercial sales environment. The workshops are equipped with a representative range of microcomputers and software on loan from manufacturers and suppliers. As a federation the centres have access to common information and can build on the accumulated range of technical and applications expertise. The Department of Trade and Industry has encouraged this by providing some support for development activities relating, for example, to training.

In addition to the workshop, each centre offers one-hour advisory sessions at economical rates and a variety of training courses for both the newcomer to computing and the experienced user. Additional services are offered at the discretion of each centre manager, depending on local demand. Further information can be obtained from The Federation of Microsystems Centres, 3 Heaton Road, Newcastle upon Tyne, NE6 1SA (tel: 091-276 6288).

Centres have been established at:

Birmingham Microsystems Centre
Business Support Centre
Wolverley House
18 Digbeth
Birmingham B5 6BJ
021-631 4940

Bristol Microsystems Centre
Bristol ITeC
St Anne's House
St Anne's Road
Bristol BS4 4AB
0272 779247

Newcastle Microsystems Centre
(Federation Administration Unit)
3 Heaton Road
Newcastle upon Tyne NE6 1SA
091-276 6288

New Forest Microsystems Centre
Connellen Computer Associates
71 Christchurch Road
Ringwood BH24 1DH
0425 479910

Business Resources Centre
Bolton Institute of Higher Education
Deane Road
Bolton BL3 5AB
0204 28851

Cheltenham Microsystems Centre
GLOSCAT
Park Campus
Merestone Road
The Park
Cheltenham
Gloucester GL50 2RR
0204 532054/5

Dorset Microsystems Centre
Ground Floor
Holland House
Oxford Road
Bournemouth BH8 8EZ
0202 595400/0202 524111

Dublin Microsystems Centre
College of Commerce
Rathmines Road
Dublin
0001 970666

Hampshire Microsystems Centre
Basingstoke College of Technology
Worthing Road
Basingstoke RG1 1TN
0256 471771

London Microsystems Centre
11 Clarke Path
Oldhill Place
London N16 6QE
01-802 1017

Norwich Microsystems Centre
Ivory House Site
All Saints Green
Norwich NR1 3NB
0603 761076

South Yorkshire Microsystems Centre
Sheffield Science Park
Cooper Building
Arundel Street
Sheffield S1 2NR
0742 738184

Strathclyde Microsystems Centre
Technology & Business Centre
Paisley College of Technology
High Street
Paisley PA1 2BE
041-887 1241/041-887 5948

Washington Microsystems Centre
Micro Technology Centre
Armstrong House
Armstrong Road
District 2
Washington NE37 1PR
091-417 8517

West Yorkshire Microsystems Centre
Leeds Polytechnic
Queenswood House
Beckett Park
Leeds LS6 3QS
0532 759741

A Microcomputer Advisory Service has been in operation at the University of Manchester since 1979, when the university's Research Consultancy Service began offering informal seminars and courses to provide help and guidance. The activities of the service have been aimed primarily at people with no prior experience of computing and in a situation where total capital spending was likely to be less than £10,000. The emphasis is on self-help.

One of the basic assumptions at the start was that few business people would want or need direct involvement in computer programming. The initial courses, therefore, omitted programming and concentrated on explanation of the function of the hardware – the actual computer and its ancillary equipment – and assessment of the software, the programs and documentation needed to carry out processes such as accounting, stock control or cash flow forecasting. It soon became apparent, however, that business people both wanted and needed to know something about programming. For the person with no previous experience of computing, acquiring the ability to understand fundamental concepts of programming helps with identifying suitable tasks for computerisation, understanding the function of components such as disk drives, and assessing packaged software.

Another consideration was that many business people have a number of tasks peculiar to their own business, for which packaged software is never likely to be produced. Such tasks would not present too much difficulty in programming even for the person with relatively little experience. Further information about the facilities offered by the Research Consultancy Service of Manchester University can be obtained from Dr David Jackson on 061–273 3333 (ext 3206/3219).

9.3   Computer security

ROBERT BOYD

The first-time business computer user has a lot to learn, but security is something he should consider at an early stage. Computer fraud may be the first risk to come to mind, but this possibility is unlikely to be important in the small installation.

When management retains control of much of the detailed work, 'adjusting' the books or programs is probably more difficult than in the corresponding manual system.

The least exciting but possibly the most important aspect of security for the small business computer user is the protection and recovery of data files. These include the most vital records of the company such as customer and supplier master files, outstanding sales invoices, order and stock records, wages records or whatever else has been computerised.

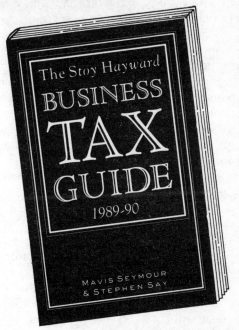

Without secure back-up procedures for these files the efficiency and profitability of the company could be seriously affected.

The smaller the computer system the more likely it is that the software will lack sophisticated checking facilities or have bugs that could lead to incorrect or corrupt data. An accidental cut in the electricity supply or a hardware fault may have the same result. In one case mysterious file corruptions were traced to winter sunshine overheating a hard disk unit normally too far back in the room for the sun to reach.

The commonest form of back-up is floppy disk although cartridge tape is sometimes available for securing Winchester type hard disks where 10 megabytes or more may have to be transferred at a time.

How often security copies are taken depends on the installation though once every day for records that have changed is really the minimum requirement. This ensures that it will never be necessary to re-input more than one day's work on a file that is found to be unusable for some reason.

The usual system is to rotate the security disks using the 'grandfather, father, son' method. By securing to each disk, or set of disks in turn, there are always at least two older versions to go back to. Early on in the use of new software, or with particularly large files a weekly or monthly version may also be advisable. It is possible that an error in a little-used part of a program, for example month or year end routines, may not be noticed for some time.

A register showing the date and contents of each disk is essential to avoid confusion if it should be necessary to re-input data. Also some form of arithmetical control should be kept on accounts data input so that output – debtors for example – can be verified in total.

Security copies of application programs will also be kept, although as these do not change the rotating copy system is not necessary. It is advisable for the security disks to be kept in a fireproof safe and an advantage of the smaller hard disks is that the complete unit can be put into the safe. For extra protection a copy may be taken home by a senior member of staff each week.

There are many firms specialising in access control equipment using either magnetic cards or digital codes. If a separate room is set aside for the computer this is a very useful way of preventing unauthorised access. However, with the advent of the micro it is common for both computer and terminals to be in the open office with consequent threat to company records.

It is not always easy for the untrained person to get useful information from a computer and although access can be prevented by passwords or log-on codes the greatest danger probably lies in the compressed and authoritative nature of the tabulations produced.

A computer listing of customers or outstanding orders is much more convenient for a competitor or salesman moving on than a bulky card index. Because of the repetitive nature of many printouts it is also much less likely to be missed. A paper shredder can be a very valuable investment.

Loss of the use of the computer is a major setback. The need for a reliable maintenance agreement goes without saying and most of the possible disasters can be insured against. There is, however, little value in cash when it is a working computer that is needed. Whether it is fire, water or civil disturbance that is being insured against, it is still advisable to take all possible steps to reduce the risk to a minimum. As computers get smaller the theft of the computer itself, data and all, must be taken into account and it may be preferable to site it off the ground floor and away from outside doors. Protection against

fire should be through the use of carbon dioxide or other gas extinguishers rather than water or foam which damage the equipment.

There may be other local users of the same type of computer. If so arrangements can possibly be made for mutual cover against disaster. Sometimes the supplier of the machine will be able to provide an alternative machine until new equipment arrives. However, in all such cases changes in specifications of current equipment could mean it was not available when needed, and the plans should be reviewed regularly.

9.4   Small business computer selection package

CLIVE WOODCOCK

Many people involved in the field of computers for the small and medium-sized business – with the exception of the computer salesmen – would probably agree that the majority of buyers approach the decision to invest in a computer from entirely the wrong direction.

The bombardment of blandishments from makers and sellers proclaiming that they have the biggest for the money, the most compact for the money, the fastest, the biggest memory, leads inevitably, not only to bewilderment, but more importantly to a concentration in the mind of the potential buyer on *which* computer to buy.

The result is the often-quoted instances of machines being bought, used for a few weeks and then abandoned in exasperation, with an expensive investment left idle and the buyer thinking of a rather different kind of hands-on interface – to use the jargon – with the seller.

The problem could, in most cases, almost certainly have been avoided if the buyer had ignored the question of *which* computer to buy and considered the question of *how* to buy – avoiding as far as possible technical considerations or comparisons in which the buyer probably had little or no expertise, and applying instead a little commercial common sense.

That, of course, is easy to say, especially as it goes beyond the normal basic response to the statement that it is important to

know what you want the computer to do now and in the future, which is to list recording functions such as purchase and nominal ledgers, sales ledger, payroll.

The main aim of a computer should be to improve the functioning of the business and so improve profitability. To achieve this a number of key factors have to be considered, ranging from the monitoring of cash flow, inventory management, the effectiveness of a salesman, to many other factors, the combination of which will vary from company to company.

The computer must provide information in the right form and frequency to help in the management of those factors.

Once those key factors have been established the prospective buyer needs to describe on paper in straightforward commercial terms the information and processing requirements of the business, including some details of accounts and transactions volumes, remembering to allow for both current needs and changes or expansions in the future.

There are two advantages to making a written statement of the key factors: first, it provides a more accurate and detailed picture of what is needed from the computer; and second, potential suppliers can be presented with the documents and asked to propose solutions and quote prices. It is then up to the supplier to provide a system to perform the defined tasks.

Again, it may sound easy in theory to follow these methods but in practice there is often a need for assistance in doing so. The opportunities for finding such assistance have been growing with, for example, the development of the Federation of Microsystems Centres, with a network of systems spread around the country offering independent advice and training, (addresses on pages 298–300).

A recent development in the field of independent advice has been the way in which the large firms of accountants, increasingly orienting themselves towards smaller firms, have started to move in, with two of the biggest, Arthur Young and Arthur Andersen, launching services aimed at the small to medium-sized business.

Arthur Young (now Ernst and Young) launched their scheme in March 1984, having recognised some time before that, as computer prices dropped, the cost of traditional management consultancy assignments for clients would become disproportionately high. At first they intended to continue giving expert guidance but to allow clients themselves to carry out much of the work, wherever practicable.

They have since moved on to develop what they call the Small Business Computer Selection Package. This is a working document supplied in conjunction with a specific amount of consultancy time from an Arthur Young specialist at a set fee, containing checklists, guidelines and other information designed to provide the businessman with a structured method of following through the microcomputer selection process, where needs can be met by standard software packages.

It covers basic business requirements, evaluation of proposals from suppliers, implementation responsibilities, and acceptance testing, as well as contractual considerations and computer terminology.

It meets the problems of the businessman who is looking at buying a computer for the first time and may not be sure of precisely which questions he should be asking. It forces him to think through the situation from a business management angle, analysing the business in a structured way to identify cost savings and profit factors, for example.

The Arthur Andersen microcomputer advisory service is called Microguide and can be tailored to suit the needs of each client. The service can be used to define the systems requirements in business terms and to assess the overall feasibility of and justification for computerisation. It also involves the selection of suitable software, hardware, and suppliers by matching outline requirements to the firm's existing knowledge of the features of the available products and inviting supplier proposals and evaluating them against a written specification.

The firm also supports the installation process, either by carrying out all the related tasks itself – such as developing the procedures, training staff, and testing and converting to the system – or by monitoring the installation work being done by a supplier.

Too often in the past the installation of a computer in small and medium-sized firms has caused problems rather than solved them. The increasing range of independent advice, particularly that which uses a 'do it yourself' approach and so leads to a better understanding of the process for the potential user, should help to reduce the incidence of such situations in the future.

Useful addresses

John Smith, Patrick Reynolds, Peter Meredith, or Paul Martin
Business Services Group
Ernst and Young
Rolls House
7 Rolls Buildings
Fetter Lane
London EC4A 1NH
01–831 7130

Clive Leyland
UK Microguide Co-ordinator
Arthur Andersen & Co
1 Surrey Street
London WC2R 2PS
01–836 1200 or 061–228 2121

9.5   Information technology disasters

LAURA GRIFFITHS

'He was a computer expert, we weren't. We didn't know what to look for. We were naive. We believed in him . . . we were done!'

This story, told by insurance broker Denis Waller, is typical of what happens when small companies try to install the latest forms of information technology (IT). They don't know where to go for advice and often spend a fortune on the wrong machines – and an eternity of a manager's time battling to understand them.

Waller thought he'd done the right thing by consulting his trade association, the British Insurance Brokers Association, who provided very general guidelines. On the basis of these he decided on a particular microcomputer. But general guidelines are not enough to see you through the computer minefield, and by the time he found out that it was the wrong machine and that the dealer had lied about its capabilities, he had paid out £9000.

'But,' he says, 'what you can't calculate is three years' man-hours looking at systems, buying one, loading in the information and then finding out over six months it didn't do what you wanted it to do – you just can't price that.' He cut his losses and junked the computer for a new system altogether.

Waller was so exasperated by the ease with which he was misled into wasting a great deal of time and money that he took part in a newly released video, *What's IT All About?* which sets out to explain information technology in practical terms and gives reasons why IT realities consistently fail to live up to the salesman's promises.

The video, made jointly by the office equipment magazine *Office Equipment Index* and the London-based TV Choice production company, makes sobering viewing. The video claims that 30 to 35 per cent of computer systems are installed at the wrong price at the wrong time – probably by the wrong people. Small businesses, keen to get ahead with the latest that technology can offer, are continually meeting with disasters, ranging from small time-wasting mysteries and mishaps to major breakdowns which lead to bankruptcy.

Who is to blame for these disasters? It's easy to blame the salesman. Cities are now full of plausible, personable young men with a slick line of patter and a charming way with secretaries, calling round on all the small businesses in their patch, selling anything from typewriters to multi-user computer systems. Methods vary from a foot in the door to cold selling on the telephone and mailshotting.

Gary Thompson, salesman with office equipment company Altus, says: 'Competition is what it's all about. You've got to want to go out there and get the business. Commission is the biggest incentive to hard work, but some people have aggressive selling techniques and this give sales people a bad reputation.'

But salesmen can't shoulder all the guilt. Major difficulties arise from managers' ignorance of new technology, and their inhibition about admitting ignorance. John Dalton Banks, who is an office equipment dealer, says, 'Nobody likes to admit they don't know something, so when the salesman starts to chunter on with jargon like "this is a 20 megabyte machine with 640k of RAM and a single floppy disk, 320k of storage . . . ," the customer tends to nod along in agreement.'

At the opposite end of the problem, there are still some people who are reluctant to look at new technology in any shape whatsoever. As he pads his city beat salesman Gary Thompson sees a lot of small companies still using old manual typewriters. The old-style bosses add parisimony to ignorance: 'They don't want to spend their money and they often don't know how letters, for example, are produced. They only see the end product and if it looks OK they don't care how long it took to produce.'

On the other hand, says Thompson, their secretaries are often keen to computerise because, 'They know more about what's going on in a company'. This sort of rift often leads to companies either not buying IT when they really need it or spending on products more to 'keep people happy' than to solve any real business problem.

But over-enthusiasm is probably the number one reason for IT disasters. People hear of the wonders computer technology can perform, they see the commercials on television, and think a computer can cure all their business headaches. One plumber's merchant had a wife who was fed up with him spending all his time on clerical work. She went out and bought him an impress-ive-looking new computer, but she didn't know that without software (computer programs) to go with it, the computer was so much scrap metal. And by the time she discovered this important fact, she found there wasn't any software available to make the new computer do what her husband wanted it to do.

Electronic mail – the sending of messages from one computer to another over the telephone lines – is another much hyped IT miracle. Like many other firms, one public relations company took up electronic mail, believing it promised instant communi-cations and that this would enable them to improve their service to their clients. A few months later they found it was taking them *eight days* to send a piece of electronic mail from London to Reading.

Getting ripped off is the easiest thing in the IT world. A com-pany of catering butchers in London asked a number of computer companies to tender for an office automation system. 'It's a minefield,' says the manager, 'we discovered that computer companies will sell you what they think you will pay for.'

Dalton Banks, office equipment dealers, say, 'The initial price of the computer may look like it's going to be £2000. Often this turns out to be £3–£4000.' The IT market may be selling the products of the twenty-first century, but it's still very much a jungle.

(*What's IT All About?*, price £96, is produced by Maclaren/TV Choice, tel: 01–379 0873.)

9.6 Where to go for help

LAURA GRIFFITHS

Faced with lines of eager high-tech salesmen and mounds of baffling computer manuals, the first-time buyer of information technology cries, 'I need help'. But finding help and advice of the right sort is in itself a major headache.

A few years ago there was an enormous shortage of people you could turn to for IT help. Now there are too many and few, if any, are genuinely helpful.

The main reason for this is that the problematic nature of IT – a complex, jargon-ridden mixture of computer and communications technology – has spawned a flourishing mini-industry designed to make you part with your money in exchange not for equipment, but information about equipment.

Consultants are the worst offenders. In theory, a consultant is an independent company or individual who will advise you on what IT, if any, you should invest in, and help you get it up and running. Not very long ago consultants were few and far between and too expensive for small companies. Now they have multiplied extraordinarily and they will take anyone's money.

Few consultants, however, are genuinely independent. Many are actually little more than computer salespeople. Others have very strong links with computer companies.

Even those who profess independence are subject to constant seduction from sales-hungry computer companies. For example, one computer consultant, having worked out what system his client wanted, put the job out to tender. He was appalled by the number of computer companies who wrote back to him offering a fee for recommending their kit.

A more useful source of help for the small business is the national Federation of Microsystems Centres which are scattered across Britain (addresses on pages 232–3). They offer advice and training to first-timers and can act as effective focal points for the experience of small businesses in local areas. But a trip to such a centre is unlikely to be very rewarding unless you know the right questions to ask.

In the first place, you need a general awareness of the pitfalls and benefits of IT, and to get this people often turn to computer magazines and books. But much of this literature is completely useless, being either aimed at computer buffs who are more interested in machine specifications than in what a piece of equipment can actually do for a company, or very general guidelines written by a journalist with a sketchy knowledge of the subject.

The printed word, by its very page-bound nature, is limited in what it can tell you about the highly visual world of IT. Television and video fare better in this department. There are several companies which provide video cassettes which explain to businesses how they can use IT, but the best – and cheapest – come from London-based TV Choice.

TV Choice produces a series of videos called 'Information Technology in Action' which concentrate on the practical aspects of the subject, and put across a lot of valuable information quickly and entertainingly. The videos show both the negative and the positive side of the IT game and make rewarding viewing for people at all stages of computerisation.

Training is one way of arming yourself for the more specific problems of putting IT theories into practice, and there is a plethora of courses on offer. But private training organisations can be extremely expensive, and as yet there is no way of checking their competence – or their independence from manufacturers. Many seedy little outfits are springing up, especially in central London, which may consist of two rooms, a couple of home computers and a large intake of foreign students paying enormous fees.

It's as well to check out the local library to find details of courses run by local colleges and polytechnics which increasingly cater for the small business, and will, at least, have qualified staff.

In addition, there is now a national network of information technology education centres, funded by the Training Agency, whose primary purpose is to train school-leavers, but which now also offer courses to local business people. But you don't have to go through the centres. The TA also offers direct grants for companies who want to train a member of staff in IT skills.

Many companies are now taking this self-help path, investing in videos and course materials and using their own staff time in order to train people in IT skills. For busy managers, this informal approach, where they take videos home and try out software packages on a computer in their living room, is much more acceptable than exposing themselves to the humiliation of being bottom of the IT class.

Sources of information

Training grants, open learning materials:

Training Agency
Moorfoot
Sheffield S1 4PQ
0742 753275

Videos:
TV Choice
80 St Martin's Lane
London WC2N 4AA
01-379 0873

Training courses:
Local libraries

Microsystem centres:
National Computing Centre
11 New Fetter Lane
London EC4 1PU
01-353 4875

9.7 Using networks

LAURA GRIFFITHS

Until recently companies getting involved in information technology had only to tussle with the problem of which computer would suit them best. As if this wasn't enough of a headache, they will increasingly have to consider what computer systems their customers and suppliers use, too.

This arises from the growing importance of networking – the ability to link one computer to another by means of telephone lines – as a crucial deciding factor in a highly competitive business world.

David Rumble, telecommunications specialist with the PA consultancy organisation, says, 'Ten years away from now, even a corner store will be at least considering the possibility that it will use a computer and a telephone line to order its goods from its wholesalers. The stores that don't do that will probably lose out . . . they won't even be in the running.'

The simple fact is that computer networks offer companies new ways of linking up with their customers and suppliers, and this offers the imaginative competitor opportunities to introduce startling innovations. Some of these innovations will succeed and put the innovators at the head of the pack. Others will fail and cost them a fortune. And, whatever happens, the companies which are unaware of the changes which networks bring will undoubtedly fall by the wayside.

One of the most colourful examples of the way in which networking has been used to transform a competitive position is that of the National Bingo Game Association. Bingo clubs began losing custom when the tabloid press started offering enormous cash prizes in daily bingo games, and for a while things looked pretty grim.

The answer was found when the National Bingo Game Association made use of a commercial computer network to link together 850 of its bingo clubs. This made it possible for people to play a bumper nationwide bingo game as well as their local ones and the clubs were able to offer prizes of up to £50,000 for countrywide winners, where the previous maximum prize was £3000. Punters began returning to the clubs and the decline was halted. This year the major bingo companies have reported record profits.

Britain's most shining example of a company using networks to gain an edge on the competition is Thomson Holidays. The holiday company discovered five years ago the competitive advantages of linking their computer system with terminals in travel agents throughout the country using a network.

Now instead of having to wait for telephone calls to get through, Thomson's agents can handle holiday inquiries and bookings via the computer. This saved Thomsons £25 million in 1987, increased staff productivity by 100 per cent and cut £1.5 million off the agents' telephone bills.

But, more important, the network became a strategic weapon to put Thomsons ahead of its rivals. A customer seeking a holiday could see the information from Thomsons first and book immediately while the enthusiasm lasted – without even looking at what the competition had on offer. Thomsons have now set the pace for the travel market and its competitors have felt obliged to imitate their system.

Thomsons themselves are experimenting with new ways of exploiting the link with the agents. TAB, Thomson Automated Banking, will enable agents not only to book holidays but to pay for them electronically. Thomsons is already a market leader in the highly competitive holiday business, and it is using these new networking initiatives to put itself further into the lead.

Networking is an extremely expensive business – not the least because it involves harnessing the very different technological worlds of computer and telecommunications – and this means that it is much more likely to be the large and dominant organisations which will be able to capitalise on it.

But smaller companies will not be able to pay any less attention to networking. On the contrary, the bigger companies will increasingly employ the networks to try to change the rules of competition, and this will have a huge impact on all players in the game.

One of the best examples of this is in the United States of America where the use of networking is much further down the road. The American drug wholesaler McKesson, for example, has given hand-held terminals to the pharmacies it supplies. These terminals are linked via McKesson's network to a central database containing details of drugs available and delivery timetables and enables the pharmacists to order up the drugs directly.

But McKesson didn't stop there. They also put computer terminals in their own suppliers' offices, enabling them to order drugs directly. These developments helped to lift McKesson's revenue by 29 per cent between 1984 and 1985. It has also brought McKesson into a new business, medical insurance, since the information they collect on drug sales is vital to the broking of medical insurance claims.

On the other hand, the companies who haven't been so quick on the networking uptake have felt a cold wind blowing. There are now far fewer drug distributors and the big four who divide the lion's share of the market between them are the ones who had the resources to set up networks similar to McKesson's.

Until recently a major problem facing companies who are trying to get in on the network game was the dire lack of information about what's possible. But now a flurry of activity has started to correct this situation. An essential book on the topic has appeared called *Competing in Time* by Peter Keen; a video on the subject has been produced by the Department of Trade and Industry and a low-cost educational package, including a video and support literature, is now available from London-based TV Choice.

The message from all these quarters is the same: networking is changing the way the business game is played and unless you learn the new rules you run the risk of losing before you've kicked off.

More information

Information Management, State of the Art Report, published by Pergamon Infotech (tel: 0628 39101).

Competing in Time, by Peter Keen, published by Harper and Row.

Networks for Competitive Advantage, by TV Choice, (tel: 01-379 0873).

Department of Trade and Industry (tel: 01-215 7877).

9.8   The Data Protection Act

LAURA GRIFFITHS

The Data Protection Act is fast becoming a new bogy in the demonology of bureaucracy confronting the small business, alongside such time-honoured figures as the VAT man and the tax inspector.

The Data Protection Act was brought in to calm the fears of people afraid that large organisations were amassing vast amounts of computerised information on individuals which might be false or be misused. The Act says that companies which process data on individuals are accountable for what they do with that data, and individuals will have the right to look at the data held on them.

However, as far as small businesses are concerned, the Act has missed its target. It has resulted in a mass of bureaucratic work, puzzlement and confusion for companies who pose little risk to individual liberties, and exempted the real sources of 'Big Brother' fears such as the police, the taxman and the security forces.

'It's a farce,' says Denis Waller of insurance brokers Croucher Reoch. 'Nobody can understand what it's for. What use has it been to us? We're registered but nobody seems to know – or care.'

All companies who process data on individuals are required to register under the Act. It's not expensive – only £22 for three years – but it is immensely time-consuming as you have to fill in a lot of complicated forms specifying the different things you use the data for. To make matters worse, the forms have all been designed with every conceivable company in mind, including very large users of computers. It's not surprising, therefore, that the smaller company is likely to come unstuck.

Denis Waller says, 'The problem for insurance brokers is that we could in theory fill in every box – but we were advised not to do that because it throws a spanner in the works of the Registrar's computer! You can't tick everything and you must tick something or you can't register. It took a whole day just to fill in the form.'

But some relief has arrived. The person who is in charge of administering the Act, the Data Registrar, has made available new, more simplified forms for the smaller business. The Registrar, Eric Howe, is aware of the problems the small business faces. 'Small businessmen have shied away from the problem and got confused because of the complicated form,' says Howe. 'But now we've reduced the list that small firms would have to handle, and we've simplified the guidelines in consultation with groups representing a variety of small firms.'

Nevertheless, there are still major uncertainties about what actually puts you in danger of the Act and what doesn't. The Act says that, for example, if you use any form of computerised equipment to process (as opposed to simply storing) data, you have to register. But does this mean that if you use a computerised telex system, you're liable? According to the Registry you probably are, but the assistant registrar, Simon Moulton, admits it's a very complex area.

And it's no easy task finding clear sources of advice on how the Act affects you. Some of the material which does exist isn't only not all that helpful, but positively dangerous. For example, *Inside Information*, a mostly accurate and trustworthy introduction to information technology published by the BBC, has a section on the Act which says that electronic mailing lists are exempt. Howe completely refutes this. This means that numberless small businesses who send out mailshots to people asking them to buy their wares will all have to register.

Even after going through the ordeal of registering, companies are left with the job of making sure they don't stray outside its provisions. For one thing, you have to make sure you don't use the data for any purpose other than the one for which you registered. For another, you have to keep the data you hold secure from misuse, theft or damage.

The need for companies and staff to understand what the issues are is therefore vital but, while larger companies can appoint full-time staff to ensure that they stay within the Act, things are much more difficult for the smaller business. The Act and its complicated requirements may well put some companies off using computers at all.

For those who do decide to battle their way through, sources of advice and help are thin and far between. There are a number of books, videos and courses now aimed at briefing people about what the Act requires them to do, but these have to be used carefully. None is recommended by the Registrar, and if they send you up the garden path you only have yourself to blame. The safest starting point is the literature published by the Registrar.

To date, about 50,000 small businesses have registered under the Act, leaving something like 100,000 organisations still in breach of the law. But Howe doesn't, at least at present, have any plans for taking businesses to court to make examples of them.

'We're using the carrot and stick approach,' says Howe. 'We're mailing a lot of small businesses with information about registration and placing notices in post offices. But we've also started doing checks on organisations, sending a simple questionnaire and following up with a visit. We're starting with the big organisations, but of course we have to deal with any complaints we may have about any size of business.'

Since November 1987, 'data subjects' have had the right to have access to data held on them. This could mean open season on mailshots. Anyone who receives something in the post that he or she suspects arises from a computerised mailing list can demand to see what information the company holds on them. Many companies which haven't registered may find themselves in trouble as the wheels of the elephantine Act slowly but surely are turned in their direction.

Further information

Books and advice:
The Registrar
Springfield House
Water Lane
Wilmslow
Cheshire SK9 5AX
0625 535777

Training courses:
Group 4 Management and
  Training Services
Farncombe House
Broadway
Worcestershire WR12 7LJ
0386 858585

Videos:
(Data Protection Act)
Video Arts
Dumbarton House
68 Oxford Street
London W1N 9LA
01-637 7288

(Data security in general):
TV Choice
80 St Martin's Lane
London WC2N 4AA
01-379 0873

10
Health and Safety

HUMPHREY NORVILL
Managing Director, Shaftesbury Health & Safety Consultants, St Ives,
Huntingdon (formerly HM Deputy Superintending Inspectorate of Factories)

10.1   Introduction

The smaller businesses are attracting increased attention from
the Health and Safety Executive and local authorities in view of
their generally poor health and safety record. Strenuous efforts
are made to identify unregistered factories and one exercise
involving 30 industrial estates revealed that 50 per cent of the
factories were unregistered. The problems discovered led to a
prosecution and a number of Prohibition and Improvement
Notices being issued.

For the owners of many small businesses, problems of premises, personnel, plant, product and marketing, to say nothing of
cash flow, take precedence over occupational health and safety.
But an Inspector knocking on the door, a serious accident, a fire
or explosion, will undoubtedly concentrate the mind on health
and safety requirements that have hitherto probably been
neglected through ignorance rather than criminal neglect.

The enforcing authorities, although under-staffed, certainly
possess teeth. HM Factory Inspectorate conducted 1975 pros-
ecutions in 1982 and over 11,500 Improvement and Prohibition
Notices were issued that year. While these Notices do not attract
the adverse publicity that surrounds a prosecution, they can
shut down a machine or an entire process, or can effectively
close down a building site, and therefore are extremely costly to
the small businessman in terms of lost production and output.
Individuals, including directors and company secretaries, face
up to two years' imprisonment under Section 33 of the Health
and Safety at Work Act 1974 for a variety of offences discussed
in later sections. The purpose of this chapter is to highlight certain
key areas of health and safety requirements with special reference
to the small business.

The first step is to register the factory with the Health and Safety Executive using Form 9, Notice of Occupation, obtainable from their area offices, the addresses of which can be found in the telephone directory. Failure to do so can result in a fine. Obviously, an Inspector's attitude on visiting will be different if he discovers an unregistered factory, compared with someone who has registered and genuinely seeks advice and assistance from the Inspectorate. Deciding not to register and hoping the enforcing authority will never find you is short-sighted and certainly not worth the eventual hassle.

Having registered, you require certain basic forms from HMSO. The General Register Form 31 is the 'passport' of your company under factory legislation; it contains details of the decoration of the premises and the employment of young persons under 18 and should be signed by the occupier. Two Accident Books are required: B1510, the Accident Book provided by the DSS and into which details of every injury, however slight, sustained at work should be entered, and Form 2509, the Register of Notifiable Accidents and Dangerous Occurrences, specifically designed for the 1980 Notification of Accidents and Dangerous Occurrences Regulations. Essentially these Regulations require the death of or major injury (a term that includes most fractures) to any person to be notified immediately by telephone to the enforcing authority followed by a completed Form 2508 within seven days. Other notifiable accidents are those that result in an employee being incapacitated for work for more than three consecutive days, excluding the day of the accident and any Sunday or rest day.

Under these Notification of Accident Regulations information can be passed between the DSS and the Health and Safety Executive and this is, of course, another method by which unregistered premises are discovered. Notifiable dangerous occurrences include the collapse or overturning of any lift, hoist, crane or mobile powered access platform, an electrical short circuit or overload attended by fire or explosion that results in the stoppage of the plant involved for more than 24 hours, an explosion or fire due to the ignition of process materials, their by-products (including waste) or finished products that resulted in the stoppage of plant or suspension of normal work for more than 24 hours, a collapse or part collapse of a scaffold more than 12 metres high and any incident in which any person is affected by the inhalation, ingestion or absorption of any substance to such an extent as to cause acute ill health requiring medical treatment. This also includes illness due to lack of oxygen. 'A Guidance Note to the Notification of Accidents and DO Regulations 1980, booklet HS(R)5, has been published by the Health and Safety Executive. Most small factories will also need a Fire Certificate, application for which should be made to your local Fire Authority.

You will also need Form 1, Abstract of the Factories Act 1961, Form OSR9, Abstract of the Offices, Shops and Railway Premises Act 1964, Form 954, the placard copy of the Electricity Regulations 1908 and 1944, and the placard indicating treatment for electric shock, obtainable from insurance companies.

If women or young persons are employed, Form 11, Permissible Hours of Work, must be completed. The Health and Safety Executive or a specialist advisory service can assist in identifying other forms that may be required for your particular industry.

10.2   General legal requirements

There is no hiding place from the Health and Safety at Work Act 1974! It embraces all work activities from safari parks to hotels, from swimming baths to fairgrounds, from primary schools to teaching hospitals, as well as the traditional workplaces of factories, mines, quarries, offices and farms. An estimated 8 million people came under this protective umbrella for the first time. In addition to safety policies, there were several far-reaching innovations in the general legal provisions of this Act.

The good news for the small businessman who may wish to buy second-hand plant or equipment is that Section 6 of the Act now imposes duties on designers, manufacturers, importers or suppliers of any article for use at work to ensure that it is so designed and constructed as to be safe and without risk to health when properly used. Plant, equipment and machinery must also be accompanied by adequate information to ensure its safe use. These same legal requirements are also applicable to any person who manufactures, imports or supplies any substance for use at work.

Having received the relevant information about the safe operation of a machine or the safe handling of a chemical, the employer has the duty to pass on this information, together with whatever relevant instruction, training and supervision may be necessary to ensure that his employees are fully aware of any risks that may be involved and the correct action to avoid such risks. This is part of the organisation of a safe system of work which will be covered in general terms in the safety policy and its arrangement discussed in section 10.5.

Another feature of the 1974 Act was the concept of self-regulation – the idea being that those living and working with potential hazards every day are given the right training, instruction and authority, and are thus better able to take remedial action before a serious incident occurs than an Inspector, who obviously only spends a fraction of his time in any one establishment. Regulations made under this Section are known as the Safety Representatives and Committees Regulations 1977, and full guidance and information on them are contained in a booklet setting out the Regulations and the Code of Practice, obtainable from HMSO.

Safety representatives are appointed by recognised trade unions, and after the employer has been notified in writing of their appointment, the representatives may undertake their duties. These include the investigation of potential hazards and dangerous occurrences, accident investigation, investigation of complaints, and routine inspections of the workplace. They are also allowed to receive information from Inspectors, including copies of correspondence sent to an employer. An employer must also, at the request of the safety representative, form a safety committee. The safety representative may make representations to an employer on any matters arising from his investigations or on general matters affecting the health and safety of the employees at the workplace. An employer must allow a safety representative such time off with pay during the employee's working hours as are necessary for the purpose of undertaking these duties and for undergoing any necessary training. Safety representatives must also be given all relevant information by an employer to enable them to fulfil their functions except where national security or personal confidentiality are involved or where information has been obtained by an employer for the purpose of, for example, defending any legal proceedings. It should be noted that failure on the part of an employer to allow a safety representative to take time off or to pay him in accordance with these Regulations enables the safety representative to present a complaint to an industrial tribunal.

However praiseworthy the intentions behind this legislation, the present economic climate has effectively muzzled many safety representatives who fear that too high a profile may lead to their inclusion in the next batch of redundancies!

The Act is also innovative in imposing a specific duty on an employer to take care of people other than his employees. This duty would extend to members of the public who might be visiting his premises or walking around scaffolding in the high street. Supplies of appropriate protective clothing should be available for visitors.

The main thrust of the 1974 Act is to extend the frontiers of occupational health and safety, placing the prime responsibility squarely on management. The small businessman must be aware of those additional duties and respond to the challenge.

10.3   Maintenance

'Maintenance is the Cinderella of the building industry, but it does not need a magic wand to transform it and dust the ashes of the dead from its rags. It needs a change of attitude on the part of those who carry out maintenance, whether building occupiers undertaking their own work or contractors brought in for the purpose, and a recognition that its problems demand a properly planned and professional approach.' This extract from the Annual Report of the Health and Safety Executive into the construction industry for 1981 to 1982 provides a valuable introduction to some of the safety problems in construction facing the smaller occupier. In the years 1977 to 1981, 169 workmen were killed during maintenance work on building operations, some 40 per cent of all fatal construction accidents. The vast majority of those deaths (151) resulted from falls, nearly 50 per cent being falls through fragile material. The trades most at risk were roofing workers and painters. The Report states that virtually all of these accidents could have been prevented by the properly planned implementation of relatively safe and simple precautions. A typical accident involved the death of one apprentice and severe injuries to another who had been instructed to clean out the gutters on the asbestos roof of a riverside warehouse. They knelt in the gutter, steadying themselves on the asbestos roof while gathering up the debris, and then walked along the walls to gain access around the roof and lower the rubbish to the ground. One of the men probably stumbled off the wall and both fell through the roof to the concrete floor some 30 feet below.

The safety precautions to be taken in roofwork are contained in Guidance Note GS10, 'Roof Work – Prevention of Falls' (HMSO), which emphasises the need for proper and sufficient crawling ladders and crawling boards, the need for roof-edge protection, and gives valuable suggestions on the use of safety belts and harnesses. There is no doubt that one of the major causes of this horrific toll of maintenance accidents is that maintenance jobs are frequently regarded as being too small to last long, and no one in management, including sometimes the professional safety advisers, gives them adequate thought and supervision. Roof maintenance is the subject of a three-part publication on all types of maintenance accidents and their prevention published by the Health and Safety Executive and available from HMSO.

Window cleaning, of course, is another aspect of building maintenance. Eight window cleaners were killed during the year 1980–81, which places window cleaners in the top ten occupations at risk. Two-thirds of the deaths were from working on unprotected window sills and this practice should be stopped by any responsible occupier. Many other safe means of access are generally available and anchorages, either fixed or portable, with suitable harnesses can be provided. Again, much detailed information on all relevant means of making window cleaning safer is given in Guidance Note GS25 (HMSO), 'Prevention of Falls to Window Cleaners'.

Figures for the construction industry show an overall increase of 16 per cent in fatal accidents for 1983 and an 8.5 per cent increase in serious accidents at a time when numbers employed in the construction industry have greatly contracted. Despite the extremely good safety films, propaganda, seminars and advisory publications produced by all sectors of the industry, this is a worrying trend. The vast majority of these fatalities and serious injuries are not at the frontiers of technology but are involved in relatively simple operations for which the safety precautions are well known and widely publicised.

Most ladder accidents occur for a job lasting under half an hour, involving a ladder that is not securely placed or fixed. Many of these accidents, caused through overreaching, overbalancing or climbing with loads, show that more suitable equipment, such as a tower scaffold, should have been used. Ladders should extend to a height of at least 3ft 6in above the landing place and should be placed at a suitable angle of about 75 degrees to the horizontal, ie about a one-in-four slope. Where securing at the top is impracticable, arrangements must be made to prevent the ladder from slipping outwards or sideways. A second person footing the ladder to prevent slipping is considered effective only for ladders under 5 metres in length overall.

Painters have a poor accident record, the main problem being safe access. Clients could assist by questioning the safety pre-cautions proposed in the tenders before awarding the contract. Typically, an industrial painting job is of short duration involving small gangs of painters. Supervision is low, with a foreman cover-ing several sites at the same time, and it is vital that a high standard of training and supervision is given to the erection and use of mobile tower scaffolds and painters' cradles.

The small occupier must remember that he has a legal responsibility for the safety of work being undertaken on his premises even if it is done by outside contractors.

10.4　Falls

Fall guys are not confined to Hollywood. 'Persons falling' are one of the categories of industrial accident known as the Big Five, accounting for some two-thirds of all occupational accidents, the others being manual handling, striking against objects, struck by falling objects, and use of hand tools.

It is probable that new regulations will be made on the manual handling of loads following the publication of a consultative document prepared by the Health and Safety Commission in 1982. Manual handling accidents in premises subject to the Factories Act 1961 have increased dramatically in the last 20 years, from 40,000 to more than 70,000 each year. Research has shown that only about 10 per cent of healthy adults can safely handle weights of between 75 and 100 lb even assuming they have benefited from appropriate specialist training, thereby highlighting the need for mechanical handling aids. There are still far too many employers who have no knowledge of the weights that are being regularly lifted by hand nor have their staff been trained in the correct lifting techniques. There are many good films on safe manual handling, and employers whose staff sustain back injuries are liable at common law if they have not provided the necessary instruction or supervision.

The latest annual statistics show that in manufacturing industry there were some 26,000 accidents caused by falls, the vast majority of which were falls on the flat, costing an estimated £180 million a year. Many of these can be attributed to worn, wet or greasy floors, often combined with unsafe footwear. The slip-resistance of most floor surfaces deteriorates when they are wet and due allowance must be made for condensation or spillage in canteens and kitchens, for wet floors in canning or meat processing factories, in abattoirs, or in wards used by geriatric patients. These are a few situations where a prudent employer must provide a flooring with a good standard of slip-resistance when wet. Advice on specialist manufacturers of safety flooring can be obtained from the Building Centre, 26 Store Street, London WC1E 7BS. Some safety floorings have an adhesive back surfacing that can simply be laid on to existing flooring or stairs. Slip-resistant coatings containing abrasive can be applied to exterior surfaces exposed to the elements and these are used on decks of warships, on outside broadcast television vehicles, and in the road haulage industry.

Floorings can also become slippery as a result of improper maintenance. Often cleaners are not supervised and fail to use the proper solvents correctly diluted. Adequate warning notices should be provided for persons approaching wet floors while cleaning is in progress. Considerable advice is contained in the publication entitled 'Watch Your Step', available from HMSO.

Striking against objects is frequently the result of bad housekeeping aided by a lack of proper safety footwear, and arises from bad stacking, congested gangways and poor layout of plant and machinery. Useful information is contained in Health and Safety at Work booklet No 47, 'Safe Stacking of Materials', obtainable from HMSO.

Neolithic man would have recognised many of the 10,000 hand-tool accidents each year, though modern technology sometimes adds a new twist: a high street shopper was injured by a stray projectile fired from a cartridge-operated tool being used on an adjacent building site! Loose hammer heads that fly off and strike the workman's colleagues, butchers' knives that slip while being used to debone a carcass and enter the butcher's groin, and the use of non-insulated pliers on live cable, have all caused death. The Court of Appeal decision in *Regina* v *Swan Hunter Ship Builders Ltd* (1981) requires employers to ensure that sub-contractors are using safe tools and proper equipment. Thus the use of a normal instead of a non-sparking tool by a contractor in an area of fire or explosion risk could have devastating consequences. Only use the best quality hand tools and check that they are properly maintained. Ensure that all portable electrical tools are regularly maintained and that this audit and control of hand tools is part of the organisation's safety policy.

Many thousands of injuries could be prevented in these Big Five categories if employers provided a full range of protective clothing to the relevant British Standard. Many eye injuries are still being caused by the use of goggles or safety glasses to BS 2092:1967, which is for general purpose safety, and not to BS 2092:1 or 2, which is the higher degree of protection for impact resistance, designed for situations where flying particles are a possibility.

Despite the Health and Safety at Work Act 1974 there was a depressing similarity between the number of Big Five accidents in the Annual Report for Manufacturing Industries for 1982 and the Chief Inspector of Factories' 1962 Report. Despite unemployment, there has been a significant real increase in these types of accident which could be dramatically reduced by some applied common sense and effective monitoring and supervision.

10.5 Safety policies

Nobel literature prizes are not awarded for safety policies. The incentive for producing a satisfactory safety policy comes, therefore, from the attitude of the enforcing authorities, either the Health and Safety Executive or the local authority, who initially decide whether the policy is appropriate for the size and complexity of the business. This is an obligation embraced in Section 2(3) of the Health and Safety at Work Act 1974. It requires each employer of more than five persons to prepare a policy setting out his or her organisation's policy for health and safety together with the arrangements for implementing that policy. A new industry was spawned in producing advisory literature and organising lectures and seminars on the requirements of the Act. Many organisations produced model 'safety policies' for their members. Frequently this approach led to embarrassing situations when member firms simply copied the 'model' safety policy without questioning its relevance in relation to their particular activities. Others, displaying a bluff John Bull independence, produced safety policies that mirrored the attitude of the author – 'this organisation will continue to protect all its assets, including its employees'.

Enforcing authorities look for a commitment from the senior people of any organisation in the general safety policy statement, and it is good practice for such statements to be signed by the Chief Executive and dated. The date is important, as the law requires that the safety policy should be revised whenever appropriate, and there have been many instances where some of the tasks referred to in existing policies were simply out of date as they referred to systems no longer in existence. It was well stated in the Health and Safety Executive's 1978 Annual Report for Manufacturing and Service Industries that, 'The policy for safety must be an expression of the firm's individual will, at the highest level, to create and maintain a safe and healthy place of work. The safety organisation must be an expression of this will in a form which is consistent with the firm's total organisation for production and profit. It should take into account the needs, the abilities and the limitations of all those members of management, at whatever level, who have to put it into effect. They should know what they have to do in the interests of safety, and know that they are provided with a means to do it.'

After the general safety policy statement clearly indicating the commitment of top management to achieving safe and healthy working conditions, there must follow details of the organisation and arrangements for implementing that policy. Clearly this will vary according to the size and complexity of the organisation in its operations. While large and medium-sized companies will embrace the safety function in job descriptions for their line and functional management, the smaller company, possibly having no written job descriptions, will probably place the responsibility on named individuals and should give them both the training and the time to undertake their safety duties. The organisation and arrangements for improving health and safety standards can only come from an awareness and reappraisal of situations within the organisation giving rise to risk, whether this be from mechanical handling, from machinery, from bad housekeeping or from people slipping on the washroom floor. These are, of course, just a very few accident-producing situations that might lead to subsequent personal injury claims.

The small firm generally does not have a full-time safety adviser and many now realise that their appreciation of risk potential is best undertaken by a professional and are 'buying in' this expertise on a contract basis in the same way as they 'buy in' their financial advice through their accountant.

Formal arrangements translate the purple prose of the general policy statement into practical reality and it is important that the provision of relevant information, proper instruction, training and supervision are all considered when detailing the arrangements required to implement the policy.

As part of the arrangements, effective monitoring should be established by a combination of 'safety sampling' – investigation of all accidents and incidents causing injury or damage – by the provision, where necessary, of internal safety rules and by arranging that safety becomes an integral part of the organisation's operations from the planning stage onwards. The arrangements should therefore include vetting of new and second-hand machinery before purchase, the questioning of suppliers on information relating to toxicity of materials entering the organisation, and thorough training on all aspects of fire precautions. Further information is obtainable from the Health and Safety Executive's booklet, 'Effective Policies for Health and Safety'.

Never neglect safe systems of work for maintenance, tool-setting and outside contractors. Experience shows that many safety policies relate only to normal working arrangements and do not allow for emergencies.

10.6   Accidents

Those injured at work each year would fill Wembley stadium for three Cup Finals and still leave an overflow along Olympic Way. Allow for a degree of under-reporting, and then consider

that each year more people are killed at work than died in the Falklands campaign, and the scale of this occupational carnage becomes apparent.

It is highly probable, therefore, that the small businessman will sooner or later be faced with an accident within his organisation. Clearly the accident must be reported and the injured person given the speediest medical attention. The purpose of this section is to concentrate, not on the reporting procedures which have already been discussed, or on the preventive measures which will be discussed in later sections, but in providing practical guidance on important actions that must be taken.

Never forget that many accidents result in litigation and it is important, when investigating an accident, to remember the possibility of the circumstances being analysed in the greatest detail in a court room several years later. Contemporary evidence is very strong evidence, and it is helpful if photographs can be taken of the scene of the accident, as well as a sketch plan showing all relevant dimensions.

Accuracy is very important: critical dimensions for woodworking machine guards, for example, are given in millimetres. If it is a lifting accident then weigh the component or item of plant involved. Take a careful note of the general environmental conditions. Was the lighting satisfactory? What was the condition of the floor? If it was slippery, what was the substance and how did it get there? Is such spillage a regular occurrence?

Having taken the necessary photographs and relevant dimensions, examine the equipment itself to see if there was a malfunction, and if so ascertain the cause. It is also very important to try to reconstruct the sequence of events leading to the accident. Were there any variations on the normal procedure for carrying out the work? If so, why were they taken?

After investigating the circumstances leading to the accident and the accident itself in detail, one must decide whether changes in the system of work are required in order to prevent a repetition of the incident. Even where an operation falls within a specified code of regulations imposing strict training procedures, it is still quite common to find, especially in the smaller factories, that these training requirements, with particular relevance to the safe operation of machinery, have been ignored, often through complete ignorance of any legal requirement.

Was the standard of supervision satisfactory? Some operations require the work to be done under immediate supervision – and this does not mean that the foreman is half a mile off site in the local 'chippy'. Should the maintenance procedures on the machinery be more closely controlled? Had there been a breakdown in communications between departments? Had protective clothing been issued and if so, was it of the correct type? What was the experience of the injured person? How long had he been doing this particular job? Had there been any previous 'near misses' or similar incidents? Had there been any previous complaints made about the system of work? Had the matter been raised by a safety representative on a routine inspection or discussed at the safety committee? If so, had such complaints and discussion been documented? Was work in hand to remedy the complaint at the time of the accident?

It is extremely difficult for a defendant to refute a claim for personal injury if investigation into the accident does not commence until the writ is served, possibly up to three years after the accident. Memories are short, witnesses may have left the company, and the maintenance records might by then have been destroyed. Any chance of establishing contributory negligence on the part of the injured person may well have been lost. As a working rule, keep all the information obtained by the investigation of accidents for at least six years, but remember that a claim for industrial ill health may be initiated up to three years of the date of knowledge of one's medical condition, which may be many years after the illness was caused. This is obviously true of asbestos and noise claims, for instance.

The same principles should also be applied to incidents producing serious internal damage irrespective of whether there has been personal injury. Thus one small firm's investigation into damage to internal partitions led to a rigorous programme of fork-lift truck driver training that resulted in a saving of many thousands of pounds each year and may well have prevented another bandaged employee passing through the Wembley turnstiles in the future. Time spent in conducting a thorough investigation is, like reconnaissance, never wasted.

10.7   Safe systems of work

Safe systems of work never, alas, appeared in Betjeman's verse. Yet the words trip obligingly off the tongue and people nod in understanding. However, many employers, both large and small, fail to grasp the varied duties imposed on them within that simple phrase.

An employer must take reasonable care to provide and maintain proper plant and machinery. Having decided whether such equipment is necessary, and then on the type of equipment, he must ensure that it is safe and in a proper state of repair. Thus there must be a satisfactory system of routine maintenance; he is responsible for careless inspection and examination of plant, poor repairs and delays in carrying out those repairs. All too frequently civil claims against an employer cannot be successfully resisted by him in the courts because he is unable to show any documentary evidence, maintenance record cards, for example, that demonstrate an effective and planned preventive maintenance system. Certain items of plant and machinery such as power presses lifting tackle cranes, lifts, air receivers, steam boilers and scaffolding require regular statutory thorough inspection but it must never be forgotten that regular inspection, testing and servicing, for which written records should be kept, are also required of other plant and equipment. An employer must also act promptly once defects in plant and equipment have been reported to him, as from that time he is deemed to be 'on notice' and has no real defence should an accident occur. Short-cuts on maintenance are a fast lane to the courts.

An employer must also provide a safe place of work together with safe means of access and egress. Particular attention should be paid to the provision of guard rails where people are likely to fall a distance of more than 6 ft 6 in, to well-lit staircases having firm and secure hand-rails, to the maintenance of unobstructed and non-slip floor surfaces. Obviously floors have to be cleaned and there will frequently be spillages. A safe system of work must include the provision of adequate warning notices to indicate that the floor is wet or that there has been a spillage, and there must be a system of coping with spillages such as the provision of oil-absorbing granules or a handy pan and brush. A man who slipped on a waxed job card on the floor of a paper mill was recently awarded over £20,000. So analyse your slipping accidents. Where do they occur? Can the floor surface be improved? Are they caused through spillage or as a result of floor cleaning? Are the correct cleaning materials being used? Working 90 ft above the ground concentrates the mind on the need for guard rails, toe boards and a safety helmet, but more falls occur on the level than from heights.

A safe system of work must also include the provision of proper protective clothing, the training of those undertaking the work and their effective supervision. Specific statutory safety training is required for certain operations, for example, those setting power presses, mounting abrasive wheels or operating woodworking machinery, but most jobs require and contain an element of safety training. Though obviously of crucial importance to young persons, it is not confined to them. A 56-year-old man sustained a severe back injury lifting a roll of paper with arms outstretched. The court found that he was adopting probably the worst posture for this lifting operation, but found in his favour because he had never received any proper instruction on the safe methods of lifting. Many fork-lift truck accidents are caused by drivers who have never been trained, while even trained drivers should be given refresher instruction when changing to a different type of lift truck.

Clearly the amount of supervision will vary according to the nature of the work and the person performing it. An apprentice requires much closer supervision than a millwright, but it should not be assumed that the millwright, because of his experience, needs no guidance or instruction. Much of a millwright's work might have been tackling a series of 'one-off' situations as they arose around the factory and each job would be different and would require considerable planning in advance as to how it could be safely tackled. Effective supervision must also ensure, for example, that protective clothing, be it goggles, helmets, gloves or shoes, is not only provided but also worn, and that supervisors and management must lead by example and wear such clothing themselves whenever appropriate.

The provision of a safe system of work requires careful pre-planning and is dependent upon effective organisation, the details of which should already have been spelt out by an employer as part of the company safety policy.

10.8 Safeguarding machinery

The combination of child labour, long hours and unguarded machinery attracted the attention of nineteenth-century social reformers. Safety provisions were included for the first time in the 1844 Factories Act largely due to the reports of the first four factory inspectors who recounted horrific accidents involving the death and mutilation of mill operatives. Happily, child labour and excessive hours are relegated to social history, but machinery accidents refuse to fade away.

I have investigated the death of a 17-year-old on agricultural machinery, the amputation of the right hand of a man aged 23 on a printing press, and two amputation accidents when operators were removing workpieces from the rear of guillotines. These represent the human face on a body of statistics that each year accounts for 15 to 20 per cent of the total of some 300,000 reportable accidents.

What is the standard required and how can it be achieved?
Essentially, the law requires that every dangerous part of machinery be securely fenced. This apparently simple sentence has caused many High Court battles. The House of Lords has stated that, 'A part of machinery is dangerous if it is a reasonably foreseeable cause of injury to anyone acting in a way in which a human being may be reasonably expected to act in circumstances which may be reasonably expected to occur.' This inter-action between the behaviour of operators and the behaviour of the machine must determine the type and extent of guarding required in order to prevent any part of the operator, or indeed anyone else, from coming into contact with the dangerous part of the machinery. One still hears the same excuses being put forward by employers who fail to appreciate that the requirement to fence securely is an absolute legal obligation. The law protects the careless and inattentive worker as well as the alert and skilled operative. It is no excuse for an employer to say that he was unaware of the legal requirement, or that he had received no warning about that particular dangerous part of machinery from the factory inspector. Similarly, the absence of previous complaints or accidents is no defence. As Lord Justice Clerk stated in *Mitchell* v *North British Rubber Co* (1945), 'Long immunity from accident may be due to good fortune, or unusual skill and care on the part of a succession of operatives, or other causes, and is quite compatible with a machine having been "dangerous" all along. Different considerations apply if a machinery accident has been caused by an operator deliberately tampering with a guard or safety device and although there would still be a breach of the absolute duty clearly there would be substantial contributory negligence against the operator.'

269

The small factory occupier should obtain a copy of British Standard Code of Practice 5304:1975, 'Safe Guarding of Machinery', obtainable from The British Standards Institution, 101 Pentonville Road, London N1. The majority of machinery accidents are not the product of the microchip but of the 'mega-clot', the person who, despite information from his trade association, enforcing authorities and outside organisations, still assumes that machinery fencing may be disregarded and that his organisation has divine protection. Inrunning nips between rollers or between belts and pulleys, traps between rotating and fixed parts, between reciprocating parts of machinery, between unfenced gear wheels, and entanglement around a rotating shaft, to name just a few dangerous parts, would unfortunately be as familiar to the first four factory inspectors appointed in 1833 as to their present-day successors. Most machinery accidents occur either because the guard provided proved to be inadequate or it had been removed and not replaced.

Section 6 of the Health and Safety at Work Act 1974 requires manufacturers, designers, importers and suppliers of machinery to ensure that the article is, insofar as is reasonably practicable, designed and constructed so as to be safe and without risks to health when properly used. They must also carry out or arrange for any relevant testing and examination to enable them to meet that obligation. This duty extends not only to new machinery but also to the suppliers of reconditioned and second-hand machinery and the employer is therefore now in a much stronger legal position than hitherto, when the main burden of guarding a new machine rested with the factory occupier. If the employer is able to control his own organisation effectively then there will be a marked reduction in machinery accidents. The key to success lies in the total commitment of management to the company safety policy, describing the necessary organisation, duties and training, together with effective 'feedback' and regular monitoring on how the policy is working. Machinery safety is the result of good design, careful training and competent supervision.

10.9   Fire

Only six people died in the 1666 Great Fire of London. Deaths of women machinists in a London East End clothing factory focused attention on the annual death and destruction caused by fire at work. Each year fire damage sets new records and frequently exceeds £30 million a month.

Fire generates smoke, fumes, heat and flames, which, if uncontrolled, will spread rapidly to every part of a building. Stairways and lift shafts offer a 'flue' effect, and lack of compartmentation, particularly in storage areas, is a major reason for fire spread. Smoke not only restricts visibility, making escape difficult, but its choking effect also produces panic. Useful information on fire risk in the storage and industrial use of cellular plastics is given in Guidance Note GS3, produced by the Health and Safety Executive.

Despite this scenario of death, damage, devastation and debt, positive action from every employer would reduce and possibly eliminate loss of life through fires at work. A speedy and safe evacuation is the result of advanced planning by the fire authorities, advice on process risk by the Health and Safety Executive, and fire drills and maintenance of safe fire exit routes by the employer.

The Fire Precautions Act 1971 and its relevant Regulations require fire certificates for factory premises in which more than 20 people are employed at any one time, or in which 10 people are employed at any one time elsewhere than on the ground floor, or which are in the same building as other factory, office, shop or railway premises and the aggregate of all employees in all the premises exceeds 20 or exceeds 10 elsewhere than on the ground floor; or if highly flammable or explosive materials are stored or used in or under the premises. The Fire Authority provide Form FP1 (Rev) on which application for a fire certificate should be made. Plans or drawings of the premises will be required and once the fire authority are satisfied that the means of escape from fire and related fire precautions are satisfactory they must issue a fire certificate specifying a safe and effective means of escape, including measures to restrict the spread of fire, smoke and fumes, emergency lighting and direction signs, means for fighting fire, fire alarms and particulars concerning the storage of highly flammable or explosive materials. The fire certificate may also impose requirements relating to the maintenance of the means of escape, the training of people employed in the premises to take action in the event of fire and the limitation on the number of people who may be in the premises at any one time. The penalty for using premises without a fire certificate or for contravening a requirement of a fire certificate, or for making structural alterations to the premises once a fire certificate has been issued without again informing the fire authority, or for beginning to store or use highly flammable or explosive materials again without consulting the fire authority is a maximum fine on summary conviction of £1000 and on conviction or indictment, a fine or imprisonment for a maximum of two years, or both.

Having obtained a fire certificate the employer must ensure that gangways remain unobstructed, and that employees recognise the sound of the fire alarm. Do not test the fire alarm on a Sunday morning when the majority of staff are absent. Similarly, given the fact that frequently the safe evacuation time is under two minutes, a padlocked fire exit door can be the difference between life and death. Regular fire drills would have saved the lives of three women who went back for their handbags and who were then trapped and killed. Advice on holding fire drills is readily available from the fire authority who, together with the Health and Safety Executive and other bodies such as the Fire Protection Association, are only too happy to give freely of their time and expertise to prevent tragedy.

Most fires costing over £25,000 in damage are caused either by an electrical fault or by arson. Automatic fire alarms, smoke and heat detectors are a worthwhile investment for any organisation. Most cases of arson are premeditated and lead to a fast build-up of heat and smoke, evidence of which is discernible to a skilled fire investigator. The best fire detection systems will actuate either a fault alarm or the fire alarm if they are tampered with and there are many types of fire protection available that are acceptable to fire insurers and which may give a worthwhile reduction in premiums. An unwanted fire can lead to lost production and severe cash flow difficulties. Keeping the home fires burning is a laudable aim but providing an impressive bonfire in the middle of an industrial estate is being over-generous!

10.10 Industrial health

Many employers have caught a cold over industrial health. Unfortunately their employees have frequently paid for this neglect with their lives.

Section 2 of the Health and Safety at Work Act 1974 requires employers to ensure the health, safety and welfare at work of all their employees. They are also required by Section 3 to conduct their undertakings so that persons not in their employment who may be affected by their work activities are not thereby exposed to health risks. Manufacturers, importers and suppliers of substances for use at work are required by Section 6 to ensure that the substances are safe and without risk to health when properly used. They must carry out such testing and examination as is necessary and must ensure that adequate information is available about the results of any such tests and that the necessary information is given to ensure that they will be safe when properly used. The standard of reasonable practicability common to these sections means that the degree of risk on one hand must be considered against the physical difficulty, time, trouble and expense involved in eliminating or minimising the risks. The greater the degree of risk, the less weight can be given to the cost of remedial measures. The reasonably practicable precaution applies alike to both prosperous employers and those on hard times. Occupational exposure limits for 1984 are set out in Guidance Note EH40 obtainable from HMSO, which additionally contains a helpful bibliography.

Apart from specific requirements relating to particular processes detailed in Regulations, Section 63 of the Factories Act 1961 requires the use of local exhaust ventilation provided and maintained as close as possible to the source of dust or fume. This is necessary for any process where either substantial quantities of dust are emitted or there is dust or fume likely to be injurious or offensive to persons employed. Atmospheric monitoring should regularly be undertaken to ascertain the degree of process control and therefore of an employee's exposure to harmful substances. It is now possible to use a video recorder and Tyndall beam which make fine dust visible by outlining it against a bright light, while infra-red equipment can now be used to examine gaseous and vapour contaminants.

One report by the Health and Safety Executive on Manufacturing and Service Industries highlights two methods of tackling dust hazards adopted by small firms: 'A small company making refractory powders found an ingenious way of solving a major dust problem. It linked a redundant conveyor to a vibratory unit and an extracted tunnel enclosure to create a highly effective bag conditioning unit. Airborne dust was reduced, the finished bags stacked better and took up less space . . . A somewhat less ingenious entrepreneur was seen, in passing, filling bags with a toxic powder in the doorway of his premises, relying on the wind to blow escaping dust away. The Inspector stopped to visit the firm.'

Despite the long awareness of the dangers of lead, incidents continue to arise which indicate that lead is still an important occupational hazard and the Control of Lead at Work Regulations 1980 have not yet been fully adopted throughout industry. The 1982 Report states that ' . . . Inspectors also had to act in the case of a number of smaller companies engaged in furniture restoration, stained glass window repair and battery breaking, for example. Often, until the Inspector identified the lead hazard, people were unaware of it.'

Despite extensive media coverage on the dangers of asbestos, the latest Report on Manufacturing and Service Industries considers that the degree of awareness of the hazard and the vigour of implementing safety precautions continues to vary widely. In discussing proper decontamination procedures in one railway carriage works where airborne fibre counts showed minimal contamination, the Report commented that, 'Present-day employees were surprised at the precautions needed for one half-crown sized piece of crocidolite or blue asbestos. They could recall stories of snow ball fights with asbestos and night shift workers sleeping among sacks of crocidolite.' The latest thrust in the fight against asbestos is to ensure that only licensed contractors carry out work involving asbestos insulation, coating and stripping.

The Classification, Packaging and Labelling of Dangerous Substances Regulations 1984 should be studied by every employer dealing in any way with such substances. These Regulations apply to explosive, oxidising, flammable, toxic, harmful, corrosive and irritant substances. They not only classify dangerous substances but also give detailed guidance on their packaging and labelling.

The second most common cause of industrial ill health is tenosynovitis and an employer in those industries likely to give rise to repetitive hand movements, and particularly those identified in Guidance Note MS10, should inform employees of the risk, undertake regular medical checks of staff and should reduce the risk of tenosynovitis by carefully supervised schemes of job rotation or job enlargement.

These examples of current problems in occupational health highlight the far-reaching obligations now placed on employers.

10.11   Noise

Being a big noise is not always socially desirable! The Health and Safety Commission has intensified its campaign to make noise reduction a top priority. The Code of Practice for reducing the exposure of employed persons to noise (HMSO), first published in 1972, specified a limit for continuous exposure to a steady sound level for eight hours in one day as 90 decibels. As a rough guide, normal conversation at three feet would measure 50 decibels, traffic 80 decibels, and a busy office some 60 decibels. Noise levels in foundries can exceed 100 decibels, those in woodworking shops 110 decibels, while the noise of jet engines or of riveting 130 decibels. Given the fact that the decibel scale for measuring sound intensity is logarithmic, then a small increase in the decibel scale corresponds to a large increase in intensity. Thus, 80 decibels is 100 times the intensity of 60 decibels, and an increase of 3 dB corresponds to a doubling of sound intensity being transmitted to the ear. Thus at high noise intensities, only a few minutes' exposure is necessary to sustain hearing damage.

In August 1981 the Health and Safety Commission published a consultative document setting out proposals for new Regulations, a draft approved Code of Practice and Guidance Notes on noise control. These proposals contained a list of requirements already adopted by many progressive employers and included the carrying out of noise surveys, the provision of personal hearing protection, preparation of an action programme by the employer, the training and provision of information for employees and a duty to appoint a qualified noise adviser. Where noise levels exceed 105 dB(A) employers would have to arrange for audiometric programmes in which employees would be obliged to co-operate. Manufacturers of machinery and equipment would also have to provide information on likely noise exposure. Certain employers already arrange for audiometric screening of employees as part of a pre-employment medical, so that any hearing loss already sustained elsewhere can be quantified.

The Woodworking Machines Regulations 1974 and the Tractor Cabs Regulations already have statutory authority for a level of 90 decibels and the EC has published a Draft Directive on noise requiring the daily sound level to which a worker is subjected not to exceed 85 decibels, and this, which is already TUC policy, would bring the UK into line with the rest of Europe, with the exception of Italy and West Germany. The standard in the USA is 85 decibels with an absolute maximum level of 116 dB(A).

In order to assist both employers and employees, the Health and Safety Commission have published *A Hundred Practical Applications of Noise Reduction Methods* (HMSO) which gives details of a wide range of noise reduction methods together with their approximate cost. The industries covered range from textiles and woodworking to plastics, food and drink, from engineering to printing, concrete and construction. The examples given are frequently capable of being adapted elsewhere.

Because one is not initially conscious of losing one's hearing, education on the effects of noise and subsequent deafness is all-important and the HSC has imaginatively equipped a caravan as a mobile roadshow. A noise simulator enables visitors to select a particular industry and exposure period, for example, a foundry after 30 years' work, and demonstrates through headphones what a normal conversation would sound like after that period of exposure. The principles of noise reduction and of noise monitoring are also shown and videos demonstrate success stories in the bottling and woodworking industries. Details of the caravan's itinerary are available from the HSE inquiry point, Bootle, Merseyside.

The first case where common law liability was established against an employer for occupational deafness was *Berry* v *Stone Manganese Marine Ltd* in 1972 and subsequent High Court cases, none of which has gone to the Court of Appeal, have established that from 1963, when the Health and Safety Booklet 'Noise and the Worker' (HMSO) was published by HM Factory Inspectorate, employers have been on notice regarding the potential dangers arising from exposing their employees to noise. The small employer may not have read the booklet but the fact that it exists makes it advisable that a prudent employer should be aware of its contents. Because it is at present considered that the greater part of hearing loss takes place in the early years of exposure to intense noise, it is vitally important for employers to advise and educate their employees as part of a total hearing conservation programme on joining the organisation.

In addition to the publications already mentioned, the small businessman is also advised to obtain a copy of the TUC 'Handbook on Noise at Work' which is an excellent guide and discusses the complex scientific subject in clear layman's terms.

10.12   The role of the enforcing authorities

Health and safety for the small businessman received, if not a citation, at least a mention in despatches. 'Lifting the Burden', the government's avowed intent to ease the bureaucratic burden on industry, indicated that, 'the government are committed to maintaining necessary protection and have no intention of down-grading health and safety standards either generally or in relation to small firms'. Suggested proposals included making a written safety policy obligatory when employing over 20 employees instead of the present five, making inspectors more aware of small firms' interests, reminding and educating employers of their right to question inspectors' decisions and designating one Health and Safety Commissioner to represent small business interests.

In an interview published in the *Director* of September 1985, John Cullen, Chairman of the Health and Safety Commission, emphasised that small businesses must register and that a significant part of factory inspectorate and local authority resources would be spent detecting unregistered businesses: 'There are a number of back-yard operations which are using quite dangerous machinery. Those are the ones we want to get to. There are still a large number of accidents which are caused by moving machinery – people getting their hands chopped off, their fingers chopped off. We could help to prevent such accidents without imposing high costs.'

Certainly, at present there is an imbalance between the resources of the Health and Safety Executive inspectorates and the local authorities who are not only able to inspect premises at a much greater frequency but who also inevitably, from time to time, place a different emphasis on aspects of the work and thus, for example, have been known to prosecute even for failing to post a placard copy of appropriate Regulations on a wall. It is probable that more responsibilities will be devolved to local authorities – an inevitable consequence of the cuts in budget and staff which have occurred within the Health and Safety Executive.

The role of the HSE is not simply one of law enforcement though, of course, this is the one that frequently makes most impact on the local business scene, particularly when serious cases can result in prosecution or indictment with unlimited fines and prison sentences. The research and laboratory services division of the HSE has an annual net expenditure of some £15 million and includes, for example, occupational medicine work on the venting of dust explosions, on exposure of flammable and toxic materials to fire, and work on the loss of control of tractors, work now under threat as a result of further financial cutbacks.

What may be of more immediate relevance to the small businessman is the amount of valuable information which can be found in the series of Guidance Notes and health and safety booklets obtainable from HMSO and HSE area offices. Ignorance of either the law or of the necessary and suitable health and safety precautions can no longer be used by the small businessman as an excuse for ignoring his legal obligations. Jim Hammer, in his Report on Manufacturing and Service Industries, said of small enterprises, 'Whether they are the sort that make no concessions to new technology, efficiency or even old-fashioned good housekeeping, or whether they are highly competent in instrument, computer or laser technology, the majority are not alert to the hazards to which their employees are exposed, and are not well briefed to health and safety legislation and practice.'

It has been suggested by the Health and Safety Commission in their 'Future Plan of Work' that companies with good safety records should have more responsibility for self-regulation in health and safety. The point was amplified by Dr Cullen in his

Director interview, where he is quoted as saying, 'We believe that you are more than capable of running health and safety. We are prepared to let you go on and run your health and safety and we will merely audit it once every two years, say, and we would carry out any investigations into a serious accident.' However, in the foreword to one Report on Manufacturing and Service Industries, HM Chief Inspector, speaking from a deep professional knowledge, commented that, 'Whilst certain industries and processes do carry a higher than average potential hazard, it is generally just these which have received and will continue to receive particularly close attention both from management and inspectors. In other workplaces, which of course form the majority there is almost always a certain risk of a serious or fatal accident in entirely commonplace and foreseeable circumstances, for example during materials handling, maintenance work and the use of internal transport. Whether such a serious injury or death occurs does not depend on chance but in large measure on the quality and competence of management in minimising and controlling risk – its ability to foresee problems and regulate its affairs safely – and on the alertness of supervisors, employees and their representatives. These, together with training, are the critical factors in the prevention of occupational accidents and disease. The unpalatable fact is that certain economic and industrial trends noted in recent years have tended to militate against the competent management of health and safety within the concept and practice of self-regulation which underlies the Health and Safety at Work Act 1974.'

One can confidently predict that there will be considerable public debate of any proposals which dilute, in practical terms, the protection given to people at work by regular, impartial enforcement in order to camouflage the true impact of the severity of government cuts in occupational health and safety.

11
Business Premises

HOWARD GREEN, PAUL FOLEY AND BRIAN CHALKLEY

11.1 The right property

Of the many problems which confront the small businessman, finding suitable premises has been shown repeatedly to be among the most serious and widespread.

For the would-be entrepreneur, the problem may indeed be finding premises at all. For the existing business, difficulties which can arise will vary from premises of the wrong size in the wrong location to ones on insecure tenure. Choosing the right premises is one of the most important decisions a small business owner will have to make.

The problem of finding suitable property is compounded by the fact that decisions about where to locate a company and which premises to choose are without parallel or precedent for many small businesses. The property problem can often look like a maze with no signposts from previous experience to offer directions or guidance.

The complexity of the problem is reflected in the bewildering array of expert professionals, solicitors, planners, estate agents, accountants, fire officers, insurance agents, to mention just a few, who may be involved in the property decision.

Choosing business premises involves a long-term commitment to a particular location and also to the financial costs associated with the premises chosen for the business. For companies buying premises the financial sums involved are likely to dwarf virtually all other commercial transactions. Even companies renting property sign a commitment which ties them to paying rents, rates, heating, lighting and maintenance costs for a fixed period.

Whether buying or renting property most companies are undertaking a long-term decision about the future of their business. Whereas spending on other items can be quickly adjusted to match the state of trade, the main way of reducing property costs is to find and move to cheaper premises. This cannot be accomplished overnight and the costs associated with moving and selling the property or a lease can be considerable.

The choice of geographical location can have a major impact on a company's prospects and profitability. For retailers the choice of location is crucial in determining levels of turnover and market potential.

But for virtually all businesses, location will influence the cost and ease of many day-to-day operations such as access to customers and contacts with suppliers. The extent of local competition, opportunities for developing new markets, ease of obtaining suitable staff and the speed of obtaining essential components or services will all be affected by a company's location.

The physical characteristics of a property may affect a company's productivity and level of trade. The size and layout of premises can be important factors in influencing productivity. Too little space imposes limitations on a business; too much space is wasteful and can be costly because the business is paying for something which is not being used.

The overall condition of a property can also have an impact on productivity. Pressures on most small businesses are quite sufficient without having the additional stresses and strains of difficult and unpleasant surroundings. Energy and enthusiasm can soon be eroded by poor conditions and it may become difficult to retain or attract staff.

The view which customers have of a company is also important. This view is greatly influenced by the quality of accommodation. Premises and their condition can create a vital business image.

These issues indicate some of the important considerations which small businesses need to resolve when searching for suitable premises. In recent years the process of searching for premises has, in itself, become more problematical, as in many parts of the country there has been a serious shortage of small business premises.

Town planners have substantially reduced the stock of old small premises through redeveloped schemes. This has removed many of the older, cheaper premises which previously provided ideal 'starter' premises for many new small businesses. Property companies have not generally been interested in building new small premises. The ending of government allowances to promote the building of small units in March 1985 did little to encourage new units to be built.

On the other hand, there is evidence from many parts of the country that demand for small 'starter' units of less than 1000 sq ft is outstripping supply.

It is essential that businesses find premises suitable for their requirements. Mistakes made in selecting premises can affect the success of any business and they can be very costly to overcome. Making mistakes on technical matters such as planning permission, building regulations or the small print on leases can create major costs and trouble.

If a serious error is made, moving to the wrong place will bring many more problems than opportunities. These may soon require you to move again thereby creating another round of disruption, cost and management headache.

To avoid many of the pitfalls it is vital for all businesses choosing property to have a clear understanding of all the property issues important to their business together with a good knowledge of how the property market operates.

11.2   Key to the right front door

Many small businesses give too little attention to their choice of location.

Some firms are, of course, compelled to accept inappropriate premises because of the absence of anything better. They are the victims of a property market which has traditionally cared little for the needs of small firms. Recent years, however, have seen a proliferation of various kinds of small business premises by a range of government and private bodies. The available property stock is still far from ideal but increasingly premises' problems must be seen as the product of inefficient business decisions rather than insufficient property opportunities.

The choice of location and premises is among the most momentous and complex of the decisions small businesses have to make but it is an infrequent, non-routine problem for which the average small business owner is ill-prepared by expertise, experience or education. (Few of the start-your-own-business courses devote much time to premises.) Given the mismatch between the significance of the problem and the resources available to deal with it, mistakes are commonplace. How can such blunders be best avoided?

The search for premises should begin with a definition of what is wanted in terms of location, size, tenure, condition, layout and access. Obviously, ambition must be tempered with realism. Estate agents, personal contacts, business advisory services can all help. Discussion with accountants and bank managers should identify what can be afforded and where the money is to come from.

Armed with clear objectives (and a good map) it is best to advance on a number of different fronts. Estate agents, especially those specialising in commercial and industrial premises, should certainly be consulted. There are, though, other agencies worth visiting. It is not sufficiently widely known that many local authorities now keep registers of small business premises. These registers are regularly updated and normally cover industrial, warehouse and workshop premises in public and private sectors.

Local newspapers and business information services can also be helpful, as can walking or driving around the target area. The latter approach can bring to light vacant properties which have not yet been formally advertised. Through local enquiries you may even discover a property which is only partly used: such spare space could perhaps provide both a place for you and some welcome extra income for the host firm.

When inspecting possible sites (before paying for a proper survey) there are four useful rules of thumb:

1. Take with you a checklist covering detailed questions about the condition and layout of the building as well as the disposition of services such as electricity, heating and lighting.
2. If first impressions are promising be sure to arrange a return visit at a different time of the day and week, when, for example, parking, traffic and daylighting conditions may be very different.
3. Take someone with you, such as a senior employee, to provide a second opinion.
4. Find out why the previous occupants left and if possible contact them to ask about their experience of the building and any problems it posed.

In making the final decision some business owners evaluate alternative premises by use of a points system in which each element of the property, such as its location and size, is weighted and scored. Others base their final judgement more on feel and intuition. Whichever method is used, it is good practice to canvass as many opinions as possible and (unless there are really compelling pressures) to allow time for careful reflection.

11.3   Living 'over the shop'

Although a large number of businesses start life in a front room or on the kitchen table, for many the owner-manager's home is the long-term permanent base. A wide range of businesses, particularly those providing a service, can operate efficiently from home. For many aspiring entrepreneurs, there is no real alternative; if they cannot run the business from home, they cannot run a business.

The disabled, those with young families, sick or elderly relatives, frequently find working from home the only practical alternative. So what are the advantages and disadvantages of taking this option?

Money is perhaps the major advantage. You will only be paying one set of housing costs. For even the smallest workshop the rent, rates, insurance, electricity and other associated charges, will cost well over £1000 a year.

The saving of time is also a very important benefit. By eliminating travelling you will have more time to build up and manage the business. For those artistic or creative professions where mood and inspiration are important, having the job and tools to hand may also prove important.

Working from home also offers the benefit of assistance from the family. A husband or wife who is prepared to deal with telephone calls or help with correspondence as and when needed is a valuable and often unpaid asset.

The intermingling of business and family life does have its drawbacks. Domestic tension can soon arise as the dining room begins to resemble a workshop or office. If at all possible separate accommodation is essential. Family life can easily become disrupted by clients visiting at awkward times or the continual interruption of the telephone. Many home-based business people have also experienced the problem of keeping young children quiet while conducting important negotiations on the telephone.

For those who do not have the self-discipline, the business can fall victim to domestic pressure. A full day's work becomes difficult if you are surrounded by domestic chores. The home environment can offer too many comforts and distractions. Many people need separate premises to provide the discipline necessary for work.

Premises create an image for business. Working from home can give the impression of a company working at the margins of profitability. Attractive premises can convey the aura of respectability and professionalism. Do not be deterred; some of the most respected groups in society 'live over the shop', including farmers, priests and the Prime Minister.

There are areas of officialdom which need to be observed. Working from home can create problems with the local planners. The attitude of the local authority will depend on the effect your activities have on your surroundings. Normally, one or two man businesses which do not generate much traffic, do not use noisy machinery and do not annoy their neighbours will not require planning permission.

Because of uncertainties with the planning authority, many small businesses deliberately operate outside the planning system. Changes currently under discussion will formalise the position of home-based business at least as far as planning is concerned, making working from home a more attractive alternative.

There are a number of other matters which the potential home-based business person will need to consider. Your building society or bank should be consulted. Although they are unlikely to object, they may wish to reassess your insurance liability.

Property deeds or leases need to be checked to confirm that business activity is not forbidden. In the case of council tenants the White Paper 'Lifting the Burden' recognised the obstacle restrictive housing management policies can pose for small businesses. Local authority attitudes to tenants have in some cases begun to change.

Using your home for business purposes can increase your rates bill slightly as 'domestic relief' on that part of the home used for the business will be lost. However, as you are not legally obliged to inform the local rating officer of your business, this question may never arise. You will, though, be able to claim tax relief on that part of your rates bill which relates to the business as well as for heating, lighting, repairing and maintaining the room used.

Working from home does have many benefits, particularly

for the new start-up or those wishing to try their hand at business part-time before making a full-time commitment. By removing the costs of premises, one of the major financial obstacles to starting in business is minimised.

11.4 Looking for new premises

There is a wide range of considerations which may encourage a firm to think about moving and to start looking round for alternative premises. Some firms move because they are compelled to do so by force of circumstances: 'push factors' such as lease expiry or a sharply increased rent may leave the business with little or no choice but to relocate. On the other hand, many businesses move in response to 'pull factors' and are enticed by the superior attraction of a different location offering better opportunities.

The most frequently occurring reasons for movement include shortage of space, too much space, inefficient building layout, problems of getting labour and the development of new markets. Additionally, some companies move premises for personal reasons, to take advantage of government assistance or to make use of capital tied up in property.

The decision to move is of such significance that it should only be taken after careful analysis. The question must be asked whether relocation is really the answer to your problems. Perhaps your existing premises could be used more efficiently or the building could be modified or enlarged. A careful examination of all the alternatives is needed before embarking on a move.

It may also be worth considering whether establishing a branch plant could be more advantageous than a complete transfer. If you are in badly organised, highly inefficient buildings then a complete move may be the answer. On the other hand, if you simply need more space, why not keep what you have and add to it elsewhere?

In considering the physical movement of machinery, equipment, stock etc you may be tempted to 'do it yourself'. For many very small businesses this will be a perfectly sensible economy. However, do think back to the last time you moved house and remember all the difficulties, the hard work and the heartache involved. Remember too that there is little to be gained from using your own specialist employees as packers and porters when they should be doing their own jobs. You may be well advised, therefore, to use professional removers who will have all the appropriate equipment. Always obtain at least three quotations as rates can vary significantly between companies.

On a more general level, in preparing for and managing the movement operation as a whole, it is a good idea to start planning early. Relocation is a complex exercise and you should not underestimate the time it will take to get things organised. Try to arrange the move for a slack period of the year. If possible this should be your normal holiday period or one of the long public holiday weekends. There may be advantages in planning the move so that both units are running simultaneously during a brief transition stage. Given the overriding importance of maintaining trading levels, production and output, ensure that all the necessary stock, materials and ancillary services will be ready and available at the new site. Remember that new machinery often takes time to commission and any new employees will need training and a 'settling in' period. If possible, appoint one person to be in charge of and co-ordinate the entire movement operation and release him from as many responsibilities as you can.

One of the major worries facing businesses which move long distances is the loss of key personnel. The degree of concern will depend on the number of highly qualified staff and the prospects for obtaining suitable replacements should this prove necessary. While for the firm and its owner the move will have positive benefits, quite frequently the workforce will see it as both uninvited and unwelcome. Bear in mind that in general we are not a very mobile nation and that moving from one community to another does not come easily. The younger employees are usually more likely to leave. As a consequence, do not rely on taking all your workforce with you. If the loss of employees is likely to be seriously disruptive, then think again about relocation and make provision to recruit and train staff at the new location well in advance of the move. You may also have to consider a redundancy policy.

There are, though, several ways in which you may encourage the workforce to move with you. These include involving staff in the search for a new site, offering an incentive package and 'selling' the new location to the staff. Do remember also to take advantage of any assistance available for transferring workers.

Whatever the reason for your relocation, it is vital that it is properly advertised and receives good publicity. It is important to publicise the move at both the old site and the new one. Inform all your suppliers and customers of your change of address. Produce a leaflet which includes a map of your new location. Ensure that the agent dealing with your former property indicates on the sale board that you have moved and not gone out of business. A 'to let' sign frequently indicates a company which has ceased trading.

For many firms moving long distances, the danger of losing contact with suppliers and customers is the key worry. These concerns, however, can be overstated. Although it is often suggested that small businesses trade over a small area this is in fact rarely the case. If you then analyse the amount of face-to-face contact involved in running your business (compared with telephone, telex and other forms of communication) you will have an assessment of the danger of dislocation. Companies who have moved longer distances usually suggest that they have few, if any, problems in keeping their business links. Indeed, many continue to trade with their former suppliers and customers as if no move had taken place.

11.5 Organising your property – the internal layout

Amid all the other pressures on small business managers, it is tempting to give only scant attention to the internal layout and interior design of premises. However, a well thought-out layout and attractive working environment can actually contribute to the effective operation of a business and hence its profitability. Careful physical planning can reduce space requirements and consequently save money.

In deciding how much time, effort and money to spend on fitting out a property, your security of tenure will be important. It makes more sense to spend money on a building which you own or on which you hold a long lease. Similarly, some businesses will need to give the problem more attention than others. Some items will be required by law. In satisfying the local fire authority, you may need to purchase some portable fire extinguishers or even install a sophisticated sprinkler system.

In the provision of basic services, most premises will have electricity, gas, water, toilets and washing facilities. In new property, electricity services may only be provided to a meter, so careful thought must be given to the number and location of sockets. Similar care will be needed with planning and layout of a heating system. You will need to take account of the building's geographical orientation and insulation qualities, as well as the level of comfort required and the costs of installation and operation. Careful choice of lighting can be used not only to compensate for inadequate daylight but also as an attractive feature of internal design.

Security is an issue which demands particular attention. How much to spend on prevention will depend on the value of the goods held in stock and the degree of dislocation which burglary or vandalism would cause. Burglary can cause an enormous disruption to trade so it is wise to use some preventive system. Risk varies considerably between different trades and locations as a glance at insurance companies' application forms will show. While expensive equipment will be useful do not forget the simple solutions. Careful internal layout can help a great deal; a reception desk or cash desk placed so that the movement of people in and out of premises can be monitored and save major losses from theft. Expert guidance in property security can be obtained from the crime prevention officer of your local police force.

A periodic review of the use of space and layout can be a great benefit to all firms. In thinking about layout, begin by identifying the various stages or sections within the firm's operation. Ask yourself, 'How much space does this activity need?', 'Does the activity have specific locational requirements?' In this way you can build up a picture of the preferred arrangement of activities and of movement requirements for employees, materials and stock. Clearly, the physical structure of the building will constrain what can be done so that you will also need to ask yourself, 'Given other present buildings, how can they be best used?'

Two areas are particularly important. One will be set aside for an office which will act both as a quiet sanctuary and as a room in which to meet clients. While a comfortable environment is important, do not isolate yourself from other areas of operation of the business. The reception area is similarly important as it is the first point of contact with the firm. It provides an ideal opportunity to show off your wares and advertise your qualifications and experience. No matter what your business, newspapers and trade papers will be well appreciated by waiting customers or clients.

Do not neglect the outside of your premises. All too often units rapidly develop a run-down appearance, not good for business image, because they are not regularly tidied up and rubbish removed. Display signs are an important part of the external image of premises. While it is tempting to erect large illuminated signs, discretion in display signs can create a better company image. In some cases signs are still subject to planning consent so it is always worth checking with the planning authority before spending money.

For older property in particular, a fresh coat of paint can go a long way towards improving the external image. In choosing colours, particularly for interior decor, take account of their psychological impact and the atmosphere they create. Blues seem cool and quiet, reds are hot and loud, greens and yellows fresh and restful. Dark tones can be depressing, light tones are more cheerful. Careful use of colour can also change a room's perceived proportions.

Decor, fixtures and fittings will all need to be maintained and cleaned to prolong their life and protect their appearance. It is essential, therefore, to undertake regular cleaning and to budget for redecoration and the replacement of carpets, furniture and fittings.

The layout and decor of your premises are not static. Adjustments which adapt to changes in the goals and nature of your business will be needed from time to time. Such changes can be refreshing and add a new stimulus to your business activity.

11.6 Keeping on the right side of officialdom

Every year a number of small businesses make the mistake of buying or leasing property which they cannot use. This often costly and catastrophic mistake arises because the premises do not have the appropriate official approval for their particular use.

Some properties have conditions associated with them which allow only certain uses. These conditions can arise from a variety of sources. Convenants or deeds drawn up when the property was first built may specify that certain types of business activity cannot take place. Town planners and building control officers designate business properties into categories such as office use, shop use and light industrial use. If uses other than those designated are carried out in the property, planning and building control officials have the power to stop the businesses concerned. Other officials such as environmental health officers and fire officers also have powers to stop businesses trading if they think the premises are a health hazard or fire risk respectively. It is important to consider the role of these officials (and solicitors in the case of examining covenants and deeds when moving) at all times when dealing with business premises.

The list of official groups involved in regulating the use of premises may seem daunting, but in reality consultations and approvals may be done automatically during the process of acquiring property. A brief review of the officials involved in regulating business property will examine the importance of each group.

Planning controls have become a highly emotive issue in the last few years. However, most businesses will only become concerned with planning officials when moving or undertaking building work at premises. Planners try to control the use of individual buildings and areas of towns and cities to ensure that incompatible users, such as houses and heavy industrial uses, are not located side by side. For this reason they designate all buildings into certain 'use classes'. All companies moving into new properties should consult the local planning authority to ensure they can use the building for their particular line of business. Remarkable as it may seem, it may be necessary to establish the 'use' for which a building has permission at present. It is one thing for tenants to be carrying out a particular activity and quite another to have established permission to do so!

The other occasion when planners have to be consulted is when construction or building work is being undertaken. However, there are some exceptions such as extensions of less than 25 per cent of existing volume (up to a maximum of 1000 cubic metres) and most types of internal alterations, painting and decorating. In considering applications, planners examine the effects of any development on road safety, noise, unsightliness and damage to the local environment. In recent years central government has advised local authority planners to take a more sympathetic approach to planning applications from small businesses.

Building regulations are perhaps the most important statutory requirement to be considered in connection with development work on a property. Whereas planners consider the effect of building work on the surrounding environment, building control officers are concerned with the structural safety of a building and means of escape from the building during a fire. Nearly all forms of building work require approval. Building control officers should also be consulted if there is to be a change of use of the building. Building regulations specify certain standards which have to be achieved in all buildings. If these specifications cannot be met it is sometimes possible to obtain a 'relaxation' (which allows a development to continue without reaching usual building standards).

Most businesses need a Fire Certificate to confirm that adequate fire prevention precautions have been taken. Even if a building has an existing Certificate it may be necessary to revalidate it if changes have taken place. The changes fall into three groups and they will usually be most important for businesses moving premises. Revalidation is required if there is a change of use (as defined by the building regulations), if there is a change in the processes used or materials stored, or finally, if there is the subdivision of premises to multiple use. Certain smaller buildings do not require a Fire Certificate, but the possibility should never be left in doubt.

The environmental health department of the local authority is responsible for the health and physical welfare of the local population. The key areas they are interested in are dust, fumes and odours from industrial premises, noise from industrial processes, food standards and food hygiene. Any businesses which might conflict in these areas, particularly new business moving into premises for the first time or existing businesses making alterations to premises, should consult the environmental health officer so that any possible problems in the subsequent use of a property can be overcome at an early stage.

The Health and Safety Executive, and their inspectors who periodically visit all business premises, are concerned with ensuring the health and safety of all employees. Their main task is to ensure that the regulations set out in the 1974 Health and

Safety at Work Act and the 1963 Offices, Shops and Railway Premises Act are properly implemented. The inspectors ensure that catering and toilet facilities are kept clean and safe, dangerous equipment is properly guarded, and floors, steps, stairs and passages are kept safe and free from obstruction. If standards are inadequate and dangerous they can serve prohibition notices to stop businesses trading and prosecute them.

Many of the official groups, described above, have a very poor public image. They are seen as constraining the growth of small businesses, towards which many of them have taken a more sympathetic view in recent years. To try to promote a better understanding of their often complex role many have published booklets outlining their function. In addition, all the groups are willing to talk to small businesses and help them to overcome their problems. It is essential to consult the appropriate officials when moving or expanding premises. This will help to prevent the costly and sometimes catastrophic event of signing an agreement which commits a company to premises which it is unable to use.

11.7 Property tenure and small business need

Traditionally, the lease has been the contract between landlord and tenant. However, in recent years other forms of agreement have slowly gained in popularity. Leases can be a liability. They are a form of property tenure in many ways out of sympathy with the needs of small businesses. Typically, small firms cannot see more than a few months ahead and so a commitment to even a five- or ten-year lease is a leap in the dark which many will not want to take. Expanding firms will quickly outgrow their premises: businesses contracting or closing down will have equally compelling reasons to leave. Whether the firm is going up and out or down and out, the message is the same: leases can be too inflexible. A dynamic small business sector needs a more adaptable form of tenure.

It is true, of course, that a tenant may be able to sell an unwanted lease but this would depend on finding a buyer who meets with the landlord's approval. In practice, assigning or disposing of leases can prove quite a headache. And if the tenant does continue in occupation right to the end of the lease, arguments about repairs clauses and 'reinstating' the property can be both troublesome and expensive. A lease nearing expiry may look temptingly cheap but could involve a liability for putting right the deterioration of the building which has occurred over the full lease term.

Some landlords do, of course, allow less onerous and shorter term leases and tenancy agreements, but there remains an often voiced fear that traditional tenure forms are an obstruction to new small firms. Freehold premises are beyond their means and even finding the money to buy a lease (and pay the solicitor's fees) can exhaust or deplete the resources of many embryonic businesses. Leases can be an unproductive diversion of limited capital and an impediment to the birth and growth of new small enterprises.

In response to this kind of critique, new forms of tenure have begun to emerge. Indeed, the increased interest in the small business sector has been an important stimulus for change. Local authorities and other government bodies have been especially keen to provide accommodation on 'easy-in, easy-out' terms. Many now offer licence agreements with notice periods of only a few weeks. There is no entrance or 'key money', only a regular weekly or monthly rental. Some even offer 'tenancy at will' under which the tenancy can be terminated by either side at any time.

These kinds of more flexible arrangement are especially common in the new small workshops or rent-a-bench schemes which also provide collective services including business advice, typing, cleaning and security. (Such collective arrangements would be difficult to formalise in a conventional lease.) In Plymouth, for example, the local authority has converted an old Rank-Toshiba factory into 92 small units each separated by shoulder-high partitions and each sharing the benefit of various collective services. There is no lease, only a very simple document which specifies the address, the rent and other basic information.

These kinds of arrangement are not only in the tenants' interests; they serve to protect the landlord. Smaller 'starter' units run an above-average risk of bad tenants. They tend to attract people with no business track record – unknown quantities without the usual references. Ease of eviction can therefore be very useful.

The private sector, with its commercial rather than job creation objectives, is generally less disposed to use licences and other less formal agreements. Developers and property companies prefer stable, long-term tenants and a guaranteed continuity of income. None the less, tenancies are increasingly being offered on short licence agreements. Where an owner has a large number of small units to let it can be advisable to offer easy terms in order to fill up the units quickly and minimise the number of voids.

The use of licences rather than leases is certainly growing but some words of caution are needed. Although for the average tenant in the public sector 'easy-in, easy-out' terms will in practice still convey good security of tenure, the same is not always true of private premises. Without a lease there is no protection from the Landlord and Tenant Act over matters such as grounds for eviction and compensation for improvements. Aggrieved tenants have only the general protection of the courts rather than the specific protection of the Act. Leases protect tenants' rights: less formal arrangements can in the wrong hands be used to circumvent the safeguards and conditions which a proper lease would specify. Getting your solicitor to look at any property document is certainly to be advised.

Remember too that a licence is not a 'valuable interest': it cannot be bought or sold. By contrast, selling a lease can yield money to fund growth or to weather economic storms. Leases can also be used as bank collateral.

In weighing up the merits of leases and licences the key element is often the landlord. If a reputable landlord is offering a licence the tenant may derive many of the benefits of a lease without the costs. If the landlord's credentials are more questionable the protection of a lease could prove very useful.

11.8 Converting property to your own requirements

Conversion and subdivision are two approaches to obtaining premises often overlooked by small businesses. If you cannot find the type of premises you want, conversion of an existing building can provide 'tailor-made' premises to meet your exact requirements. If you need less space than you currently possess and are thinking of moving to smaller premises, subdivision can avoid the problems and costs of relocation. By leasing out your spare space you can obtain an additional income and provide a useful means of diversifying your firm's activities. For the business willing to turn its hand to small-scale property development both conversion and subdivision can bring quick economic returns.

Conversion can be possible in a wide range of buildings. It is not always necessary for the premises to have been used previously as business accommodation. Residential houses, old tram depots, schools, churches and even mortuaries have all been converted into various types of small business premises.

Although the market for small premises has remained relatively buoyant, medium and larger-scale properties have found fewer buyers. This has led to a fall in prices and has created the opportunity to purchase cheap larger properties for conversion into the smaller units which are more in demand.

The process of subdividing premises and renting out spare space can take many forms. It may involve simply separating off an unused area by a chalk line on the floor. More substantial schemes involve the construction of walls, doorways, toilets and washing facilities. It might be thought that subdivision is only useful for declining firms which are no longer making full use of their premises. This is not necessarily the case. Even expanding firms often find that technological innovation and the introduction of new plant and machinery allow increased production from a reduced floor area.

Next time you are at work look at the space around you and assess whether it is fully used. Is any spare capacity needed for business expansion (an entirely legitimate use of space) or is it simply surplus to requirements? A tidying up and reorganisation of your premises and the removal of redundant machinery or furniture might give you the extra space needed for a subdivision scheme. If you are unsure about the benefits of subdivision, calculate how much in rates, insurance, maintenance, heating, lighting and either rent or interest repayments your underused space is costing. You might well be surprised.

Because many leases do not permit substantial internal reorganisation or subletting, it is usually necessary to own premises before you can consider undertaking conversion or subdivision. But some landlords have agreed to rewrite leases and to allow tenants to create smaller units. The main advantage for the landlord is that his premises are converted, at no cost to himself, into the size of units currently in demand by the market.

Most small firms regard a move into property management as a quantum leap in business practice. A fear of the unknown and concern about high costs are common reasons for a lack of action. Certainly, worries about costs need not be justified. By avoiding expensive construction work and doing some jobs in-house costs can be kept to a minimum and may even be recovered within the first year or two of operation. In this way you will ensure a long-term income from the property as well as a purpose designed for your business.

This chapter is based on the authors' books – *How to Choose Business Premises* (Kogan Page) and *Redundant Space: A Productive Asset* (Harper and Row).

12
Further Information

Action Resource Centre
Cap House
3rd Floor
9–12 Long Lane
London EC1A 9HD
01-726 8987

**Alliance of Small Firms
& Self Employed People**
33 The Green
Calne
Wiltshire SN11 8DJ
0249 817003

**Association of British
Chambers of Commerce**
Sovereign House
212 Shaftesbury Avenue
London WC2H 8EW
01-240 5831

**Association of Independent
Businesses**
Trowbray House
108 Weston Street
London SE1 3QB
01-403 4066

British Technology Group
101 Newington Causeway
London SE1 6BU
01-403 6666

BSC (Industry)
Canterbury House
2–6 Sydenham Road
Croydon CR9 2LJ
01-686 2311

Community of St Helens Trust
PO Box 36
Canal Street
St Helens
Merseyside WA10 3TT
0744 28882

Co-operative Development Agency
Broadmead House
21 Panton Street
London SW1Y 4DR
01-839 2985

Co-operative Union
Holyoake House
Hanover Street
Manchester M60 0AS
061-832 4300

Crafts Council
12 Waterloo Place
London SW1Y 4AT
01-930 4811

**Development Board for
Rural Wales**
Ladywell House
Newtown
Powys SY16 1JB
0686 626965

Enterprise North
Durham University Business School
Mill Lane
Durham DH1 3LB
091-374 2000

Forum of Private Business
Ruskin Chambers
Drury Lane
Knutsford
Cheshire WA16 6HA
0565 4467

Highlands and Islands Development Board
Bridge House
Bank Street
Inverness IV1 1QR
0463 34171

Industrial Common Ownership Movement
Vassalli House
20 Central Road
Leeds LS1 6DE
0532 461737

London Enterprise Agency
4 Snow Hill
London EC1A 2BS
01-236 3000

Northern Ireland Development Agency
Maryfield
100 Belfast Road
Holywood
Co Down
02317 4232

Northern Ireland:
Local Enterprise Development Unit
LEDU House
Upper Galwally
Belfast BT8 4TB
0232 491031

Rural Development Commission (CoSIRA)
141 Castle Street
Salisbury
Wiltshire SP1 3TP
0722 336255

Scottish Development Agency
Small Business Division
120 Bothwell Street
Glasgow G2 7JP
041-248 2700

Small Business Unit
Thames Polytechnic School of
    Business Administration
Beresford Street
London SE18 6BU
01-316-9022/9023

Small Firms Centres:
Dial 100 and ask for
Freefone Enterprise

Scotland
21 Bothwell Street
Glasgow G2 6NR
041-248 6014

Wales
16 St David's House
Wood Street
Cardiff CF1 1ER
0222 396116

Northern Region
15th Floor
Cale Cross House
156 Pilgrim Street
Newcastle upon Tyne NE1 6PZ
091-232 5353

North-West Region
26-28 Deansgate
Manchester M3 1RH
061-832 5282

Liverpool Sub-office
Graeme House
Derby Square
Liverpool L2 7UJ
051-236 5756

Yorkshire and Humberside Region:
1 Park Row
City Square
Leeds LS1 5NR
0532 445151

East Midlands Region:
Severns House
20 Middle Pavement
Nottingham NG1 7DW
0602 506181

12. Further Information

West Midlands Region
Ninth Floor
Alpha Tower
Suffolk Street
Queensway
Birmingham B1 1TT
021-643 3344

Eastern Region
Carlyle House
Carlyle Road
Cambridge CB4 3DN
0223 63312

London and South-East Region
Ebury Bridge House
2–18 Ebury Bridge Road
London SW1W 8QD
01-730 8451

Abbey Hall
Abbey Square
Reading RG1 3BE
0734 591733

South-West Region
The Pithay
Bristol BS1 2NB
0272 294546

Welsh Development Agency
Small Business Unit
Treforest Industrial Estate
Pontypridd
Mid Glamorgan CF37 5UT
0443 85 2666

13
Select Bibliography

Business Rip-offs and How to Avoid Them, Tony Attwood, Kogan Page

Buying for Business: How to Get the Best Deal from your Suppliers, Tony Attwood, Kogan Page

Choosing and Using Professional Advisers Revised Edition, Paul Chaplin, Kogan Page

Complete Guide to Managing Your Business Managing Your Business Ltd, 7 Cromwell Road, London SW7

Cooperatives and Community David H. Wright, Bedford Square Press

Croner's Reference Book for the Self-Employed and Smaller Business Croner Publications Ltd, Croner House, London Road, Kingston-upon-Thames, Surrey KT2 6SR

Debt Collection Made Easy, Peter Buckland, Kogan Page

Essential Business Law series (paperback), Sweet and Maxwell

Export for the Small Business 2nd Edition, Henry Deschampsneufs, Kogan Page

The Genghis Khan Guide to Business, Brian Warnes, Osmosis Publications, 8 Holyrood Street, London SE1 2EL

The Good Franchise Guide, 2nd Edition, Tony Attwood and Len Hough, Kogan Page

How to Deal With Your Bank Manager, Geoffrey Sales, Kogan Page

Getting Sales Richard D Smith and Ginger Dick, Kogan Page

Importing for the Small Business 2nd Edition, Mag Morris, Kogan Page

Law for the Small Business 6th Edition, Patricia Clayton, Kogan Page

Make a Success of Microcomputing in Your Business Pannell, Jackson and Lucas, Enterprise Books

Raising Finance: The Guardian Guide for the Small Business 3rd Edition, Clive Woodcock, Kogan Page

Rapid Company Growth A C Hazel and A S Reid, Business Books
Running Your Own Cooperative, John Pearce, Kogan Page
The Small Business Action Kit 2nd Edition, Kogan Page
The Small Business Guide 3rd Edition, Colin Barrow, BBC Publications
So You Think Your Business Needs a Computer? Khalid Aziz, Kogan Page
Starting and Running A Small Business Alan Sproxton, United Writers Publications, Zennor, St Ives, Cornwall
Taking up a Franchise 6th Edition, Colin Barrow and Godfrey Golzen, Kogan Page
Tax Facts Joe Horner, Mistsave Ltd, 20 Victoria Avenue, Cheadle, Stockport, Cheshire
Understand Your Accounts 2nd Edition, A St J Price, Kogan Page
Working for Yourself 11th Edition, Godfrey Golzen, Kogan Page

Index

Abbreviations: *add* = address

Abbey National Building Society
190
accidents 263–6; caused by falls
259–61; construction industry
258; ladders 258–9;
maintenance precautions 257–
9; notification of 254; painters
259
accountant 18, 26
accounts 30, 49–55; annual 49;
as management tool 49
Action Resource Centre 20, 91;
add 298
administration, legislation 178
advertising 154–6; elements of
155; management 155–6
advertising agencies 156
advice sources 18–22, 88
Advisory, Conciliation and Arbitration Service (ACAS) 216,
217, 218
Advisory Council for Applied
Research and Development
143
advisory schemes 26
Alex Lawrie Factors 103, 136
Alta Berkeley Associates 133
Altus 243
Andersen, Arthur & Co 108,
240, 241
asbestos hazards 274
Association of British Factors
133–6; *add* 137
Association of Independent
Businesses 37; *add* 298
Avon Enterprise Fund 130

Balance sheet 49, 55
bank loans 24
bank manager 18, 58–61
bankruptcy 13, 29, 30
banks 87–8, 92–5; borrowing
from 55–64; export facilities
103; export finance 103–5
Barclays 93, 94, 103, 131
Barrow, Colin, *The Small Business
Guide* 22
Berry v *Stone Manganese Marine
Ltd* 276
bingo clubs 248
Birmingham Action Resource
Centre 91
Birmingham City Council 133
Birmingham Technology 133
Bolton Business Ventures 91
British Coal Enterprise 141; *add*
20
British Franchise Association
183, 192, 201, 203; *add* 206
British Institute of Management
167
British Insurance Brokers Associ-
ation 242
British Overseas Trade Board
104–5, 160; *add* 105
British Steel 20, 163
British Technology Group 133;
add 298
British Venture Capital Associ-
ation 108, 109, 131
Broughton, Frank 97
BSC (Industry) 20, 141; *add* 20,
298

budget 17
budgetary control 73–4
budgets 59; capital expenditure
73, 78; cash 74; operating 73,
78; overhead 17, 75–7; sales
74–5
budgets and budgeting: cash
77–81; profit 73–6
Building Regulations 177, 178,
292
Burger King 190
Business Capital Connection
(BCC) 101
Business Expansion Scheme
. 99–103
Business in the Community 21;
add 21, 105
business plan 16–18, 22, 24, 71
business premises 280–97; basic
services 289; combined with
living accommodation 284–6;
conversions 295–7; customers'
view of 281, 285; decision
making 283–4; 'easy-in, easy-
out' terms 294, 295; geographical location 282–4;
information and advisory
services 283; insurance 285;
layout 288–90; leases 293–5;
licence agreements 295; lighting 289; moving 282, 286–8;
organisation 288–90; overall
condition of 281; physical
characteristics 281; planning
permission 285, 290–93;
property tenure 293–5;
searching for 281, 283, 286–8;
security 289; selection of 280;
site inspection 283; starter
units 294; sub-dividing 296;
tenants' rights 27–9
Business Start-up Scheme 99

Capability dismissal 214–16
capital 24
capital base, bank manager's
assessment of 59

capital expenditure 73, 80;
budgets 78
capital ledger 31, 32
Cardiff and Vale Enterprise 91
cash book 31, 32
cash budgeting 77–81
cash flow 35; forecasting 18, 59,
77–81, 83; planning 30; problems 42
cash resources, allocation of 41–2
Centre for Physical Distribution
Management add 167
Century Belting 145–6
Chancery Corporate Finance
Division 110–29
City Action Teams 90
college courses 22, 27
Community of St Helens Trust
21, 102; add 298
Competing in Time 249
competition 163
computers 226–52; back-up
facilities 236; breakdowns
228; decisions concerning
228; finding help and advice
245–7; information sources
228; main aim 240; main-
tenance agreements 237;
networks 247–50; problems
experienced by users 228;
reasons for considering 228;
security issues 234–8; selection packages 238–41; service
contracts 228; software problems 228–30; training 228;
upgrading 230
Confederation of British Industry
211
construction industry, accidents
258
constructive dismissal 211–14
continuous service calculation
208–9, 210–11
Co-operative Bank 37, 87, 94,
99, 103, 106, 107
co-operative development
agencies (CDAs) 99

Co-operative Development Agency 33; *add* 34, 99, 298
Co-operative Union 34; *add* 298
Co-operative Venture Capital (Scotland) 98
Co-operative Wholesale Society 190
co-operatives 32–5; basic elements 35; failures 33; finance 97–9; legal forms of 35; marketing 35; neighbourhood or community 34; operating problems 33; profitability 33
Cornerstone estate agency 190
corporate strategy 22
corporate success 81–2; key to 82
corporate venturing 109
cost of sales stock 54; budget 75
costs 17
Council for Small Industries in Rural Areas (CoSIRA), *see* Rural Development Commission
Cranfield Institute of Technology 131
credit: insurance 104–5; medium-term 63
credit industry 48
creditworthiness, assessment of 136
Cullen, John 277, 278
Curran, James 86

Dalton Banks 243
dangerous substances regulations 274
Dartington and Co 130
Data Protection Act 250–52
debt collection by telephone 35–7
debtors: controlling 64–7; investment in 64–7; management of 66–7; significance of 65–6
delegation of duties 25
Deloitte Haskins and Sells 87
Department of Employment 19, 26, 87

Department of Enterprise 140
Department of Trade and Industry 105, 140, 232
Development Agencies 141
Development Board for Rural Wales 20; *add* 298
direct labour 80
dismissal 207–18; definitions 210, 211
distribution 164–7; as marketing tool 164; management 165; management involvement 165–6; special problems of 166
Duffield, Jim 165
Durham University Business School 20
dust problems 273–4

Early payment 40–42
80/20 rule 70, 82–3
Electra Investment Trust 109
Electricity Regulations 255
electronic mail 244
electronic typewriters 172
Employers' Liability Act 177, 178
Employment Appeal Tribunal 207
employment contracts 212, 219
employment law 207–25
Employment Protection (Consolidation) Act 1978: 208, 220, 221
Enterprise Allowance Scheme 87–9, 91
'enterprise cheques' 132
Enterprise Funds for Youth Scheme 91
Enterprise Initiative 140–42
Enterprise North 20–21; *add* 298
Entré Computer Centres 200
entrepreneurial attitudes 13
Entrust 85
environmental health 292
Equipment Leasing Association *add* 140

'equity gap', filling the 130
Ernst and Young 240–41; *add* 242
European Coal and Steel Community 94, 141
European Community 94
European Foundation for Management Development 43
European Small Business Seminar 43
Exfinco 104
Export Credits Guarantee Department (ECGD) 64, 104
export factoring 103–4
exporting 159–61; elements of 160; finance 103–5; organisation 160; potential for growth in 161

Factories Act 1844: 269
Factories Act 1961: 255, 273
factoring 133–7; export 103–4, 136; non-recourse 135; recourse 135–6
Fairbridge Society 90
Falkirk Enterprise Action Trust 91
falls 259–61; prevention of 258
Federation of Microsystems Centres 232, 240, 245; *add* 232–3
finance 61–4; co-operatives 97–9; exporting 103–5; for young people 89–92; planning 23–4; sources of 24, 85–142
financial control 24
Fire Certificate 255, 292
fire precautions 178, 271–2
Fire Precautions Act 177, 178, 271
Fire Protection Association 272
flooring, safety 260
Franchise Consultants Association 206
franchising 183–206; advertising 197; basic questions concerning 201–3; categories of 186–8;

Code of Ethics 203–4; decision making 197; effectiveness of 194–200; entrepreneurial 192–4; entry costs 200; failure rate 205–6; fees 193; forms of relationship 183; franchisor-franchisee communication 199; franchisor-franchisee disagreements 205; franchisor-franchisee relationship 194–9; future trends 203–6; growth of 188–90, 206; manufacturer-retailer 186; manufacturer-wholesaler 186; marketing 193; pioneers of 184; risk profiles 205; in service sector 169; setting-up 190–94; statistics 188, 205, 206; strengths of 194; tips for potential franchisees 199–203; trade-name 188; in USA 186; wholesaler-retailer 188

Government bodies 140–42
government regional aid 105
Grabner Sports 43
Grabner, Wolfgang 43–4
Greater London Enterprise Board 98, 133
Greater Manchester Economic Development Corporation 106
gross profit percentage 50–52
Guardian 14
Guide to Local Authority Assistance 107

Hambros 90
Hammer, Jim 278
Hankinson, Alan 86
Harris Queensway stores group 90
Harris, Sir Philip 90
Hasty Footwear 155
health and safety 177, 253–79; enforcing authorities 253;

environmental 292; Guidance Notes 278; industrial health 273–5; legal requirements 255–7; role of enforcing authorities 277–9

Health and Safety at Work Act 1974: 172, 176, 253, 255, 261–2, 270, 273, 279, 292–3

Health and Safety Commission 259, 275, 277

Health and Safety Executive 253, 254, 257, 258, 261, 262, 263, 272, 273, 278

Heinz 163

high technology, funding for 131–3

Highlands and Islands Development Board 20, 142; *add* 299

Holland and Barrett 190

Howe, Eric 251–2

Hundred Practical Applications of Noise Reduction Methods 276

IDA 45

independence 24

Industrial Common Ownership Finance (ICOF) 97–9; *add* 99

Industrial Common Ownership Movement (ICOM) 34, 97; *add* 35, 299

industrial health 273–5

inflation 49

information: effective use of 147–8; for marketing 147–9; sources of 19–22, 149

information services 283

information technology 232; disasters 242–4; education centres 246; finding help and advice 245–7; training 246; *see also* computers

Information Technology in Action 246

Inland Revenue 29–30, 32, 100, 208

innovation 152–3

Inside Information 251

Institute of Practitioners in Advertising 156

insurance 178, 285; credit 104–5

interest on outstanding payments 47

International Factors 103, 136

investors' clubs 101

invoices: dating 39–40; discounting 136; outstanding 36; processing 38–40

Irish Development Bank 45

Jackson, David 234

Jenny Craig Weight Loss Centre 190

job creation 88, 96, 100

Job Ownership organisation 34

Jobcentres 87, 89, 91

Johnston Group: Johnston Development Capital (JDC) 130

Jones, George 33

Keen, Peter, *Competing in Time* 249

Kellock Factors 137

Kent Economic Development Board 106

Kentucky Fried Chicken 188, 190

Kreiger, Ian 108

Labour costs 80

ladder accidents 258–9

La Mama franchise 200, 203

Lancashire Enterprises 109

landlord: obligations of 293–5; responsibilities 28

Landlord and Tenant Act 27–9, 295

Late Late Supershops 190

late payments 24, 46–7

laying off workers 219–20

lead hazards 274

leases 293–5

leasing 137–40; finance 139; operating 139; sales aid 139

leasing facilities 64
Legal and General 92
legal requirements 176–9
libraries 149
limited companies 31
liquidity, adequate levels of 84
liquidity ratios 54–5
Livewire 92; add 92
Lloyds Bank 93–4, 103, 131, 133
Lloyds Bank Factoring Guarantee Scheme 136
Lloyds Bowmaker 136
Loan Guarantee Scheme 94, 95–6, 107
local authorities 86, 91, 105–7
Local Authorities (Miscellaneous Provisions) Act 1982: 107
local enterprise agencies 26, 85
Local Enterprise Development Unit (LEDU) 141–2
local enterprise trusts 20
Local Investment Networking Company (LINC) 130
London Building Acts 177, 178
London Chamber of Commerce 107
London Co-operative Development Fund 98
London Enterprise Agency 37, 85, 91, 101, 130; add 299
London Research Centre 107

Machinery, safety 269–70
McKesson 249
maintenance 178; for accident avoidance 257–9; short-cuts on 267
Managed Technology Investors 132
management, bank manager's assessment of 58–9
management accounting 26, 82
management buy-ins 108–9
management buy-outs 108, 109
management information 74, 81–4

management team 25–6
Manpower Services Commission 88
Market Entry Guarantee Scheme 159
market research 149
marketing 23, 143–69; co-operatives 33; for small firms 143–6; franchising 193; information for 147–9, 154; planning 150–54; service sector 167–9; start-up firm 161–4
maternity leave 222, 223
maternity pay 221–2
maternity rights 207, 221–3
Medical Engineering Ltd 153
Metal Box 163
MFI 108
Microcomputer Advisory Service 233
microcomputers, advisory services 230–34
Mid Wales Development 142
Midland Bank 87, 93, 94, 103; Credo 93
Midland Furnishings 145, 146
Milton Keynes Business Venture 106
misconduct dismissals 216–18
Mitchell v *North British Rubber Co* 269
Moffett, Carol 45
Moffett Engineering 45
Moffett Multicast System 45
Morgan Grenfell 132
Moulded Plastics Ltd 150–52

National Bingo Game Association 248
National Computing Centre 232; add 247
National Economic Development Office (NEDO) 109, 130
National Insurance 207–8, 221
National Westminster Bank 93–4, 131
net profit percentage 52–4

New Business Guardian 14, 19
New Technology Based Firms (NTBFs) 164
noise control 275-7
nominal ledger 31-2
Northern Ireland 19, 141-2
Northern Ireland Development Agency 141; *add* 299
Northern Ireland Local Enterprise Development Unit 19, 142; *add* 299
Northern Youth Venture Fund 90

Occupiers' Liability Act 177, 178
Oceania Motors 148
Octagon Investment Management 133
office: accommodation 173-6; acoustics 181; automation 172; decorations 181; equipment 173; expansion 175-6; floor covering 182; heating 182; interior design and fitting out 180-82; layout 171; legal requirements 176-9; lighting 181; organisation 170-72; planning 170-82; reception area 171; space considerations 171-2, 173-5; storage equipment 171-2; *see also* business premises
Office Equipment Index 243
Offices, Shops and Railway Premises Act 177, 178, 255, 293
Ogilvy, Benson and Mather 156
order numbers 39
overdrafts 61-3
overheads 17, 80; budgeting 75-7
overload 27

PA Consulting Services 132
painters, accidents 259
Paperback 97
Pareto's Law 82

part-time workers 25
payment: demanding 24; early payment 40-42; enforcing 46-8; late payments 46; slow payers 37-40; techniques of avoiding 37; withholding 47
Peat Marwick 100, 108
performance analysis 50-55
petty cash book 31
Pilkington Group 21
Pizza Hut 190
planning 16-48; case for 70-73; finance 23-4; first steps in 16-18; future 22-4, 58-9; implementation 72; making room for 27; marketing 150-54; overall 22, 70-73; products and 150-54; relevance of 70-73; strategic 42-6
Policy Studies Institute 223
premises, protection of 27; *see also* business premises
price decision 156-8
price of product 17, 158
pricing policies 156-8
Prince's Youth Business Trust 89-90; *add* 90
product development 150-54
product management 153
products: bank manager's assessment of 59; sources for new ideas 153-4
profit 30; assessment of 17; budgeting 73-6; gross profit percentage 50-52; net profit percentage 52-4; ploughing back 17
profit and loss account 49, 54
profit and loss report 82-4
profitability 82-4
profitability ratios 50-54
Project North East 90; *add* 90
Prontaprint 188
property management 296-7
prospects, bank manager's assessment of 59
protective clothing 261, 268

Prudential Venture Managers 132
public relations 156
purchases 80
purchases ledger 31, 38-9

Rank Xerox Pension Fund 85
ratio analysis 50-55
records 29-32
redundancy 87, 207, 209, 219-20
Reedpack 108
Regina v Swan Hunter Ship Builders Ltd 261
Research Corporation 132
resource mobilisation 160
risk taking 11
roofwork, safety precautions 257-8
Royal Bank of Scotland 94
Rumble, David 247
Rural Development Commission (CoSIRA) 20, 94, 142; add 299

Safety 177, 178; flooring 260; machinery 268-70; policies 261-3; systems of work 266-8; see also health and safety
Safety Representatives and Committee Regulations 1977: 256
sales 78; budgeting 75; forecast 16-17; promotion 154-6
sales/debtors 55
sales ledger 31, 32, 36; administration and factoring 136
Scottish Co-operatives Development Committee 98
Scottish Development Agency 19, 20, 91, 141; add 299
Selby District Council 106
self-employed 207
selling 16; start-up firm 161-4
service sector, marketing 167-9
Sheffield City Council 106
Shell Enterprise Loan Fund 85, 91
Shell UK 85-6

sickness absence 215-16
Sketchley 190
slow payers 37-40
Small Business Centre 20
small business clubs 27
Small Business Computer Selection Package 241
Small Business Guardian 14
Small Business Guide, The 22
Small Business Research Trust 86
Small Computers in Small Companies 226
small firms: activities designed to encourage 11; fight for survival 11; mortality rate 11; pitfalls in 11
Small Firms Centres adds 299-300
Small Firms Counselling Service 19, 141
Small Firms Service 19-20, 26, 88, 105
solicitor 18
Sources of Venture Capital 110-29
South Bank Technopark 132
specialist skills 25
Sperrings 190
Springfield Furnishings 165
start-up firms: basic questions for 164; marketing 161-4; selling 161-4
start-up funds 87-9, 130
start-up technology enterprises 131-2
statutory sick pay 223-5
stock: control of 165-6; investment in 67; management of 67-70; valuation 82
stock-turn ratio 70
stores manager 165
strategy 14, 42-6
structural alterations and improvements 179
supplementary benefit 87

TAB (Thomson Automated Banking) 248

taxation 88; *see also* Inland
  Revenue
technical advisory points
  schemes 131
technology: appraisal schemes
  131; funding 131–3
telephone cash collection 35–7
tenancy: expiry 28; new 28–9
tenants' rights 27–9
tenosynovitis 275
terms of payment 47
Thomas White Foundation 91
Thompson, Gary 243–4
Thomson Holidays 248
Thomson McLintock 87
3i: 94, 109, 132
time utilisation 25–6
TNT 190
Tractor Cabs Regulations 276
Trades Union Congress 211
traffic manager 165
Training Agency 246; *add* 247
trial balance 32
TSB 94
TV Choice 243, 246; *add* 247
Tyneside Enterprise Agency 85

Unemployment benefit 87
unfair dismissal 207–11, 214–18

VAT 30, 138
venture capital 24, 86, 98,
  108–30; sources 110–29

Waller, Denis 242, 250

Wandsworth Youth Develop-
  ment 92
warehousing 165
welfare 177; *see also* health and
  safety
Welsh Development Agency 19,
  141; *add* 300
West Midlands Co-operative
  Finance 98; *add* 99
West Midlands Enterprise Board
  130
West Yorkshire Enterprise Board
  106
Western Excavating (ECC) v *Sharp*
  212
Wimpy 188, 200
window cleaning, safety precautions 258
Winkler, John, *Winkler on Marketing Planning* 154
Woodworking Machines Regulations 1974: 276
word processors 172
working capital 60–61
working conditions 178
Worknorth scheme 106

York City Council 106
York Enterprise Agency 106
Young Entrepreneurs Fund 90
Young's Franchise Group 203
Youth Business Initiative 89
Youth Business Trust 89–90
Youth Enterprise Scheme 90

Index of Advertisers

AES Carphones *38*
Albany Chemicals Ltd *191*
Amberchem *187*
B + B Technics *231*
Barclays Bank *Facing title page*
British Telecom *Inside front cover*
Business Box *237*
Carissima Ltd *196*
Cleshar WP Plus *62*
Delta Five *151*
Dyno-Locks *195*
Euro-Connect Ltd *204*
Fineline Communications Ltd *76*
Gruber Levinson Franks *53*
Holmes *198*
Hotel and Catering Training Board *264*
Institute of Chartered Accountants in England and Wales *12*
Johnson Hall Publishing *51*
Kendall Motor Oils *193*
Lloyds Bank *Facing half title*
Midland Bank *8*
Mundays *15*
Norfolk House Promotions *202*
PIP Printing *185*
Printdesigns *184*
Prontaprint plc *189*
Shearwater Executive Communications *144*
Small Firms Service *Back cover*
Transam Express Courier Parcels Ltd *186*
Vanguard Telecommunications Ltd *21*
Venture Factors plc *134*
Zenith Data Systems *227, 229*